Political Ideology in the Arab World

Arab nationalism and Islamism have been the two most potent ideological forces in the Arab region across the twentieth century. Over the last two decades, however, an accommodation of sorts has been developing between liberals, socialists, and Islamists, to protest unpopular foreign and domestic policies, such as those aimed at cooperation with Israel or the war in Iraq. By examining the writings of Arab nationalist, socialist, and Islamist intellectuals, and through numerous interviews with political participants from different persuasions, Michaelle Browers traces these developments from the "Arab age of ideology," as it has been called, through an "age of ideological transformation," demonstrating clearly how the recent flow of ideas from one group to another have their roots in the past. *Political Ideology in the Arab World* assesses the impact of ideological changes on Egypt's Kifaya! [Enough!] movement and Yemen's Joint Meeting Parties.

MICHAELLE L. BROWERS is Associate Professor in the Department of Political Science at Wake Forest University. Her recent publications include *Democracy and Civil Society in Arab Political Thought: Transcultural Possibilities* (2006) and *An Islamic Reformation?* (with Charles Kurzman, 2004).

Cambridge Middle East Studies 31

Editorial Board

Charles Tripp (general editor)

Julia Clancy-Smith, F. Gregory Gause, Yezid Sayigh, Avi Shlaim,
Judith Tucker

Cambridge Middle East Studies has been established to publish
books on the nineteenth- to twenty-first-century Middle East and
North Africa. The aim of the series is to provide new and original
interpretations of aspects of Middle Eastern societies and their
histories. To achieve disciplinary diversity, books will be solicited
from authors writing in a wide range of fields, including history,
sociology, anthropology, political science and political economy. The
emphasis will be on producing books offering an original approach
along theoretical and empirical lines. The series is intended for
students and academics, but the more accessible and wide-ranging
studies will also appeal to the interested general reader.

A list of books in the series can be found after the index.

Political Ideology in the Arab World

Accommodation and Transformation

Michaelle L. Browers

Wake Forest University

CAMBRIDGE
UNIVERSITY PRESS

CAMBRIDGE UNIVERSITY PRESS
Cambridge, New York, Melbourne, Madrid, Cape Town, Singapore, São Paulo, Delhi

Cambridge University Press
The Edinburgh Building, Cambridge CB2 8RU, UK

Published in the United States of America by Cambridge University Press, New York

www.cambridge.org
Information on this title: www.cambridge.org/9780521749343

First published 2009

Printed in the United Kingdom at the University Press, Cambridge

A catalogue record for this publication is available from the British Library

Library of Congress Cataloguing in Publication data
Browers, Michaelle, 1968–
    Political ideology in the Arab world : accommodation and
    transformation / Michaelle L. Browers.
        p.   cm. – (Cambridge Middle East studies)
    Includes bibliographical references and index.
    ISBN 978-0-521-76532-9 (hardback) – ISBN 978-0-521-74934-3 (pbk.)
    1. Ideology – Political aspects – Arab countries.   2. Arab countries – Politics and
    government – 1945–   I. Title.   II. Series.
    JQ1850.A58B76 2009
    320.50917′4927–dc22

ISBN 978-0-521-76532-9 hardback
ISBN 978-0-521-74934-3 paperback

Contents

Acknowledgments

The International Institute for the Study of Islam in the Modern World in Leiden, the Netherlands, proved a hospitable and stimulating environment for working through some of the conceptual questions that initiated this project. The recent closure of this institute represents a great loss. The scope of the project was further sharpened through participation in a workshop at the Mediterranean Social and Political Research Meeting on "Cooperation across Ideological Divides: Comparative Locales within Arab Public Spheres" that was led by two outstanding scholars, Jillian Schwedler and Bassel Salloukh, and sponsored by the European University Institute in Florence, Italy. The Fulbright Middle East, North Africa, South Asia Regional Research Program; the American Institute for Maghribi Studies; the American Center for Oriental Research in Amman, Jordan; and the William C. Archie Fund Grant at Wake Forest University, provided funding for research completed in Yemen, Egypt, Lebanon, Jordan, and Morocco.

Earlier versions of portions of this manuscript were published as the following journal articles: "Origins and Architects of Yemen's Joint Meeting Parties," *International Journal of Middle East Studies* 39 (2007), 565–586; "The Egyptian Movement for Change: Intellectual Antecedents and Generational Conflicts," *Contemporary Islam: Dynamics of Muslim Life* 1 (2007), 69–88; and "The Centrality and Marginalization of Women in the Political Discourse of Arab Nationalists and Islamists," *Journal of Middle East Women's Studies* 2 (2006), 8–34.

I will not attempt to list all of the intellectuals and activists whose thoughts and experiences contributed to the completion of this work and to whom I owe many debts of gratitude, for fear that I will leave some out. However, I would be rather negligent if I failed to note the generosity of a few friends, colleagues, and comrades on whom I leaned particularly heavily while in the region, on my way to the region, or in those times where I had to locate something from home: Raghida Abou Alwan, Melani Cammett, Daniel Corstange, Hossam al-Hamalawy,

Khayr al-Din Hasib, Muhammad 'Abd al-Malik al-Mutawakkil, Ridwan al-Sayyid, Nabil al-Soufi, Joshua Stacher, Fawwaz Traboulsi, Stacey Philbrick Yadav, Murad Zafir, and the late and great Ahmed Abdalla, to whom I dedicate this book. All shortcomings or errors in what follows remain the author's alone.

Glossary

ahl al-dhimma: protected peoples, non-Muslim subjects of Islamic governments

asala: authenticity

azma: crisis

da'wa: calling or inviting to Islam

fiqh: Islamic jurisprudence

hadatha: modernity

ijtihad: independent reasoning, particularly in regard to interpreting religious texts

'ilmaniyya: secularism, from *'ilm* (science); also rendered *'almaniyya*, from *'alam* (world)

jahiliyya: ignorance or barbarism; usually used in reference to the pre-Islamic era, though in modern times it has come to be used in reference to individuals, systems and societies not following Islam; also known as the "age of ignorance"

kafir, plural *kuffar*: unbeliever, one who rejects Islam

khuruj: literally, coming out or rising; Zaydi principle of rising up against an unjust ruler

kifaya: enough; slogan of and nickname for the Egyptian Movement for Change

mu'asira: contemporaenity

muwatin: citizen

Nahda: awakening or renaissance; name given to the period of intellectual creativity and reform from the late nineteenth to the early twentieth centuries; often seen as the Arab and Islamic counterpart to the European Enlightenment

qawmiyya: nationalism, usually referring to pan-Arab nationalism, as opposed to *wataniyya*

salafiyya: movement claiming to follow in the way of the righteous ancestors (*salaf*); used to describe traditionalist and puritanical Islamic movements in various parts of the world

shariʿa: body of Islamic law; literally, the way or path

shura: consultation, used by some Islamic thinkers as a synonym for democracy

turath: heritage

umma: community

wasatiyya: an intellectual trend characterized or claiming characterization as centrist or moderate (*wasti*), or said to occupy the middle (*wasat*) between extremist alternatives

watan: homeland, nation

wataniyya: nationalism, usually referring to state-based nationalism, as opposed to *qawmiyya*

Introduction: Ideological thought and practice in the Arab region

Arab nationalism and Islamism[1] have proven two of the most potent ideological forces in the Arab region over the past century. On the one hand, the two trends would seem to possess a number of natural affinities. Muslims are keenly aware of the central role played by Arabs and Arabic in the development of Islamic civilization. In the words of the founder of the Muslim Brotherhood, Hasan al-Banna (1906–1949): "Islam arose among Arabs and reached other nations through the Arabs. Its noble book is in Arabic. It is found in the traditions that 'when Arabs are denigrated, Islam is denigrated . . . Arabs are the guardians of Islam'."[2] So too, Arab nationalists have acknowledged the special place Islam occupies in Arab civilization: not only is Islam the religion of the vast majority of Arabs, but Islam's golden age corresponds with one of the most celebrated periods in Arab history. Ba'th Party founder Michel 'Aflaq (1910–1989) affirmed this relation in claiming that "Islam . . . was an Arab movement and its meaning was the renewal and completion of Arabism."[3]

However, even when Arab nationalists and Islamists have found themselves facing a common enemy – such as corrupt and authoritarian regimes that seek their marginalization or suppression – they have most commonly proven to be each other's worst enemy. Throughout the contemporary period their relationship has been better characterized as competitive and hostile than as cooperative and complementary, as each of the two ideologies has fought for pride of place in the hearts and minds of people in the region. Islamists have denounced the achievements of Arab nationalists as superficial and pursued at the expense of the religiosity and unity of the *umma* (Islamic community) – tantamount to a "modern *jahiliyya*," in the words of the Egyptian Shaykh Muhammad al-Ghazzali (1917–1996).[4] They have sought to delegitimize Arab nationalists as atheistic servants of external powers or, in the words of the popular Islamist thinker Yusuf al-Qaradawi (Egypt/Qatar, b. 1926), as misguided advocates of "imported solutions" (*hulul mustawrada*).[5] Many Islamists cite Arab nationalism as the cause

1

of Arab and Islamic weakness in the face of its religious and civilizational opponents, particularly Israel, various European powers, and, most recently, the United States. The central role played by a number of Christian thinkers in the formulation of Arab nationalism has contributed to the ideology's secular focus, to the chagrin of Islamists. Ghazzali once speculated that "non-Muslims, of course, have welcomed nationalism enthusiastically for the obvious advantage it has of lending itself readily to the destruction of Islam."[6]

For their part, Arab nationalists – including Sati' al-Husri (1880–1967), whom many consider the father of the ideology – have denied that religion could ever constitute the fundamental element of national solidarity because of linguistic and cultural differences that exist among Muslims throughout the world. Islam, according to this argument, exists across too vast a geographical expanse and is too permeated with competing forms of identity. Some Arab nationalists have attempted to place blame for political and economic stagnation upon what they characterize as backward or reactionary ideas touted by Islamists. Islamists, they say, want to drag society back to the Middle Ages. They lack understanding of the myriad problems facing – and solutions required for – "modern society." More recently, many nationalist thinkers have sought to criminalize Islamist groups by labeling them as fanatics or terrorists.

Arab nationalists and Islamists have both been at odds – politically and ideologically – with socialist and communist forces in the region as well. Although socialism was appropriated by Arab nationalist regimes in the 1970s, the relationship between the two has not been without tensions, as those regimes often considered the marginalization, if not eradication, of Marxist influences the *sine qua non* for their consolidation of power. Communists were persecuted, imprisoned, and tortured for many years in Egypt under Gamal 'Abd al-Nasir's rule. Socialism has had an even more troubled relationship with advocates of Islamic politics. Most Islamists are avowedly hostile to socialism, both for its atheism, and for its emphasis on material (as opposed to spiritual) development. Classical Marxism criticizes religion as a factor of alienation, a form of false consciousness, and an opiate of the people. Both religion and nationalism, according to socialists, tend to lead people to heed obligations and prohibitions that hamper human development, to accept submission, inequality, and cultural backwardness, and to affirm national or religious unity over class struggle.

Arab leaders, for their part, have often traded repression and cultivation of one ideological grouping at the expense of the other to diminish the capacity of each to act as a significant oppositional force vis-à-vis the state and further deepening the lines that divide political groups. In the 1950s, Jordan's King Husayn viewed Islamists as a strategic ally against his Arab nationalist and socialist critics; in the early 1970s, Egyptian president Anwar al-Sadat bolstered the Muslim Brotherhood in his campaign against leftists and Nasirists; in the early 1980s, Algerian president Chadli Bendjedid facilitated the rise of the Islamist movement as an auxiliary force in his purge of leftists and Boumédiennists; and, throughout the 1990s, Yemeni president 'Ali 'Abdullah Salih pitted Islamists against socialists to weaken the political influence of the latter – to cite just a few of many such examples from the region.

In light of the political and ideological tensions that have dominated much of the contemporary period, one might not expect to see many instances of cooperation between Arab nationalists and Islamists – let alone with socialist forces in the region as well. Yet a growing number of researchers are beginning to note precisely this: Arab socialists, nationalists, Islamists, as well as some liberals, protesting alongside one another – and, at times, coordinating protest activity – against policies, for example, aimed at normalization with Israel and supportive of US intervention in Iraq.[7] As early as 1992, Jordan's leading Islamist group, the Islamic Action Front (the political party of the Muslim Brotherhood), allied with seven nationalist and leftist organizations to form the "Popular Arab Jordanian Committee for Resisting Submission and Normalization," which aimed at opposing the drive to normalize relations with Israel. Among the joint actions achieved by this alliance was the staging of a series of sit-ins to protest against the opening of the Israeli embassy in Amman. In 2000, thirteen Palestinian organizations, including Fatah, the Popular Front for the Liberation of Palestine, Hamas, the Democratic Front for the Liberation of Palestine, and Islamic Jihad, aligned to form the "National and Islamic Forces," which subsequently cooperated in staging general strikes and public demonstrations, as well as in issuing joint statements. The "Cairo Anti-War Conference," which has held conferences and demonstrations against the war in Iraq annually since December 2002, has brought together members of Egypt's Muslim Brotherhood, the banned Egyptian Communist Party, the Islamist Wasat Party, the pan-Arab Karama Party, the Organization of Revolutionary Socialists, and the Socialist People's Party, as well as an ideologically wide array of international activists and intellectuals.

On occasion, these cross-ideological alliances have adopted more overtly oppositional forms by challenging existing governments on issues such as election reforms, limitations on press freedoms, or the regulation of civil society organizations, as is the case with the two groups that receive the most attention in the present work's final chapters: the Egyptian

National Movement for Change (better known as Kifaya! [Enough!]), and Yemen's Joint Meeting Parties. And, in some cases, ideologically disparate and historically opposed forces have formalized their cooperation by forming new political parties or organizations: Egypt's Socialist Labor Party, established in 1979 as a socialist-oriented movement, joined forces with the Muslim Brotherhood and the right-of-center Liberal Socialist Party to form the Labor Islamic Alliance for the parliamentary elections held in 1987. By 1989, the Labor Party formally adopted an Islamic line. A number of other smaller parties claiming to straddle historical ideological divides have formed in a number of countries and sought official recognition. For example, the Arab Islamic Democratic Movement gained party status in Jordan in 1993. Also known as *al-Du'a* (the call), the party characterizes itself as a "modern Islamic alternative" and espouses five potentially incongruous principles: Islamic-Arabism, democracy as *shura*, the correspondence of reason and spirituality, Muslim and Christian coexistence, and Islamic economic policies.

These cross-ideological exchanges and actions raise several questions of significance for analysis of the history of Arab political thought. What are their historical and intellectual antecedents? Do they constitute merely a temporary convergence of interests, cooperation undertaken purely for opportunist reasons, or are these alliances evidence of more significant convergences among – and transformations within – competing ideological traditions in the region? Is much thought given to the significance of these collaborations – that is, how do the participants rationalize and justify working with groups they have anathemized in the recent past? What are the implications of ongoing dialog for the thought and practice of the ideological traditions that inform the engagements? More broadly, the aim of the present work is both to analyze the intellectual changes that have facilitated the emergence of cross-ideological alliances, and to assess the significance of the crossing of ideological boundaries by individuals and groups for the political and intellectual landscape of the Arab region.

Assessing the ideological terrain

A number of works have provided differing accounts of the latest events and impending prospects of the ideologies that have animated the Arab region during the period under study here. Some studies suggest new ideologies have emerged to replace the old. In the most recent and expanded edition of his influential study of *Arab Nationalism*, Bassam Tibi characterizes Islam and nationalism as ideological rivals, and maintains that "this tension characterizes the turn to the twenty-first century: to despise Arab nationalism *fi mizan al-islam* (on the balance of Islam), while reviving Islamic universalism."[8] Tibi maintains that the delegitimation of the ideology of Arab nationalism was accelerated by the Arab defeat in the Six-Day War of 1967, and that its demise both caused and was completed by the rise of political Islam, which "was not only a challenge to secular Arab nationalism and the project of its Pan-Arab state[, but also] . . . presents its own alternative: the Islamic state."[9]

This view of the incommensurability of Islam and Arab nationalism is reiterated in Emmanuel Sivan's study of electronic preachers (audio-cassettes of Islamist preachers and activists that circulate in the Middle East) for whom Arabism assumes the "frightful bogey" and "the equation Arabism = state police is . . . experiential and affective."[10] In other cases it seems Arab socialism, whether in its nationalist or Marxist forms, plays the role of bogey. For example, the Islamist prosecutors of the liberal Egyptian thinker Nasr Hamid Abu Zayd (b. 1943) repeatedly criticized him for his "Marxian analysis," which alone seems enough to substantiate his presumed apostasy in the minds of his detractors.[11] In the assessment of a number of scholars, political Islam has emerged as the final negation of secular and socialist Arab ideologies.

In contrast to Tibi and Sivan, Leonard Binder, in his classic work, *Islamic Liberalism*, noted what he understood to be a "convergence" between the orientations of "modernists" and "fundamentalists:" "the modernists are becoming more 'Islamic' while the fundamentalists are becoming more liberal."[12] While Binder considered this convergence to be largely "verbal," he also suggested that "the possibility of bringing these two groups together is a tempting political goal. The liberal modernists believe that they know how to run a modern state and how to build effective administrative institutions, but the fundamentalists or the authoritarian modernists seem to be able to mobilize and move the masses."[13] Such a possibility offers both promise and potential pitfalls. The task, Binder argues, is for liberal Muslims to "appropriate religion as part of a new ideology before it is appropriated by some rival force." Islamic fundamentalism poses the most threatening rival in Binder's assessment. But the predicament for Islamic liberals, Binder argues, is that they must at once avoid too close association with Western culture (in which case they run the risk of being stigmatized with inauthenticity or sacrilege) and avoid foolhardy coalitions with the fundamentalists (lest they fall into the same trap as their counterparts in Iran).[14]

Other works have pointed to a striking number of intellectuals who have crossed the line and fallen into the trap of which Binder warns. Sivan notes "the number of former Arab nationalists and Marxists who

[have] converted to radical Islam from the late 1970s on," such as the Egyptian thinker 'Adil Husayn (1932–2001) and the Palestinian thinker Munir Shafiq (b. 1936), both of whom migrated to Islamism from the more decidedly socialist wing of Arab nationalism and the latter of whom converted to Islam from Greek Orthodox Christianity.[15] 'Adil Husayn was the secretary-general of the Labor Party until his death and played a central role in its eventual transformation into an Islamist party. Munir Shafiq was director of the Palestine Liberation Organization's Palestine Planning Center until 1992. Today Shafiq is a spokesperson for Hamas. Based on such cases, François Burgat declares that "Islamism is effectively the reincarnation of an older Arab nationalism, clothed in imagery considered more indigenous."[16] The Egyptian law professor, Hussam 'Issa (b. 1939), provides a similar assessment:

After the defeat, people would say: we tried liberalism before the revolution in 1952, then we tried Arab nationalism, and then we had to find another form of identity. Then the Islamists came and said: before we are Arabs we are Muslims. And this approach, after 1967, can explain part of the [Islamist] phenomenon ... It's a change of identity. Now the Muslim intellectuals are coming to say: we are Arab Muslims. Meanwhile, the Arab nationalists are coming closer to the Islamists, whereas the Islamists are becoming more Arab.[17]

Another competing perspective is offered by Paul Salem's 1994 study, *Bitter Legacy: Ideology and Politics in the Arab World*. Working from an understanding of political ideologies that associates ideological thinking with periods of "rapid social, economic, political, and cultural change," which contribute toward "considerable psychological strain" and openness to "ideological formulations of reality," Salem identifies three phases of ideological upheavals, each of which corresponds to a twenty-five-year generational shift. The liberal and conservative regional nationalist ideologies that emerged after the collapse of the Ottoman Empire were opposed by the revolutionary pan-Arab nationalism that emerged after the loss of Palestine. Radical Arab nationalism was in turn challenged by the Islamic revivalism that gained strength after the 1967 defeat.[18] However, rather than concluding that Islamism would begin to ebb at the end of its twenty-five-year cycle (presumably by the mid-1990s), Salem detected the rise of a middle class that began to drift away from ideological thinking as they began to achieve political dominance in the mid-1970s. This leads him to conclude that the rise of Islamic radicalism "does not represent the beginning of a new phase of ideological effervescence but the last throes of an age of ideology that is gradually coming to an end, and which may give way to a period of more widely pragmatic politics in the not-too distant future."[19]

Olivier Roy's book, *The Failure of Political Islam*, seems to combine the conversion and post-ideological theses. In Roy's account, rather than leftists becoming Islamists, Islamists have reformulated a 1960s Third Worldism, appropriating its anti-imperialism and models of economics and revolution. However, the ideology's inability to formulate a distinctively Islamic model for society that could provide an alternative to Western modernity is what Roy claims ultimately results in the "failure" of Islam as a social movement and revolutionary force in the 1980s, and accounts for what he identifies as a current drift into a form of neofundamentalism, a more individualized and less politicized form of Islam.[20]

Thus, we face several alternative accounts of the transformation of Arab ideologies in the contemporary period: Arab nationalism and socialism have been supplanted by political Islam (Tibi and Sivan); an intellectual or ideological convergence is taking place, whether through the formulation of Islamic liberalism (Binder) or by virtue of various conversion experiences toward political Islam (Burgat); or we have reached a post-ideological age, characterized either by increasingly pragmatic thinking (Salem) or by post-Islamism (Roy). None of the views discussed above consider the possible emergence of a simpler ideological rapprochement among the various contending political groups in opposition – let alone their joining forces despite enduring ideological differences in order to challenge the regimes in power. Without dismissing some aspects of the supplantation, convergence, conversion, and post-ideological pragmatism theses, I argue that the relationship among competing ideologies of opposition in the contemporary Arab region is best characterized as accommodationist, with strategic alliances forming among more pragmatic and moderate wings of otherwise opposed ideological factions of marginalized groups. Further, alliances are as much a product of, as they are a source for, shifts (but not an end) in ideological debates that have occurred over the past several decades.

Based on analysis of works by Arab nationalist and socialist intellectuals who draw from Islamic sources in their discussions of national unity and liberation; the writings of Islamic thinkers associated with what has come to be called the *wasatiyya* (centrist or moderate) trend; the published proceedings of a variety of meetings that have put members of diverse political persuasions in dialog; interviews with scores of participants and organizers of such forums; and various other documents, such as media coverage of the cross-ideological dialogs and actions and joint statements released by cross-ideological political groupings, this book provides a historical and analytical account of the development of Arab ideological writings from the end of what some have called the "Arab Age of Ideology" through the outset of what might be termed the "Arab Age of Ideological Transformation."[21] The evidence provided here suggests that the level of ideological transformation that has occurred is significant but limited, falling far short of the "end of ideology" Salem anticipates, the liberal-Islamic convergence Binder hopes for, and the "post-Islamism" Roy announces. Rather, historically opposed ideological trends and groups have found mutual enemies more than common political visions, and related political goals rather than shared understandings of basic political and social concepts.

Accounting for changes in thought and practice: moderates and moderation theses

The account of ideological accommodation and transformation offered here has implications for the now considerable political science literature that engages what Jillian Schwedler has termed "the inclusion-moderation hypothesis" – that is, the idea that participation in multiparty political processes leads toward an increased willingness to work within existing systems.[22] Most of the early works that examine this hypothesis in the context of the Arab region tended to be too narrowly focused on Islamists and on formal political processes – typically confining analysis to Islamist participation in national elections.[23] The conclusions of such studies usually suggest either one half of Binder's convergence thesis (with Islamists becoming more liberal) or a part of Salem's pragmatism thesis (with Islamists becoming less doctrinaire or more self-limiting in their political aims). Recent studies by Schwedler, Clark, and others have shifted much of the debate from the question of whether inclusion results in moderation toward the question of whether working across ideological divides contributes toward moderation and, in the process, their work has broadened analysis previously focused on party–state relations to encompass a wider range of interactions among ideologically opposed parties.[24] This change in focus largely results from Schwedler's important contribution to our understanding of the "mechanisms" by which moderation – "in the sense of being relatively more open and tolerant of alternative perspectives" – is likely to occur.[25] Schwedler finds that the key element lies in the extent to which a party's leadership has engaged in the deliberations necessary to justify changes in strategy. Inclusion can contribute to moderation, but only when the party manages to develop "modes of justification" for engaging in political practices with other political (and ideologically opposed) political groups. However, the results of cross-ideological cooperation tend to be mixed when viewed from the level of parties. Schwedler's own comparative work between the two main Islamist parties in Jordan and Yemen concludes that while Jordan's Islamic Action Front (IAF) has become more open and tolerant of alternative perspectives through participation in pluralist political processes, the inclusion of Yemen's Islah Party in similar processes has not.[26] Janine Clark's study of the Higher Committee for the Coordination of National Opposition Parties in Jordan "questions the degree to which cooperation leads to ideological moderation" on the part of the IAF.[27]

In fact, these works have pointed to the importance not only of ideology, but also to individuals and groups of individuals in the formulation of ideology and the forging of cross-ideological cooperation. Political parties do not work for moderation, individuals within and outside of parties do. Further, while the moderation of individuals and groups of individuals can have an impact on the discourse and practice of political parties, it need not. As Michael Freeden has noted, "parties operate at the mass production end of the long ideological production line. Ideologies *emerge* among groups within a party or outside of it. Those groups may consist of intellectuals or skilled rhetoricians, who themselves are frequently articulating more popular or inchoate beliefs or, conversely, watering down complex philosophical positions."[28] Thus, focusing on inclusion or cooperation at the level of parties may miss both the impetus and the outcome of cross-ideological interactions. They miss the impetus when they focus on structural conditions – such as the democratic openings of the early 1990s, which are said to have brought more groups into political processes – but neglect the intellectual context, often the result of exclusion and closings and conflicts (rather than inclusion and openings), that precede observable moments of cooperation and provide some of the discursive and ideational elements that enable the interaction to take place. They run the risk of mischaracterizing the outcome when they look too exclusively to political parties as the locus of change, rather than focusing on networks of individuals, which might indicate possibilities for intellectual transformations, generational changes, or even nascent political movements. The present work is intended to contribute to the inclusion-moderation and cooperation-moderation debates by further shifting the focus from structural to intellectual and ideological contexts, and from parties to individuals and networks of individuals that cross or work outside party lines. Attention to a broader array of ideological forces offers a fuller and more complex picture of the character of contentious politics in the Arab region. While many scholars are asking whether Islamists have become more moderate through participation in electoral and governing processes or through cross-ideological engagement, considerably less attention has been paid to what my study demonstrates: that those processes many scholars deem central to moderation processes required moderates – that is, thinkers with no small measure of pragmatism and creativity of thought. Attention to the intellectual "back-story" of recent cross-ideological engagements is essential for beginning to understand such questions as:

1 why groups and individuals from other, competing ideological trends choose to engage Islamists;
2 why Islamists choose to engage;
3 how such engagements are articulated and justified and whether these articulations and justifications constitute "moderation"; and
4 what impact such engagements have had (and not only on Islamists).

While cognizant of the observation, articulated by Muhammad Habib (b. 1943), the supreme guide of Egypt's Muslim Brotherhood upon the killing of Abu Musab al-Zarqawi (1966–2006) by US forces in Iraq – that Americans always make the mistake of focusing on individuals – training in intellectual history leads me to attempt to identify particular figures who have been central to the various intellectual reformulations that have made these alliances possible, though in addressing the role of the Islamist parties and political groups I focus more on generations and trends of thinkers.[29] In analyzing both the writings of central intellectual figures of Arab nationalism, Arab socialism, and Islamism, as well as instances of dialog among them, I conclude that by constructing largely oppositional frameworks that focus attention on broad issues of concern, such as the Palestine–Israeli conflict, US intervention in the Middle East and, to some extent, on the need for democratization and respect for human rights in the region – and by avoiding substantive discussion of areas of disagreement – a broad spectrum of intellectuals and activists reveal a growing number of overlapping concepts emerging amidst persisting and often intense ideological conflict. These points of overlap have proven significant in fostering cross-ideological interactions in a number of Arab countries. While in many respects the points of agreement achieved have been partial and temporary, it is also possible to detect a significant morphology of the various political concepts that comprise not only Arab nationalism and Islamism (though it is seen most clearly in those two traditions), but also socialist and liberal strands in the region. This analysis demonstrates that rather than Arab nationalists and socialists becoming more Islamist, or Islamists becoming more Arab nationalist or socialist, a wide variety of ideological groupings are developing a shared store of concepts increasingly dominated by rhetoric traditionally associated with liberalism, and based on notions such as democracy and human rights.

Yet the increasing prevalence of the liberal paradigm in the Arab political discourse reveals its own paradoxes. Where one might expect that the experience of cross-ideological engagement would contribute toward increased liberalization within these trends, one should not mistake the use of liberal rhetoric for a more categorical transformation toward liberal thought and practice. Rather, what the evidence reveals is something more tenuous: the persistence of those oppositional frames that permit these alliances to take place hinders discussion of various issues – particularly gender and religion, but also other forms of difference – which might contribute to a fuller articulation and more meaningful embrace of liberal and democratic values among the main oppositional forces in the Arab region. While substantive discussion, let alone agreement, on issues of gender and religion has proven nearly impossible in the context of cross-ideological dialogs, tensions created by the persistence of such issues have contributed toward some liberalization in at least two contexts. The personal relationships and use of liberal concepts fostered in these dialogs has provided space sufficient for development of an oppositional movement that is both cross-ideological and inter-religious in the context of Egypt, and a cross-ideological alliance that has proven susceptible to women's call for expansion of their political role in the context of Yemen.

Outline of the book

The book's chapters move from examination of intellectual antecedents (Chapters 1 and 2), to analysis of achieved points of agreements and remaining points of divergence revealed in a series of meetings aimed at aligning historically opposed ideological groupings (Chapter 3), to consideration of the development and character of cross-ideological alliances that have emerged within two national contexts (Chapters 4 and 5). The historical account provided in the first three chapters suggests that some Arab nationalists and socialists have reached out to Islamists in recent decades, that some Islamists have responded to these overtures, and that interaction, collaboration, and dialog has contributed to significant reformulation not only of Arab nationalism and socialism, but also of Islamism. Chapter 3 and the case studies in the book's final two chapters both substantiate and qualify that conclusion by critically assessing the overall project to build political consensus across ideological divides and its development in particular national contexts.

While the structure of the book moves from intellectual history, to discourse analysis, to examination of contentious politics in national contexts, the aim is to establish an organic relationship between thought, dialog, and practice. The debates that animated and the trends that emerged within the late 1960s/early 1970s through the 1980s provided the foundation for a more direct and sustained dialog that began in the 1990s. The primary authors of the transformation of thinking in Chapters 1 and 2 are the leaders of the dialogs that are examined in Chapter 3, and their wider band of interlocutors are in turn the main architects of the national political alliances analyzed in Chapters 4 and 5.

The book's first two chapters examine the political and intellectual foundations of contemporary attempts to forge political alliances across historically opposed ideologies. Chapter 1 examines the writings of various leftist and Arab nationalist thinkers, among whom I trace a distinct retreat from secularism, especially since the Iranian revolution in 1979. I locate this in the debates over authenticity and how to approach the Arab-Islamic *turath*, in the emergence of an Islamic left, and in the articulation of notion of unity based on an Arab-Islamic civilizational idea. With particular thinkers one can detect development over time, from recognition of the Islamic contribution to the national awakening in the Arab region in their early works (in the 1960s and early 1970s), to a more conscious attempt to synthesize aspects of Islamism and Arab nationalism in more recent writings (since the late 1970s and early 1980s). Chapter 2 looks at the writings of Islamic thinkers of the *wasatiyya* trend, which are presented as alternatives to extremist and violent interpretations of Islam and has recently encouraged dialog with non-Islamist – even secular – political forces. While consisting primarily of Egyptian Islamists, at least one Egyptian Copt espouses similar ideas and has aligned himself politically with this trend, and the influence of these thinkers extends far beyond Egypt.

While the analysis presented here of *wasatiyya* intellectuals is indebted to the work of Raymond Baker, who has succeeded in articulating the reformist agenda of these new Islamist intellectuals for an English-speaking audience, it goes beyond his work by engaging these authors more critically, and by assessing their impact in contributing to the cross-ideological character of protest activity aimed at political reform in the region.[30] In dealing with *wasatiyya* figures as a distinct school of "new Islamists," Baker fails to analyze more fully the collective and individual relationships of the figures he discusses with existing political and ideological trends, perhaps most importantly, the Muslim Brotherhood. In addition, the present work differs from Baker's in treating one key individual, Tariq al-Bishri (Egypt, b. 1933), as a nationalist thinker – that is, Bishri's thought is treated primarily in Chapter 1 rather than Chapter 2. This is important for tracing the role of his rich corpus in facilitating Arab nationalist and leftist overtures to liberal Islamic thinkers. Not only do I argue that Bishri is more rightly understood in the context of the tradition out of which his thought developed, but treating him as such is important because less systematic attention has been paid to the transformation in thinking on the part of a number of leftist and Arab nationalist thinkers than has been paid to developments in Islamist thought.[31] My study begins with these secular intellectuals because, in many respects, it is from there that the impetus for dialog across ideological divides stems.

All of the intellectuals discussed in the first two chapters have been involved in some aspect of the series of forums, dialogs, and conferences discussed in Chapter 3, the largest and most sustained of which have been the five National-Islamic Conferences (*al-mu'tamar al-qawmi al-dini*, NIC) convened in Beirut between 1994 and 2004. These conferences have brought together Arab nationalists and Islamists and have succeeded in putting individuals and groups from these and other ideological trends into regular contact for over a decade. Chapter 3 outlines the contours of the points of agreement and strategies of accommodation that draw together and sustain dialog among the various groups represented at the conferences. I also outline here areas in which the shared understandings have proven difficult or even impossible to forge. Discussion of democracy in particular has proven rather thin, only occasionally moving beyond a critique of authoritarianism and political corruption or a general call for party pluralism and free and fair elections, toward fuller articulation of democratic values. Topics such as the political status of women and religious minorities and the question of the role of secular and Islamic law in politics and society are only occasionally broached – and never approach consensus – at these forums. In general, among those individuals and groups most consistent in their call for building an ideologically inclusive movement for revival and reform of Arab society, one finds that the reliance upon far-away enemies (such as Israel and the United States) to sustain these fragile alliances often detracts from activism aimed at concerns closer to home, such as building domestic institutions to cultivate and sustain more democratic values. This critical assessment holds in regard to all three components analyzed in the book:

1 the intellectual antecedents (those trends of thinking on the left and among Islamists and Arab nationalists who focus on the reconceptualization of a more inclusive union at the expense of recognition of – and critical engagement with – the reality of Arab politics and society);

2 the cross-ideological engagements and dialogs (where issues that might divide this fragile alliance are shelved in the name of unity); and
3 the political manifestations of the alliances (those acts of opposition and protest where the publication of political programs are sacrificed to the imperatives of maintaining a visible and united opposition front).

At the same time, incongruence between nationalist, socialist, and Islamist conceptions of the role of Islamic law, religious minorities, and women, as well as the persistence of secularists, non-Muslims, and feminists both within and outside the NIC, have kept these issues from being fully subsumed, or forgotten, in the context of this now over decade-long series of discussions. The remaining chapters explore how alternative possibilities for non-Muslims and women are being negotiated in two national contexts (Egypt and Yemen), where cross-ideological collaborations have been significantly fostered by the intellectual trends discussed in Chapters 1 and 2 and participation in the National-Islamic Conferences and various other forums. While the extent of the impact those organizations and individuals discussed in these chapters will have on political life in Egypt and Yemen is not yet known, the consistency of themes and language between the intellectual trends discussed in the book's first two chapters and the cross-ideological discussions analyzed in Chapter 3, on the one hand, and the particular political contexts discussed in the book's final two chapters, on the other hand, reveal the character and status of ideological politics in the Arab region today. But there are also differences between the two cases. The protest activity that began in Egypt in the latter half of 2000 provided space for further development and deepening of relations (as well as for foregrounding of significant limitations) among the Arab nationalists, leftists, Islamists, and liberals. Thus, the momentum of the demonstrations accounts at least as much for the expansion and character of the cross-ideological cooperation that emerged in Egypt as does the dialog among intellectuals and ideologues that preceded these actions. On the other hand, the case of Yemen seems more clearly an outgrowth of the intellectual and ideological discussions, transformations, and personal relationships that form in these dialogs. Political generations are more important in the former case, where individuals are more significant in accounting for the latter.

In light of the fact that many of the intellectual precursors to – and instigators of – the cross-ideological forums and dialogs that have emerged can be traced to Egypt, it is not surprising that some of the more successful cases of cross-ideological alignment have developed there as well. Chapter 4 examines the emergence and character of a number of groups and actions, focusing in particular on the Wasat Party and the Kifaya (Enough) movement, each of which represents not only a case of cross-ideological political mobilization, but also ones in which non-Muslims (Copts) have managed to occupy important positions. George Ishaq (b. 1939), one of Kifaya's most prominent leaders, is a Copt, as is Munir 'Abd al-Nur (b. 1945), an economist and vice president of the liberal Wafd Party, and Rafiq Habib (b. 1959), who is not only active in Kifaya but perhaps more importantly founded the Wasat Party with a number of former members of the Muslim Brotherhood. The Kifaya movement's bold entry onto the Egyptian political landscape has not only pushed the Muslim Brotherhood into a more confrontational stance vis-à-vis the Egyptian state, but has also spurred actions of varying sorts under the slogan of "Enough!" in Lebanon (*Kafa*), Morocco (*Baraka*), Tunisia (*Yezzi*), Yemen (*Irhalu*), and Palestine (*Kafa*). However, it is only in Egypt that a movement calling for comprehensive political reform has succeeded in incorporating both secular and non-secular Christians and Muslims.

While the issue of women's status has always provided a point of difference among Islamists, socialists, and nationalists, in the context of Yemen, a cross-ideological oppositional alliance has placed the issue of women's political participation on the agenda of all political parties. Chapter 5 looks at the role of Jaralluh 'Umar (1942–2002) of the Yemeni Socialist Party (YSP), Muhammad 'Abd al-Malik al-Mutawakil (b. 1942) of the liberal Islamic Union of Popular Forces (UPF), and a number of modernists in the Islamist party, the Yemeni Reform Gathering (Islah) – such as Muhammad Yadumi, Muhammad Qahtan and 'Abd al-Wahhab al-Anisi – in forging what has come to be known as the Joint Meeting Parties (JMP), a coalition which includes not only the YSP, Islah, and UPF, but also the Popular Nasirist Unity Organization and the conservative Zaydi Party (al-Haq). While talks among JMP members stalled many times over the issue of women's status, as well as over questions regarding the role of Islamic law in the Yemeni constitution, issues upon which Islah and the YSP in particular could not agree, in November 2005 the group published "The Program of the Joint Meeting for Political and National Reform," which listed the promotion of women among its goals, though Islah had not yet formally decided whether they could support women running for public office. Subsequent statements from Islah leaders affirmed their commitment to women's political engagement. The JMP alliance was further consolidated with the choice of a single candidate to oppose President Salih in the election held in September 2006.

The book's concluding chapter returns to the central question that animates this study (What are the implications for the thought and practice of the groups and actors who enter into such coalitions?), and offers the following conclusion: rather than ideological convergence or end, what these examples of cross-ideological alliances and the discussions at the National-Islamic Conferences over the past decade represent is a significant attempt at rapprochement and accommodation, one that reveals both the increasing impact of liberal discourse on a wide variety of groupings, and the persistence of various illiberal oppositional frames that both enable cross-ideological collaboration and limit the formation of a more progressive political opposition.

NOTES

1. The use of the term "Islamism" throughout this work refers to an ideological understanding of Islam that actively seeks to apply Islamic precepts to all spheres of life. See Michaelle Browers. "The Secular Bias of Ideology Studies and the Problem of Islamism," *Journal of Political Ideologies* 10 (2005), 75–93.
2. Hasan al-Banna. *Risala al-mu'tamar al-khamis* (Letter of the Fifth Conference) (Cairo: Dar al-kitab al-'arabi, n.d.), 47. Yet Banna also proves critical of nationalist perspectives that take secular forms, that involve a revival of pre-Islamic traditions, or that divide Arab Muslims from non-Arab Muslims.
3. Michael 'Aflaq. *Choice of Texts from the Ba'th Party Founder's Thought* (Florence: Cooperativa Lavoratori, 1977).
4. Muhammad al-Ghazzali. *Our Beginning in Wisdom*, tr. Ismail al-Faruqi (Washington, DC: American Council of Learned Societies, 1953), 35. Originally published as *Min huna na'lam* (Cairo: Dar al-kitab al-'arabi, 1950).
5. Yusuf al-Qaradawi. *al-Hulul al-mustawrada wa kayfa janat 'ala ummatina* (How Imported Solutions Disastrously Affected our Community) (Cairo: Maktaba wahba, 1977).
6. al-Ghazzali. *Our Beginning in Wisdom*, 81.
7. See the summary of such cooperation in Egypt, Jordan and Yemen by Jillian Schwedler and Janine A. Clark. "Islamist-Leftist Cooperation in the Arab World," *ISIM Review* 18 (Autumn 2006), 10–11.
8. Bassam Tibi. *Arab Nationalism: Between Islam and the Nation-State*, 3rd edn (New York: Saint Martin's Press, 1997), 202. Tibi's phrasing is a reference to Munir Muhammad Najib's 1981 work, *al-Harakat al-qawmiyya al-haditha fi al-mizan al-islam* (The Modern Nationalist Movements on the Balance of Islam).
9. Tibi. *Arab Nationalism*, 217.
10. Emmanuel Sivan. "Arab Nationalism in the Age of Islamic Resurgence" in Israel Gershoni and James Jankowski (eds.), *Rethinking Nationalism in the Middle East* (Columbia University Press, 1997), 210, 213.

11. See Fauzi M. Najjar. "Islamic Fundamentalism and the Intellectuals: The Case of Nasr Hamid Abu Zayd," *British Journal of Middle Eastern Studies* 27 (2000), 177–200. In 1995 an Egyptian court declared that Abu Zayd's academic writings proved he was a heretic (*murtad*). Facing threats from Islamists and the annulment of his marriage (since a Muslim woman cannot be married to a non-Muslim man), Abu Zayd fled his homeland for the Netherlands. He is currently a professor of Arabic and Islamic Studies at Leiden University.
12. Leonard Binder. *Islamic Liberalism: A Critique of Development Ideologies* (University of Chicago Press, 1988), 244.
13. Binder. *Islamic Liberalism*, 245. Binder also suggests that "the idea of an oppositional alliance between the left and the Muslim Brotherhood [in Egypt] may already be an anachronism because the ideal target for such a collation was Sadat, and the ideal moment was the time of his assassination. That moment came and went, and Egypt was rid of Sadat without the need of the leftist intellectuals who have once again been set back on their heels and have taken to musing about what might have been." Alliances that have emerged over the past decade do not bear out Binder's assessment. Events in Egypt in particular suggest that the moment for cooperation between the Muslim Brotherhood and segments of the left has not, in fact, passed.
14. Binder. *Islamic Liberalism*, 17, 359.
15. Sivan. "Arab Nationalism," 219.
16. François Burgat. *Face to Face with Political Islam* (London: I. B. Tauris, 2003), xiv.
17. Quoted in Mark Huband. *Warriors of the Prophet: The Struggle for Islam* (Boulder: Westview Press, 1999), 105. 'Isa is associated with the Nasirist party in Egypt.
18. Paul Salem. *Bitter Legacy: Ideology and Politics in the Arab World* (Syracuse University Press, 1994), 26–27, 260.
19. Salem. *Bitter Legacy*, 276.
20. Olivier Roy. *The Failure of Political Islam*, tr. Carol Volk (Harvard University Press, 1994), 97, 269.
21. Salem describes the period following the *Nahda* as the "age of ideology" in the Arab world – with the 1950s marking the "heyday of ideology" and the end of ideology commencing by the early 1970s. *Bitter Legacy*. 2, 6.
22. For a full review of this literature, see Jillian Schwedler. *Faith in Moderation: Islamist Parties in Jordan and Yemen* (Cambridge University Press, 2006), ch. 1.
23. This is noted by Janine A. Clark. "The Conditions of Islamist Moderation: Unpacking Cross-Ideological Cooperation in Jordan," *International Journal of Middle East Studies* 38 (2006), 541.
24. Schwedler and Clark organized two conferences to study Islamist–leftist cooperation: at the European University Institute and the Robert Schuman Center for Advanced Studies Mediterranean Programme in March 2004, and at Rockefeller Foundation Conference Centre in Bellagio in August 2005. My own work benefited tremendously from participation in the 2004 workshop.

25. Schwedler. *Faith in Moderation*, 192.

26. Schwedler. *Faith in Moderation*, 195.

27. Clark. "The Conditions of Islamist Moderation," 539–560. See Clark for a useful overview of a number of studies that test the cooperation-moderation relation.

28. Michael Freeden. *Ideology: A Very Short Introduction* (Oxford University Press, 2003), 79, his emphasis. Freeden's more extended account of the workings of ideologies is found in *Ideologies and Political Theory: A Conceptual Approach* (Oxford University Press, 1998).

29. *The Egyptian Gazette* (June 9, 2006). Habib and other Islamists note that their leaders always operate within the strict organizational structure and parameters of the group. While Habib considerably overstates the conformity within his ranks, his statement does contain a measure of truth when one compares the unity achieved by the Brotherhood with the internal conflicts that plague most other political groups.

30. Raymond William Baker. *Islam Without Fear: Egypt and the New Islamists* (Harvard University Press, 2003).

31. Binder's remains the most important work for capturing this transformation on the part of secular thinkers. Thus, despite some differences between our interpretations of particular thinkers, my understanding of Bishri's trajectory of thought follows that first outlined in *Islamic Liberalism*.

1   Retreat from secularism in Arab nationalist and socialist thought

Secular ideologies, particularly Arab nationalism and socialism, dominated the landscape of Arab political thought throughout much of the
1950s and 1960s. But as early as 1966, the Palestinian political scientist, Ibrahim Abu-Lughod (1929–2001), had begun to detect signs of a
"retreat from the secular path" among intellectuals in the Arab region.[1]
The waning appeal of secular ideologies became increasingly apparent in the wake of the Arab–Israeli war of 1967, even though many of
the first criticisms that emerged as part of the "self-criticism after the
defeat"[2] remained largely secular in character, with some intellectuals on the left asserting an even more uncompromisingly anti-religious
stance. With the Arab–Israeli war of 1973, the idea that a unified Arab
front was a precondition for successfully confronting Israel was challenged by state-based or more particularist Arab approaches to overcoming the weakness of Arab states vis-à-vis Israel.[3] However, it is in
the aftermath of the Islamic revolution in Iran that one sees most clearly
not only a sharp rise in Islamist critiques of secular ideologies, but also
the emergence of "new partisans of the heritage" (*turathiyyun judud*)[4]
from a seemingly unlikely source: within the ranks of Arab nationalists
and socialists.

   This chapter examines the political thought of various Arab nationalist
and socialist intellectuals in whose writings one can detect development
over time from a decidedly secular perspective to a reconsidered position
that either places greater emphasis on Islamic authenticity as a necessary
component of a national awakening or attempts to synthesize aspects of
their thinking with Islamism. I am fully aware that dealing with these
particular thinkers under the heading of "Arab nationalists and socialists," while treating another set of thinkers under the title of "Islamism"
in Chapter 2 – including Muhammad al-'Imara (Egypt, b. 1931) and
Muhammad Salim al-'Awa (Egypt, b. 1942), who began their intellectual careers as leftists but now subscribe to political Islam – will not go
uncontested. No scheme of classification can be adequate, especially in
dealing with intellectuals whose careers span so many decades – in some

cases, half a century – and whose desire for progressive political change has had to account for so much turmoil and tumult. However, as will be demonstrated, among the thinkers discussed here, neither those who prioritize issues of authenticity (*'asala*) and the Arab-Islamic heritage (*turath*), nor the theorists of Arab-Islamic civilizational unity, have joined the ranks of the Islamists. Although Ahmad Sidqi al-Dajani (Palestine, 1936–2003), Muhammad 'Abid al-Jabri (Morocco, b. 1936) and Anwar Abdel-Malek (Egypt, b. 1924) have distanced themselves from Western secularism, they do not subscribe to the political programs of the main Islamist opposition groups, in contrast to the intellectuals discussed in Chapter 2. Many thinkers, such as Jabri and Abdel-Malek, continue to keep Islamist groups and spokespersons at arm's length. Tariq al-Bishri (Egypt, b. 1933) and Abelwahab Elmessiri (Egypt, 1938–2008) both began their careers on the left, but have recently been more closely associated with moderate groups among the Islamist trend, primarily through their recent association with – and contributions to – the journal *al-Manar al-jadid*,[5] and the writings of each are distinguished by their lack of reliance on Islamic sources. The relatively recent duration of their association with Islamist groups and their intellectual approach distinguish these thinkers from figures like 'Imara and 'Awa. Those former socialists and communists who sought to establish an "Islamic left" through their conversion to an Islamist political project tend to be viewed with suspicion by the core of Islamists, accused of continuing to subscribe to Marxism or materialism, as has been the case most recently with Hasan Hanafi (Egypt, b. 1935) and has been the case in the past with 'Adil Husayn (Egypt, 1932–2001). Most of the moderate Islamist intellectuals discussed in Chapter 2 find advocates of the Islamic left position to be too radical for their liking. Munir Shafiq (Palestine, b. 1936) may provide the only real exception to this general rule. Not only does he now appeal primarily to Islamist audiences, but recent moderation of his stance has placed him, like Bishri, into sustained conversation with the Islamists discussed in Chapter 2. As a result, Shafiq and Bishri are discussed across both chapters.

Arab nationalist thought and the 1967 defeat

According to Albert Hourani, "the tendency to secularism" has been strong in modern Arab nationalist thought.[6] Although Arab nationalism has never been completely secular, it has based its principle of unity around such factors as language and geography rather than faith. The classic historical account of "the formation of the Arab nation" was penned by the Iraqi historian, 'Abd al-'Aziz al-Duri (b. 1919).[7]

Like Hourani, Duri attributes considerable importance to Islam in the early development of an Arab nationalist consciousness. "Islam," he writes, "united the Arabs, for the first time in history, within the framework of a single state."[8] However, Duri gives the Arab component greater weight in development of the "nationalist awakening." According to his account, Arab consciousness both pre- and post-dates Islam. The Arabic language contributed to development of Arab consciousness prior to the emergence of Islam. While "Islam introduced the idea of the *umma*, the 'Community' of different peoples and tribes bound together by the creed ... the political unity of the Islamic Community was only realized in the period when the Arabs were in power."[9] Although the paths of Islam and Arabism "were closely linked at first," they "subsequently followed separate courses." Further, "while both remained important to Arab development," Duri argues that "it was the successes and failures of Arabism that determined the eventual geographic and human boundaries of the Arab nation."[10] Duri maintains that the *umma* that developed in the region was fundamentally Arab: a community based on the Arabic language and Arabic culture.

However, one must qualify somewhat both Hourani's broad assessment of the secular tendency in early Arab nationalist thought and Duri's account of the shifting priority toward the Arab over the Islamic identity in the modern Middle East. While, in eastern parts of the Arab region (*al-mashriq*), formulation of a concept of nationalism that was not heavily dependent on Islam proved important for incorporating the significant and active Christian minorities into the vision of an Arab nation, in the western Arab regions (*al-maghrib*), the general absence of a Christian minority, along with the presence of an ethnic bifurcation between Berber and Arab, meant that Islam remained a central component of national cohesion. Secularism dominated nationalist thought in the Mashriq to a much greater extent than in the Maghrib. So, too, the impact of the June 1967 Arab–Israeli war was felt most keenly in the Mashriq, though it also reverberated in the Maghrib and raised the question of the relationship between Islam and politics anew in both contexts. In explaining the defeat, two broad trends emerged among Arab nationalist and socialist thinkers. Some, including several of the earliest commentators, suggested that the Arabs lost the war because their military, political systems, and people had not achieved sufficiently high levels of modernization. After the defeat, many young Arab nationalist and socialist intellectuals began to move in a more radical direction than their predecessors in criticizing "traditional" social structures and mentalities, and especially in their rejection of Islam's dominating influence in Arab political thought.

This staunchly secular perspective was articulated most forcefully in the writings of Marxist thinkers, such as Sadiq Jalal al-'Azm (b. 1934) and Nadim al-Baytar. A left-leaning Arab nationalist from Lebanon, Baytar was known as an outspoken critic of religious traditions. Some of his comments brought death threats from Islamic extremists, which, at one point, led Baytar to flee to the United States for a short period. Baytar maintained that ideologies grew out of historical circumstances and were of two types: those ideologies that consider radical society change necessary and those traditional (religious) ideologies that seek to maintain the status quo. In light of pressing needs in the present, Baytar argued that revolutionary ideology must serve as "a new religion to compete with other religions for control over the spirit of the people. Thus, its very birth is tied to its final victory, which must be achieved over the religious."[11] Like many socialists, Baytar understood Islam to form an antithesis of socialism and, thus, viewed attempts to reconcile socialism and religion as self-defeating. Baytar maintain that Arabs were imprisoned by outmoded religious ways of thinking.

The idea that Arabic thought remained in a primitive or supernatural phase and yet to achieve scientific mode of thinking has been restated in a number of later works. One of the most systemic and influential articulation is found in two books written after 1967 by a young radical Syrian philosopher, Sadiq al-'Azm. In *Self-Criticism after the Defeat*, 'Azm compared the 1967 defeat with the Russian defeat by Japan in 1904. In both cases, he argued, the defeat was not just a military one, but also based in the economic, cultural, and scientific conditions of the defeated. In this work, 'Azm placed much of the blame for the defeat on the empty slogans of the Nasirist and Ba'thist representatives of "petty bourgeois Arab nationalism."[12] *Self-Criticism after the Defeat* was followed a year later by *Critique of Religious Thought*, in which 'Azm shifted the target of his critique from regressive nationalism to what he deemed the "religious obscurantism" of Muslim and Christian thinking in the region. Religious thought, 'Azm argued, remained the primary obstacle to development of scientific and rational thinking and, thus, to the social transformation and liberation of Arab society.[13]

The prioritizing of identities or bases of community classically articulated in Duri's historical work has been challenged by the weakness of Arab nationalist regimes and parties. Yet the impact of the Arab defeats is only part of the story. As Sami Zubaida has argued, one must also consider relations of power between secular and religious forces and the ideological transformations taking place within the various groupings. Zubaida notes that "when nationalism ... became state and statist projects ... it became intolerant of any political or ideological initiatives not subordinated to its controls and objectives. Nationalism then did not supplant Islam, but became politically and ideologically differentiated from it."[14] One must add that socialism, in contrast, did not become so clearly differentiated from the state, as Arab nationalist regimes looked to socialist programs – and the Soviet Union – to give substance to their economic politics. Intolerant nationalism gave birth to – and came to confront – a form of Islamic politics that departed significantly from the reformist Islam of Muhammad Abduh and the *Salafiyyun*, which could accommodate nationalist aspirations. The political form of Islam that began to be articulated by Egypt's Muslim Brotherhood in the 1960s was based on a more exclusivist Islam, intolerant of secular nationalism and insistent on seeing Islamic law established as the basis of an Islamic state.

Many Arab nationalist and socialist intellectuals, rather than heeding the criticisms of Baytar and 'Azm, sought instead to tap into the growing popular appeal of political Islam and undertook a project to reformulate their conception of the basis of national unity in a way that draws upon and incorporates aspects of the Islamic heritage. Some secular opposition figures began to advocate cooperation with more progressive elements in the Islamic movement as a way of pursuing nationalist and revolutionary goals. In many cases, alliances were undertaken for solely strategic purposes, and viewed as temporary or limited compromises with an increasingly significant political current. However, some on the left began to articulate positions that suggested a more decided relationship, one that went beyond alliance, or even sympathy, toward a fundamental reconsideration – and some cases, conversion – that included incorporation or legitimization of the Islamic political program, in part, if not as a whole. The Islamic revolution in Iran provided an important juncture for revealing these points of accommodation and transformation.

The formation of an Islamic left: Munir Shafiq, 'Adil Husayn, and Hasan Hanafi

After the Iranian revolution, the lines between secular and religious political visions remained and, in some cases, deepened. However, the voices of those seeking to tie together the strands of Islamic and Arab nationalist thought that had separated and frayed under the post-independence states could also be heard more loudly. Mona Abaza has noted how, in the 1980s, in the wake of the Arab defeats, and inspired by the triumph of the Islamic revolution in Iran, a number of Arab intellectuals on the left began to think it necessary "to revolutionize Islam as a prolongation of a nationalist project."[15] A new trend among Arab socialists emerged as a number of well-known Marxists "converted" to a religious-based notion of revolution and liberation. Sami Zubaida notes how the ideas of the Iranian sociologist 'Ali Shari'ati (1933–1977), who drew concepts of Islamic activism and revolution from reading Marx, Franz Fanon, and Jean-Paul Sartre, as well as from (shi'i) Islam, proved "enormously attractive to a generation of intellectuals and activists seeking revolution and liberation, but with an 'authentic' cultural lineage," including a number of Egyptian socialists and Nasirists who sought to tap into the popular appeal of political Islam and/or looked to religion "as the authentic vehicle of popular contestation and national liberation."[16] Many of these newly Islamicized revolutionaries attempted to merge Third Worldist dependency theories – which emphasized resistance to dependence upon the world market and global capitalism, economic planning, social justice, and welfare – with the ideology of Islamism that was gaining popular appeal in the 1980s.

Perhaps the most dramatic conversion to an Islamist position was undertaken by Munir Shafiq, a Christian Palestinian from Jerusalem. Shafiq began as a Marxist–Leninist revolutionary, active in the Democratic People's Front for the Liberation of Palestine. His earliest works bore such titles as *Marxism–Leninism and the Theory of Revolutionary War* and *Science of War*.[17] In the wake of the Arab defeats, Shafiq began to undertake an analysis of the breakdown of Arab unity and the failure of pan-Arab ideals to bring about fundamental social, political, and economic transformations. Shafiq sought a new and more solid basis for unity than either Marxism or Arab nationalism seemed capable of providing.[18] Around 1980, he converted to Islam and proclaimed his new religion's role as the "civilizational center" for renewal and unity.[19] During this period and while working at the Fatah headquarters in Tunis, he joined the Palestinian Islamic Jihad group. Today Shafiq acts as an important ideologue and spokesperson for Hamas.

Shafiq came to understand the Arab world as divided into two sectors: a modernized, secular, Westernized elite, on the one hand, and a more traditional – or what he terms "original" – segment of society, on the other hand. The former collaborate with the West in order to divide the Arabs and increase the region's dependence on the West. Shafiq accuses the ruling elites of imitating foreign ways of living and of modeling Arab states according to the dictates of Western powers, to which they then remain subservient. In contrast to the Westernized elites, he maintains that inhabitants of the "original societies," who constitute the overwhelming majority of Arabs, remain rural and solidly grounded in traditional, Islamic ways of life. It is in the latter, more rooted identity that Shafiq locates a dynamic force with revolutionary potential. In the language of Shafiq's Islamic understanding of dependency theory, the Arab masses exist on the periphery, alienated and dominated, but a revolutionary revival of Islamic values can mobilize them against the center – that is, the secular West and their representatives who rule the Arab countries – in order to achieve true independence and social justice.[20]

Both the path of Shafiq's intellectual development, as well as the revolutionary Islamist position he comes to advocate, bear many similarities with two Egyptian intellectuals, 'Adil Husayn and Hasan Hanafi. Husayn was the youngest half-brother of Ahmad Husayn, the founder and leader in the 1930s of Young Egypt (*Misr al-fatat*), a right-wing nationalist movement modeling itself in part on European fascist groups. Ahmad Husayn began his political activism fighting against British occupation and later joined the underground communist movement. As a result of his activism, Husayn was imprisoned between 1953 and 1956 under the Nasser regime's policy of suppressing any vocal or independent elements in the opposition. After his release he obtained a university degree before being jailed again. (Husayn would be jailed again in 1994, thus earning him the dubious distinction of having served time under three Egyptian presidents.) After his release in 1964, he began working as a journalist and writer and began his first intellectual shift, from communism to a radical Arab nationalist stance that drew from dependency theory approaches. Among his early major works is a two-volume study, entitled *The Egyptian Economy from Independence to Dependency, 1974–1979*, which offered a critical examination of economic conditions wrought by the "Open Door" policies of Anwar Sadat.[21] This controversial study was followed by two more that looked at economic relations that were beginning to develop between Egypt and Israel, one of which carried the provocative title of *Normalization: The Zionist Plan for Economic Hegemony*.[22]

Already in the mid-1970s, Husayn could be heard calling for an end to what he termed the "absurd polarisation" between Marxist and Islamist political forces in Egypt, which he saw as responsible for weakening the opposition as a whole vis-à-vis the regime.[23] According to Husayn, the left must ally with more radical segments of the Islamic movement in order to increase the strength and appeal of both trends. After the Iranian revolution, however, Husayn came to believe that socialism, when understood from the perspective of Marxism, was no more relevant to the specificities of Arab-Islamic societies than capitalism, since both socialism and capitalism were offspring of the West. In a 1985 work, entitled *Toward a New Arab Thought: Nasirism, Development and Democracy*,

Husayn urges Arab intellectuals to break free from Western domination and to develop authentic models of development and democracy that draw from the particular historical experiences embedded in the Arab-Islamic heritage and that appeal to – and are anchored in – the religious sentiment of the masses.[24] As Zubaida notes, "Hussain's model is essentially that of a national Arab state, in which Islam is a crucial element," but does not offer any particular institutional mode.[25] Rather, Islam in Husayn's revolutionary project seems to be most significant as a rhetorical framework that permits distinction from the West and appeals to the masses. Only an authentic (that is, Islamic) vision can bring about a rebirth and establish balance in Arab society, in Husayn's view. But only the most general contours of the "post-revolutionary" and Islamic aspects of Husayn's new project are provided.

Husayn's intellectual and religious transformation had a significant impact on Egypt's Labor Party, which he joined in 1984. He served as editor of the party's newspaper, al-Sha'b, between 1985 and 1993. As Salwa Ismail has demonstrated, prior to Husayn's arrival the paper emphasized the party's relationship to Nasser and to socialist principles, but, beginning in the mid-1980s, paper and party increasingly articulated Islamist themes and stressed its similarities to Muslim Brotherhood principles and positions.[26] Under Husayn's editorship, al-Sha'b's pages were opened to leaders and members of the Muslim Brotherhood. This shift in ideology culminated in an alliance between the Labor Party, the Muslim Brotherhood, and the Liberal Party (Hizb al-ahrar) in 1987 under the slogan "Islam is the Solution." While the Labor Party has remained generally Islamist ever since, Ismail notes that subsequent to the 1987 alliance, more conservative forces within the Brotherhood have sought to force more leftist elements out of the Labor Party, and were largely successful in doing so. At the same time, differences between the Labor Party and the Muslim Brotherhood began to emerge, particularly in regard to the stance toward the Mubarak regime.[27] It is only in the past decade that Egypt's Muslim Brotherhood began to recover from the backlash over Sadat's assassination and came to occupy a position of rapprochement with the government and, in the wake of a series of bombings of tourist sites by radical Islamists, the party's leadership proved more conservative than revolutionary during this period.

Husayn maintained his claim to be part of the Islamist current throughout the 1990s, despite the fact that the Muslim Brotherhood seemed to keep him at arm's length. Whereas many of his earlier books were published by Arab nationalist and socialist organizations, like the Center for Arab Unity Studies in Beirut and the Future Studies Center in Cairo, throughout the 1990s many of Husayn's books were published in a new series, entitled "Islam and Issues of the Age," by the Arab-Islamic Center for Studies in al-Sayyida Zaynab, and covered themes such as the *Arab-Iranian Front Against the American-Zionist Alliance, 1991–1993.*[28] He also oversaw the compilation and publication of various writings on women by Shaykh Muhammad Mutawalli Sha'rawi (1911–1998), a popular Egyptian preacher who held many high profile positions, including President of al-Azhar, Head of Graduate Studies at King 'Abd al-'Aziz University in Mecca, and Minister of Awqaf (religious endowments) in Egypt (1976–1978).[29] Sha'rawi became a popular figure largely through his radio and television broadcasts, including appearances on Egypt's first Islamic discussion television program, *Nur 'ala nur* (Light on Light).

The coining of the phrase "Islamic Left", and the attempt to develop a synthesis between socialism and Islamism in a manner akin to liberation theologies in Latin America, can be credited to Hasan Hanafi, a professor of philosophy at the University of Cairo. Trained in philosophy at the Sorbonne, where he studied with Paul Ricouer and received a doctorate in philosophy in 1966, Hanafi returned to Egypt a left-wing phenomenologist. By Hanafi's own account, like Sayyid Qutb, whose experience in America contributed to his development of an Islamist sentiment, Hanafi's four years in America initiated a shift in his academic and political focus toward what he calls "revolutionary religion," a concept that acquired additional impetus after the revolution in Iran.

Between 1979 and 1980, Hanafi edited, wrote the introduction to, and supervised the translation into Arabic of two books by Imam Khomeini: *Wilayat-i faqih* (translated as "Islamic Government" [*al-Hukuma al-islamiyya*], rather than the more literal – and distinctly Shi'i – "guardianship of the jurist"), and *Jihad al-nafs, aw jihad al-akbar* (Struggle with the Self, or the Greatest Jihad).[30] In his introduction to Khomeini's *Islamic Government*, Hanafi characterizes the Iranian revolution as not exclusively a Shi'i revolution but as embodying a broader revival of Islam in the tradition of Afghani, Mawdudi, and Qutb – a revolutionary Islam that affirms the necessity of Islamic government in the contemporary age as a means of confronting imperialism and Zionism and for overcoming the exploitation and oppression of Muslims throughout the world.[31]

In 1981, Hanafi issued the first and only issue of a journal, called a*l-Yasar al-islami* (Islamic Left), in an effort to fuse leftist and Islamist ideologies and as the first step in launching an Islamic left movement to bring about a revolution.[32] Hanafi characterized his movement as a combination of Islamic and Nasirist elements: "Islam is in the heart of the masses and Nasserism is in their need. Islam without Nasserism falls into formalism, as in the case of Islamic groups. Nasserism without Islam will fall into secularism and will always be threatened by an Islamic movement."[33] Hanafi maintains that had Qutb not been imprisoned and tortured under the Nasir regime – the circumstances that Hanafi argues account for Qutb's conservative turn – he would have lived out his life according to its more natural course, continuing to develop and carry on a form of scientific socialism that corresponded with his Islamic faith. In fact, Hanafi further speculates that, had he lived, Qutb would have become "one of the pillars of the Islam Left in Egypt."[34]

Hanafi has also produced comprehensive interpretations of religion and philosophy, including a multi-volume work, under the title *The Heritage and Renewal*, that aim at the radical reconstruction of religious thought in relation to particular, concrete, historical existence – an approach he characterizes as "phenomenological," thus, drawing upon his philosophical training. This reading offers an "anthropocentric," as opposed to "theocentric," view of Islam, in which human beings and their needs form the center of the interpretation. The aim of this reading is to reconstruct "Islamic culture at the level of consciousness in order to discover subjectivity. Instead of being theocentric, it becomes anthropocentric. [It] provides the method for analyzing lived experiences and describing the process of linguistic pseudo-morphology."[35] Hanafi seeks to contribute to a revolutionary religious consciousness capable of confronting modern conditions of inequality, poverty, underdevelopment, domination, Westernization, and alienation. The heritage provides the "psychological storehouse" of the masses, the basis for the renewal of the dynamic aspects of Islamic civilization, and can be put into the service of solving the crisis and addressing the needs of the present age.[36]

Hanafi's project further encompasses an explicit critique of the West. His call for renewal of the heritage is put forth as an alternative to modernization understood as Westernization, a sort of "modernization from within" – that is, a way of moving forward by retaining the national, cultural, and religious specificities (*khususiyya*). In order to encourage Muslims to be producers rather than merely consumers, Hanafi seeks to construct a science of Occidentalism through which social scientists from the Orient can explore Western civilization in a way that rises from being an object of Orientalism toward devising it as a subject of their own. The contents and structures of Western consciousness must be "relativized," he argues, in order to curtail their influence, while the content and structures of the East's won heritage are emphasized. Hanafi insists that European modernity should not be considered the only route to civilization, but as merely one of a number of parallel points and paths in history, including Egypt, China, and other civilizations of the ancient Orient. Hanafi's method of Occidentalism seeks to draw from both the Arab-Islamic heritage and the experiences of Europe, but in a way that mediates the authority the latter has claimed throughout history, while still managing to address the modern age. Looking at religion and culture from a global perspective, Hanafi believes, restores the historical dimension to Western thought – that is, it refutes its claim to universality and dominance, and thus returns European civilization to what he terms its "natural size."[37] This theme of relativizing and historicizing Western civilization has been reiterated by a number of other Arab writers. For example, in a 1983 book, the Egyptian Coptic writer and Marxist, Anwar Abdel-Malek, argued that the "winds of history" are moving East – that is, the center of world history is moving from the West (Europe and the United States) to a center in East Asia and China that is in the process of shaping a new world.[38] He has further argued that more recent conflicts in the Middle East provide evidence for his theory.[39] Malek represents another Marxist intellectual who praised the revolutionary force of the revolution that took place in Iran and has revealed an increased sympathy to Islamist groups over the past two decades (though he has fallen far short of converting to Islam or the Islamic left).

In the writings of the Islamic left, an "authentic" collective identity is to substitute for Marxist class consciousness. "Foreignness" comes to occupy the position of enemy previously held by "backwardness."[40] Authenticity, in the sense Hanafi and Husayn understand it, lies in the Islamic heritage, which is embedded in the hearts and minds of the masses, and stands in contrast to the imported political and cultural ideas of Western intellectuals and ideologies. In this sense, the construction of an Islamic left shares much with another, related strand of Arab political thought, which situates its critique of the present constellation of political and intellectual forces in the tradition of the Arab *nahda* (enlightenment), but also seeks to renew Arab society through a critical engagement with both the West and the heritage.

The challenges of authenticity and renewal: reinterpreting the heritage and the West

In a context where the present was perceived as a period of decline, return to the past heritage (*turath*) validates that sense of decline by providing a point of reference against which the present can be measured. The present offers an inauthentic mode of being, an un-Arab or un-Islamic state from the perspective of the past. Although *turath* studies predate the series of disasters and defeats experienced between 1967 and 1973, in the post-1967 period these studies increase, the ideological range of intellectuals undertaking such studies broadens and the debate over the heritage becomes increasingly centered on engagement between Islamist and non-Islamist thinkers. While for Islamists this authenticity (*asala*) is measured in terms of Islam, the sense of crisis (*'azma*) – a general sense of dissatisfaction with the state of the present – was said to require a more authentic response than those offered in the past, and even Arab nationalist and socialist intellectuals began to study the Arab-Islamic *turath* as a way of overcoming present problems. As Robert D. Lee has rightly noted, the concern for authenticity among Muslim thinkers need not be about Islam nor provide religious arguments, but is most fundamentally a response to "a context in which modernity has eroded cultures, values and identities without repairing what has been damaged."[41] While none of these intellectuals can be said to have adopted an Islamist position (unlike the "converts" discussed above), their engagement with the heritage constitutes an engagement with Islamist discourses and a response to the rise of Islamic movements as the mass appeal of secular ideologies was waning. And through their engagement with the Arab-Islamic heritage, Arab nationalist and socialist intellectuals began to find meeting points and to develop a shared language with Islamists, even as considerable ideological differences remained.

One of the most significant similarities lies in the way in which authenticity comes to be measured against the West. Jaques Waardenburg has identified five conceptualizations of "the West" that have been articulated by Muslim intellectuals in the Middle East: the West as an essentialized Occident; the West as a political power and potential enemy; the West as the source of modernity; the West as a way of life unburdened with traditions; the West as a modern *jahiliyya* (barbarism), "a disintegrating society in which egoism and human solitude prevail."[42] While each of these different "Wests" could be found in different phases and places and with different connotations in Muslim writings during the latter half of the twentieth century, Waardenburg detects a shift from many more positive or neutral conceptions of the West toward a more anti-Western discourse. While this shift first became apparent among Islamists, such as Sayyid Qutb and Abu A'la Mawdudi, who viewed the West as the embodiment of modern barbarism and godlessness, it has become increasingly apparent in some of the writings of Muslim intellectuals who had earlier considered the West an object of admiration, and a source of inspiration for political, social, and economic progress as well. The concern for authenticity and the call for re-examination of the Arab-Islamic heritage fuel this negative image, by imbuing the encounter between the West and the Arab region in cultural terms.

According to the Moroccan philosopher, Muhammad 'Abid al-Jabri, the general sense of crisis (*azma*) that today pervades the Arab context can be traced back to the failure of the *nahda* project and the profound uneasiness brought about by the disjuncture this project created between Arab thought's fundamental framework of reference (the Arab-Islamic heritage) and the demands of the contemporary historical situation.[43] The crisis, Jabri argues, is something experienced at the level of consciousness, as a form of cultural disorder in which the individual becomes increasingly unable to relate social and political ideas and values to his or her life situation.[44] Although Jabri criticizes Arab thought for glorifying the past and seeking within it ready-made solutions to present problems, his project is, in large part, an attempt to reform Arabic thought from within the context of the *turath*, to reinvest the heritage in the present.

Non-Islamist intellectuals who undertake the renewal of the *turath* tend to include an analysis of the pre-Islamic period as part of their privileging of the Arabic element in the heritage and their historicization of Islam, which becomes a social phenomenon that takes place within a particular time, with particular social, economic, and linguistic context. Aziz al-Azmeh articulates this approach in arguing that "Islam is not an essence that determines the cultural, social and political particularity of society." But, rather, a given society has its own specificities of which Islam forms one part.[45] Similarly, Jabri argues that "existence precedes essence" in the sense that the essence of Islam is not fixed but always in the process of formation within given historical and empirical circumstances.[46] In an early study of how Arab thought should view its intellectual heritage, the Lebanese Marxist Husayn Muruwa (1910–1987) argued that one should not privilege the past over the present (as Islamists tend to do), but one also cannot see the present independent of the past.[47] In his two-volume work on *Materialist Tendencies in Arab Islamic Philosophy*, published in 1975, Muruwa argues that Arabs should approach their intellectual heritage in light of the revolutionary orientations of the present, through a historical materialist approach that sees the dialectical relationship between the past with its social structure and the present with its social structure.[48]

Jabri's approach also comprises a dialectical understanding of the re-reading of history, but focuses more attention on how that history emerges in the Arab-Islamic engagement with the West that begins with Islam's encounter with Greek philosophy. According to Jabri, the task before Arab intellectuals necessitates recovery of the rationalist dimensions of Arab thought, which both precede and are embodied in this productive period of Islamic philosophy and hold continuing relevance in the present. This does not mean that one should adopt a European cultural frame of reference, something Jabri faults early Muslim liberals of doing in their attempts to modernize. Rather, Jabri locates his model for rationalism in the thought of Ibn Rushd (Averroes), who he credits with presenting an alternative to the separation of religion and philosophy by locating a rationalist (rather than spiritualist or fundamentalist, both of which he deems "subjective") understanding of religion.[49] For Jabri, Ibn Rushd's approach is in this sense pre-secular and, thus, preferable as a mode that allows achievement of both authenticity and contemporaneity. Following Ibn Rushd, Jabri maintains that there exists a correspondence (*tawafuq*), not harmonization (*tawfiq*), between religion and reason, and the two will always remain distinct but not opposed as two modes of apprehending a single truth.

While some analysts have located a form of rationalism in Jabri's critique that they have characterized as "secular," Jabri does not refer to it as such; rather, he calls it "objective." The other main "referential authority" Jabri seeks to deconstruct is the Western Enlightenment and the secular Marxist and liberal ideologies it gave birth to. Implicit in Jabri's question of "how should we deal with the heritage?" is the question of how to remain authentic in a way that both engages both the Arab-Islamic heritage and addresses the needs of a contemporary reality that has inherited the legacies of Western colonialism and domination. While clearly Jabri is working to connect Arab-Islamic and Western political thought, he also takes great pains to distinguish his thinking from conventional understandings of both traditions. On a number of occasions, Jabri has maintained that efforts to position one's self and one's opponents under the banner of "secularism" or "Islamism" are a way of avoiding other, more pressing concerns.

The question of secularism in the Arab world is a false question (*masala muzayyafa*), insofar as expresses real needs by reference to categories which do not correspond to them: the need for independence within a single national identity, the need for a democracy which protects the rights of minorities and the need for the rational practice of political action. All of these are objective – even reasonable and necessary – needs in the Arab world. However, they lose their justification and necessity when expressed through the use of dubious slogans like "secularism."[50]

Democracy, according to Jabri's formulation, consists of the protection of rights, both individual and collective rights; and rationalism means a political practice based on logical and ethical standards, "rather than on identity, fanaticism, or fickleness." Thus, the exclusion of Islam from politics is neither democratic, nor rational, in his view.[51]

"Islam," Jabri argues, "is not a church that we can separate from the state."[52] While in some respects, Jabri's position echoes those Islamists who maintain Islam is both a religion and a state (*Islam din wa dawla*), it is also clear that Jabri means something else. Jabri maintains that it is a historical fact that Islam formed Arabs into a religion and a state. But it is also a fact, he says, that that state and its form was not designated in the text of the Qur'an or in the accounts (*hadith*) of the prophet. Rather, the form that the state ultimately took was a decision made by Muslims. What Jabri means in asserting that "Islam is not a church that we can separate from the state," is that just as historically the Arabs constituted the "matter of Islam," so too Islam is part of the "spirit" of the Arabs. As such, Islam becomes a basis for the Arab community: "the spiritual Islam for the Arab Muslims and the civilizational Islam for all Arabs – Muslims or non-Muslim."[53] Jabri's recent work suggests that Islam and Arabism are the basis of a renewed identity – one that will be realized through democratization of the region.[54]

Jabri is not the only Arab intellectual willing to go to great lengths to differentiate his or her perspective from that of secularism. In a recent essay, Abelwahab Elmessiri, a former professor of English Literature at 'Ayn Shams University in Egypt, attempts to bypass problems associated with a secular stance in a climate dominated by the discourse of Islamic authenticity by establishing a distinction between two forms of secularism: partial secularism and comprehensive secularism. Partial secularism, he argues, "can coexist with absolute moral values, and even with religious values, as long as they do not interfere with the political process."[55] While many Christians and Muslims would accept, and some even welcome, this form of secularism, since it frees religion from the compromises of politics and economics, they would not accept what he calls "comprehensive secularism," which aims "at the separation of all values (be they religious, moral, human) not only from 'the state'; but also from public and private life, and from the world at large."[56] Whether or not Elmessiri's assessment is correct, it is clear that he wants to distinguish his position from the secularism that was separated from, and has proven difficult to reconcile with, contemporary Islamist discourses.

Toward an Arab-Islamic unity: Dajani and Bishri

The Palestinian historian Ahmad Sidqi al-Dajani is often credited with being among the first Arab nationalist intellectuals to undertake a concerted effort not only to reach out to Islamists after they had been criminalized and anathemized by Arab nationalist regimes, but also to assert a concept of Islamic community (*al-umma al-islamiyya*) as an integral element of Arab unity. A member of the Palestinian National Council (PNC) since its inception in 1964, Dajani served on the Executive Committee of the Palestinian Liberation Organization from 1966–1977 and again from 1977 to 1985, when he was the chair of the education and culture department. He was also chair of the PNC's Culture, Science and Literature Committee. Dajani has been associated with the cause of pan-Arabism and Palestinian liberation throughout his life. Dajani responded to the October 1973 war by rearticulating an understanding of the Palestinian cause as the central component of struggle of the "Arab nation" (*al-watan al-arabi*).[57] Shortly after the war, Dajani began to act as a PLO representative in a series of Euro-Arab dialogs held between 1973 and 1978, which aimed to improve relations between the neighboring regions. In an article analyzing these dialogs and outlining the Arab attempt to convince Europe to "adopt an unambiguous and even-handed attitude to the Arab cause," Dajani places blame for the failure of the talks squarely at the feet of the United States, which, he argues, sought to limit Europe's political role in the Arab region so that it would be free to pursue its own interests there.[58] After the Iranian revolution, Dajani seemed to have become considerably less interested in dialog with the West and more convinced that there was a cultural divide that would not be soon or easily traversed. In his writings during this period, Dajani began a process of reframing the Palestinian struggle from an Arab nationalist framework to one that saw the conflict as the central component in the confrontation between Islam and the West.[59] In 1990, Dajani published the book that is credited with coining the phrase "Arab-Islamic Civilizational Circle" and with offering a first formulation of the way in which a cultural nationalism could embody both Arab nationalist and Islamist perspectives.[60] By 1997, the tent of this cross-ideological grouping became even more broadly conceived when Dajani, along with 'Isam Muhammad Hassan and Muhammad Sayyid Ahmad, composed a study of *The Renewal of Political Thought in the Framework of Democracy and Human Rights: Islamic, Marxist and Nationalist Trends.*[61]

After September 11, 2001, and the US "war on terror" that followed, Dajani's critique became even more precise. The United States' support of Israel was part of the former's confrontation with Islam. A war of globalization, he argued, was being waged under the leadership of the United States to impose its hegemony on the world and rob the Middle East of its natural resources, such as oil. This war was being waged, Dajani argued, against all who would oppose the United States. Dajani's analysis of how Islam had come to embody the civilizational "other" in the American crusade offers an illustration of the way in which notions such as the "clash of civilizations" carry within them a sort of self-fulfilling prophecy. In a book entitled *Jerusalem, the al-Aqsa Intifada and the War of Globalization*, Dajani adopted the language of Islamic *jihadis* in characterizing suicide bombings as "martyrdom in the name of God" and praising such actions as a legitimate form of resistance against Israel and the United States in their quest for domination and hegemony.[62] Dajani's ideas were widely discussed in the Arabic press and resonated with a public increasingly frustrated by US intervention in the region.

Dajani's ability to work across ideological divides in the Arab region was vital to the success of many of the forums that are discussed in Chapter 3 of the present work, such as National-Islamic Dialogue held in Cairo in 1989, an important precursor to the National-Islamic Conferences, which he helped establish in 1994, and for which he served as the first coordinator-general, a position he held until poor health (and his passing) forced him to pass that role onto Muhammad ʿAbd al-Malik al-Mutawakkil of Yemen. Dajani's delivery of the opening address to the first National-Islamic Conference was supported by both sides, and his relentless emphasis on the Palestinian issue kept the most uncontested issue of common ground in plain sight of conference participants.

Development of a cultural, Islamic emphasis in nationalist thinking is also seen in the work of the Egyptian Tariq al-Bishri, who is the author of some of the most sustained attempts to formulate an ideological framework that reconciles Islamic and nationalist concerns. Like Dajani, Bishri also has played a particularly important role in the series of forums that have put Arab intellectuals and activists from diverse ideological trends in dialog. Although often cited as a historian based on his early works, which covered the modern history of Egypt, Bishri graduated from the Faculty of Law at Cairo University, where he also taught before becoming a judge. During the Nasir years, Bishri held a number of positions. From 1998 until his retirement in 2001, Bishri served as the first deputy chair of the *Majlis al-dawla* (Council of State), an administrative court and advisory body to the state on matters of constitutional legality modeled after the French *Conseil d'Etat*. Bishri's grandfather was Shaykh al-Azhar from 1900 to 1918, which may add to his credentials among Islamists.

The corpus of Bishri's thought constitutes a project aimed at creating a shared conception of the past as a basis for political unity in the present. Yet his work also reveals a move away from more socialist-inspired analysis toward greater appreciation of the role of Islam in Arab society.

In the 1960s and for most of the 1970s, Bishri's intellectual project provided a secular nationalist perspective on the history of Egypt, understanding secularism to be the separation of public and private affairs and characterizing religion as a private matter – that is, Islam as a faith, not a law. While, in most respects, Bishri was more Egyptian than Arab nationalist, many of his early writings were first published in the Marxist review *al-Tali'a* (The Vanguard). The centerpiece of Bishri's thinking was a concept of national independence, and his political aim was to contribute to a national struggle against imperialism by foreign powers and despotism by domestic powers.[63] His understanding of national independence had both political and economic dimensions and entailed liberation from colonialism and establishment of a national economic system based on principles of social justice, as well as (to a lesser extent) Arab unity.

The 1967 war began a long process of critical reflection that would eventually culminate in a shift in thinking on Bishri's part. The defeat led him to conclude that independence is not achieved through political and economic independence alone, but also needed civilizational and religious dimensions. By the early 1980s, Bishri began attributing similar goals to nationalist and Islamist movements, specifically, the goals of unity and liberation.[64] Bishri's terminology and political aims shifted toward an Islamic perspective, as he offered a reinterpretation of his earlier work in order to account for failure of the *umma* to achieve its promise. Bishri acknowledges development of his thinking in a new introduction penned for the second edition of his first book, published in 1972 and entitled *The Political Movement in Egypt, 1945–1952*:

I now have begun to understand what I did not understand clearly in the 1960s when I prepared this book: that there is a general and important principle for demarcating the socio-political map and historical context of Egypt during the past century. This principle is that the course of Egyptian history and the social movement in any particular period are not only produced by the struggle between the nationalist movement and imperialism, nor by the social struggle between classes with different interests, but they are also determined by the ideological struggle between that which comes from outside (*al-wafid*) and that which is inherited (*al-mawruth*).[65]

Bishri came to believe that the recovery of the *turath* (the heritage) or the *mawruth* (that which is inherited), which "consists of values, organizations, ideas, customs, morals and culture which have been passed down to the present society by previous generations," is imperative for Arab-Islamic civilization.[66] According to his analysis, the *turath* finds its most potent articulation in religious – that is, Islamic – sources. Imperialism tried to obliterate this heritage. True independence will not be obtained without a recovery of this heritage in the present. Bishri demonstrates a considerable faith in the "healthy instincts" of the masses, which he sees as awakening to the call of Islam and the Muslim Brotherhood in Egypt. Bishri encourages the elites to listen to and heed these popular instincts, generally criticizing elites of all ideological bents for having failed to establish an authentic and independent society. However, Bishri singles out for particular criticism the communist movement in Egypt, which he suggests has a foreign, Jewish influence not far removed from the Zionist movement that created the state of Israel and with setting the communists against the trend of political Islam, led by the Muslim Brotherhood.[67]

In a critical study of Western discourse on the concept of modernity (*al-mu'asira*, literally "contemporaenity"), Bishri identifies what he sees as a tendency of that which is foreign in origin (*al-wafid*) to suppress the Arab-Islamic heritage and to divide society against itself. Bishri seems to prefer the term "*al-mu'asira*" to the word more commonly used for modernity – "*al-hadatha*" – since the former refers to a period of time occupied by all, as opposed to a cultural value from which some can be excluded and which is, he argues, most commonly used to differentiate Western from Eastern – and especially, Islamic – societies. However, according to Bishri, the notion of modernity in general has been used to divide societies against themselves by uniting some sectors of society with the West and its interests under the guise of modernity, while excluding and depicting as alien and unnatural those traditional people who not only are the preservers of the heritage and the land, but also represent those forces from which resistance to Western powers and foreign incursions is most likely to arise.[68] Bishri maintains that this is what took place during the colonial period. Colonialism was not merely a military or political occupation, but struck at the very basis of the social structure and imposed a foreign value system on local culture.

Bishri argues that his aim is not to reject Western thought or modernity but, rather, to address the dilemma that he believes Egypt currently faces: "what to take and what to leave from *al-mawruth* and *al-wafid*." In many respects, he writes, this is not a new matter,

but it is possible to say that the "choosing" implied in this question carries different ramifications today than it did one hundred years ago. In the past, we occupied the ground of *al-mawruth* and discussed what was of use to us from western civilization. Then we came to occupy – or most of us did – the ground of *al-wafid* (the foreign), or a mixed ground, so that we engage the heritage while conscience of its absence (*bi-dhamir al-gha'ib*), pondering what we can summon from it. We ask now what we recover from *al-turath* after our forefathers had asked what they could appropriate from *al-wafid*.[69]

The elements of the West that became part of Egypt were imposed, not chosen. Egyptians were not free to select according to what suited their needs and their value system; they were not free to formulate a course of development that employed their own historical legacy and heritage. Bishri affirms that Arab and Islamic civilization can benefit from European institutions, values, and thought, but warns that one must remember that these stem from – and correspond to – the collective cultural, economic, political, and social circumstances of Europe in the modern age. Thus, "the function of any element will change once the circumstances and conditions that are active in it change."[70] In short, historical context, Bishri seems to be telling us, is everything. And the historical context that Arabs must address is the popular appeal of the Islamic project. According to Bishri, while earlier generations were not sure whether they wanted to adopt from Islamic traditions or from Western modernity, the picture is clear: Islam constitutes Arab society's primary point of reference.

In the introduction to a more recent work, suggestively entitled *Between Islam and Arabism*, Bishri notes that "we do not choose Arabism and we do not choose Islam, rather they are determined for us." So too, Bishri continues, "state nationalism is determined for us as well in Egypt, Iraq and Morocco."[71] We do not choose these things, Bishri argues, in the same way that we do not choose our parents or our nationality or our mother-tongue. Yet we do have a choice in the sense that we can place one identity ahead of another, we can put these two identities in conflict, or we can try to integrate them. Bishri unambiguously champions this third option, what he terms the "historical reconciliation" (*al-mula'ama al-ta'rikhiyya*) of Arabism and Islam.

In view of this attempt at reconciliation, Binder's attribution of convergence between Islamic and modernist thinking in Bishri's thought seems apt. There is certainly some measure of convergence here. But is it complete? And does Bishri perhaps move even too far into the Islamist camp and, thus, fall into the trap of illiberalism of which Binder warns?

In Bishri's most recent political thought, he continues to think critically about the failures of the Egyptian state in terms of democracy. Since the period of Muhammad 'Ali, Bishri argues, the strong state has completely dominated "communal society" (his term for "civil society," which he worries posits an opposition between the civil and the religious): whether under feudalism, capitalism, or socialism, state power has consistently overwhelmed civic and social action. But the problem Bishri identifies is that there exists a disjuncture between state power and national purpose that results from the state's refusal to draw from the inherited Islamic framework for legitimating state power, preferring instead to rely upon imported Western secular models. The result, according to Bishri, is an authoritarian and arbitrary system of rule that lacks organic links to larger social purposes. Whereas in an Islamic state, the power to legislate is constrained by the higher purposes of Islam, secular states lack such moral restraints. Neither do secular states have the checks that a democratic system provides since, Bishri argues, Arab leaders imported Western models but not the democratic principles of popular sovereignty and accountability that underlie the mechanism of rule. This has resulted in a strong state in domestic matters and a weak state in foreign affairs, one that could not resist domination from foreign powers.

Bishri prefers an Islamic state with moral restraints over a secular state that is authoritarian in character – a state legitimated by, and unified under, the banner of Islam that can oppose foreign domination over one that is subject to external powers. However, in a 1998 reissued edition of his 1977 study of the Egyptian nationalist politician and leader of the Wafd Party, Sa'd Zaghlul (1860–1927), Bishri adds a new introduction that begins:

When I am asked who I am, I say that I am a son of the national movement in Egypt and from this generation that was reared on the lap of the 1919 revolution. Our generation was born after this revolution, in the thirties, but we are sons of those who rose with this revolution and were raised in their laps and we heard the sweeter melody in our childhood about the independence of Egypt. The picture of independent Egypt in our dreams is the picture of the ideal city (al-madina al-fadhila).[72]

It is my contention that Bishri did not so much convert from a leftist to an Islamic political project as he sought within Islam a new way to articulate nationalist aspirations, which Binder aptly characterizes as "bureaucratic authoritarianism plus Islam."[73] Certainly he shares with those thinkers who have exchanged their leftist revolutionary garb for something more akin to an Islamic liberation theology a project of revision aimed at accommodating a new reality that includes a strong Islamist movement with popular appeal. Yet Bishri's shift is one focused on historical continuity and conformity with the dictates of the status quo, rather than revolution, and, as such, reveals a philosophical conservatism that has characterized his historical writings throughout his career. He accommodates the new reality by contextualizing his understanding of national independence in light of the strength of political Islam. He also becomes slightly more comprehensive in his thinking: although he never really loses his Egyptian focus, his attention to Islam leads him to pay closer attention to a larger Arab and Islamic *umma*. In this sense, it is less an intellectual or even ideological shift, than a shift in political orientation, brought about through the continued attempt to integrate thought and reality. "Thought," he writes, "like any other living being, cannot be protected by placing it in isolation. The best way to defend its existence is by renovating it in interaction with lived reality."[74] In light of the fact that Bishri is so often termed a moderate Islamist and listed along with the likes of Muhammad al-'Imara and Muhammad Salim al-'Awa, among others, I do not expect that this interpretation of his corpus will go unchallenged. There is much to be said for paying attention to both the characterizations that a thinker is given by others in his context, as well as to the thinker's self-characterization. While Bishri's transformation and influence may be best gauged in reference to development of a cultural form of nationalism and authenticity that embody a retreat from secularism among Arab intellectuals over the course of the past three decades, one suspects that the illiberal aspects in Bishri's thinking are less a result of his "historical reconciliation" of Arabism and Islam (though perhaps exacerbated by this) than something that preceded and continues subsequent to his shift in thinking.

Secular critics: orientalism in reverse

The debate between secular and Islamic intellectuals, especially among those writing on issues of authenticity and the heritage aimed at formulating more expansive bases of unity, began to increasingly take place on the grounds of the Islamist after the Arab defeats and the Islamic revolution in Iran. A recent assessment made by Nelly Lahoud in regard to a group of intellectuals she characterizes as "Apologists" could be said of these new "partisans of the heritage:" "the Apologist current is condition by the Islamist current and is in essence a reaction to it."[75] Those who Lahoud characterizes as "Apologist" are thinkers like the Egyptian Shaykh Muhammad Sa'id al-Ashmawi and the Syrian engineer Muhammad Shahrur, but her characterization of the appropriation of Islamist discourse involved in "liberal" responses to the rise of political Islam is also apparent among at least some of the "Intellectuals" she discusses, including Jabri, even though, as she points out, they do not base their arguments primarily in religious texts. In many respects, this move away from secularism is what Binder suggested was (or at least should be) taking place. Binder's *Islamic Liberalism* calls for Muslim intellectuals to refashion their religious heritage into a liberation theology. His engagements with the writings of various Muslim intellectuals aim at showing how far they have gone toward this aim and how much farther they must still go in building a new cultural consensus based on an Islam that is practical, rational, and tolerant. Recall, in this context, his critical engagement with the work of the Islamic judge 'Ali 'Abd al-Raziq (Egypt, 1888–1966). Binder sees the rejection of 'Abd al-Raziq's call for a separation of religion and state in his controversial 1925 study, *al-Islam wa usul al-hukm* (Islam and the Principles of Rule), by practically all sectors of society as constituting an affirmation of the position that political alternatives have to be found within Islam – and liberalism in the Middle East has to come in an Islamic form.[76] But Binder also maintains that this Islamic liberalism has to contend with strands of Islamic fundamentalism which oppose political and religious pluralism.

Yet these reconceptualizations of liberation and authenticity, undertaken in response to and, in some cases, with inspiration from, Islamism, run the risk of being used in an intolerant fashion by others and, at times, seem to reveal illiberal modes of thinking on the part of those intellectuals who articulate them. Arab nationalist and socialist thinkers who had previously drawn from secular European ideologies in their struggles for liberation and in their calls for political reform and modernization have come to reject these sources as inauthentic, inapplicable, or insufficient to the Arab region. Yet, as Sami Zubaida points out, in many respects their doing so still constitutes "the rejection of Western thought using its own devises."[77] That is, these intellectuals continue to operate within frameworks of Western discourses of liberation even as they develop their own "authentic" forms of what Zubaida rightly characterizes as "cultural nationalism." Their projects are culturalist in that they focus on cultural bases of resistance to foreign domination and to the failing and authoritarian states that rule over them, where previous movements for liberation and modernization had emphasized political and economic forms of independence and reform. However, often what is legitimized as "cultural" carries a rejectionist, exclusionary, intolerant, illiberal, or undemocratic character. Roel Meijer, for examples, notes that most of the institutions that Bishri deems "authentic" are also "hierarchical" and, thus, antithetical to Bishri's own call for democratization.[78] As Radwan al-Sayyid has noted, authenticity often serves as "a means of seclusion," in that it encourages cultural differentiation and particularism.[79] The extent to which Jabri incorporates an exclusionary Islam in his philosophical perspective became apparent in (the admittedly low point of) a debate with the Syrian intellectual, Georges Tarabishi, and reveals rather illiberal implications. Responding to Tarabishi's insistence on a secular stand, Jabri replied that Tarabishi had no place criticizing a project based in Islamic tradition, since he was a Christian.[80]

These intellectual shifts toward Islam and retreats from secularism have not been without critics. One of the earliest rejections of projects that undertook studies of the *turath* as a route to renewal and reform came from Sadiq al-'Azm, who called instead for a definitive rupture with the Arab-Islamic heritage which, he argued, constituted an obstacle to modernization, progress, justice, and freedom.[81] In a more recent work, George Tarabishi has taken on a number of thinkers, including Jabri and some of the moderate Islamic intellectuals who will be discussed in Chapter 2, for "massacring the heritage" and substituting a general willingness to understand "the other" with a call that goes beyond the dictates of independence from "the other" to a more destructive position that entails declaring war on all "others."[82] 'Azm has charged what he characterizes as a "revisionist Arab line of political thought," inspired largely by the Iranian revolution, with constituting a form of "orientalism in reverse." According to 'Azm, the central thesis of these reverse-orientalists is: "The national salvation so eagerly sought by the Arabs since the Napoleonic occupation of Egypt is to be found neither in secular nationalism (be it radical, conservative or liberal) nor in revolutionary communism, socialism or what have you, but in a return to the authenticity of what they call 'popular political Islam'." This trend proves "no less, reactionary, mystifying, ahistorical and anti-humanist than ... Orientalism proper," 'Azm argues, but only reverses the point of reference from the West to Islam.[83]

NOTES

1. Ibrahim Abu-Lughod. "Retreat from the Secular Path: Islamic Dilemmas of Arab Politics," *Review of Politics* 28 (1966), 447–476.
2. Sadiq Jalal al-'Azm. *al-Naqd al-dhati ba'd al-hazima* (Self Criticism after the Defeat) (Beirut: Dar al-Tali'a, 1968).
3. Avraham Sela notes the shift toward state-based approaches to Israel in the writings of Arab intellectuals and elites. "Politics, Identity and Peacemaking: The Arab Discourse on Peace with Israel in the 1990s," *Israel Studies* 10 (2005), 25.
4. Alexander Flores. "Egypt: A New Secularism?" *Middle East Report* 153 (1988), 27.
5. Established in Cairo in 1998, *al-Manar al-jadid* provides a forum for various moderate Islamists who aim to revise and revive the reformist vision articulated in Rashid Rida's periodical, *al-Manar*.
6. Albert Hourani. *The Emergence of the Modern Middle East* (University of California Press, 1981), 187.

7. Duri is Professor Emeritus of History at Jordan University in Amman and former president of Baghdad University (1965–1968).

8. 'Abd al-'Aziz al-Duri. *The Historical Formation of the Arab Nation: A Study in Identity and Consciousness*, tr. Lawrence Conrad (London: Croom Helm, 1987), 29.

9. Duri. *Historical Formation of the Arab Nation*, 326.

10. 'Abd al-'Aziz al-Duri, *The Rise of Historical Writing among the Arabs* (Princeton University Press, 1983), 1.

11. Nadim al-Baytar. *al-Iydiyulujiyya al-thawriyya* (The Revolutionary Ideology) (Beirut: al-Mu'assasa al-jami'iyya, 1982), 742–746.

12. 'Azm. a*l-Naqd al-dhati ba'd al-hazima*.

13. Sadiq Jalal al-'Azm. a*l-Naqd al-fikr al-dini* (Critique of Religious Thought) (Beirut: Dar al-Tali'a, 1969).

14. Sami Zubaida. "Islam, Cultural Nationalism and the Left," *Review of Middle East Studies* 4 (1988), 5.

15. Mona Abaza. *Debates on Islam and Knowledge in Malaysia and Egypt: Shifting Worlds* (London: Routledge, 2002), 22.

16. Sami Zubaida. "Trajectories of Political Islam: Egypt, Iran and Turkey," *Political Quarterly* 71 (2000), 61.

17. Munir Shafiq. *al-Marksiyya al-lininiyya wa nazariyya al-hizb al-thawri* (Marxist–Leninism and the Theory of Revolutionary War) (Beirut: Dar al-Tali'a, 1971) and *'Ilm al-harb* (Science of War) (Beirut: al-Mu'assasa al-'arabiyya, 1972).

18. See Munir Shafiq. *Fi al-wahda al-'arabiyya wa al-tajzi'a* (On Arab Unity and Fragmentation) (Beirut: Dar al-Tali'a, 1979) and his collection of writings appearing under the title *al-Qawmiyya al-'arabiyya bayna waqi' al-tajzi'a wa tatallu'at al-wahda* (Arab Nationalism between the Reality of Breakdown and the Aspirations of Unity) (Jerusalem: Wakalat Abu 'Arafat, 1980).

19. See the first full statement of his revolutionary Islamist position in Munir Shafiq. *al-Islam fi ma'raka al-hadara* (Islam at the Center of Civilization) (Beirut: Dar al-kalima, 1982); also *al-Islam wa tahaddiyyat al-inhitat al-mu'asir: qadaya al-tajzi'a wa al-sihyuniyya – al-taghrib wa al-taba'iyya* (Islam and the Challenges of the Current Despair: The Issue of Fragmentation and Zionism – Alienation and Dependency) (London: Dar Taha, 1983); and *al-Fikr al-islami al-mu'asir wa al-tahaddiyat: thawra, haraka, kitaba* (Contemporary Islamic Thought and the Challenges: Revolution, Movement and Writing) (Kuwait: Dar al-qalam, 1986).

20. Beginning in the 1990s, Shafiq embarked upon yet another transformation, which he characterized as "a critical perspective from within" in regard to the Islamic revival. He has begun to call for a transformation of Islamic thinking along more democratic and liberal principles. He has called for a serious effort of *ijtihad* (independent reasoning) to reinterpret Islamic law and rethink such notions as *shura* (consultation, understood to be an Islamic notion of democracy) so that they conform to contemporary principles of pluralism, tolerance, respect for human rights, and alternation of political power. See Munir Shafiq. *al-Nizam al-duwali al-jadid wa al-khiyar al-muwajaha* (The New World Order and the Alternative Choice) (Beirut: al-Nashir, 1992), for one of his earliest engagements with these

themes; and more recently, *al-Dimuqratiyya wa al-'imaniyya fi al-tarjriba al-gharbiyya* (Democracy and Secularism in the Western Experience) (London: al-Markaq al-maghribi lil-buhuth wa al-tarjama, 2001). As such, his thinking has developed along with the *Wasatiyya* intellectuals discussed in Chapter 2.

21. 'Adil Husayn. *Iqtisad al-misri min al-istiqlal ila al-taba'iyya, 1974–1979* (The Egyptian Economy: From Independence to Dependency), 2 vols. (Beirut: Dar al-kalima lil-nashr, 1981). Husayn characterizes his stance as "radical," but arguably his shift is better characterized as a reaction to Sadat's liberalization and normalization policies.

22. 'Adil Husayn, *al-Tatbi': al-mukhatta al-sihyuni lil-haymana al-iqtisadiyya* (Normalization: The Zionist Plan for Economic Hegemony) (Cairo: Madbuli Bookstore, 1985); and *al-'alaqat al-iqtisadiyya bayna misr wa isra'il* (Economic Relations Between Egypt and Israel) (Beirut: Institute for Palestinian Studies, 1984).

23. 'Adil Husayn. "Islam and Marxism: The Absurd Polarisation of Contemporary Egyptian Politics," *Review of Middle East Studies* 2 (1976), 71–83.

24. 'Adil Husayn. *Nahwa fikr 'arabi jadid, al-nasiriyya wa al-tanmiyya wa al-dimuqratiyya* (Toward A New Arab Thought: Nasirism, Development and Democracy) (Cairo: Dar al-mustaqbal al-'arabi, 1985).

25. Zubaida. "Islam, Cultural Nationalism and the Left," 24. Zubaida provides an insightful and critical discussion of Husayn's various transformations, 15–27.

26. Salwa Ismail. "Confronting the Other: Identity, Culture, Politics and Conservative Islamism in Egypt," *International Journal of Middle East Studies* 30 (1998), 217.

27. Ismail. "Confronting the Other," 218, 225 (n.120).

28. 'Adil Husayn. *al-Jabha al-'arabiyya al-iraniyya didda al-hilf al-amriki al-sihyuni, 1991–1993* (The Arab-Iranian Front against the American-Zionist Alliance) (Cairo: Arab-Islamic Center for Studies, 1998).

29. Muhammad Mutawalli Sha'rawi. *Fiqh al-mara al-muslima* (Jurisprudence for Muslim Women), ed. 'Adil Husayn (Cairo: al-Dar al-'alimiyya lil-kutub wa al-nashr, 1998).

30. Ruhollah Khomeini. *al-Hukuma al-islamiyya* (Islamic Government) (Cairo: n.p., 1979) and *Jihad al-nafs, aw al-jihad al-akbar* (Struggle with the Self, or the Greatest Jihad) (Cairo: n.p., 1980).

31. However, Hanafi also notes some reservations as to the model of Islamic government outlined by Khomeini. See the discussion of this by Nazih Ayubi. *Political Islam: Religion and Politics in the Arab World* (London: Routledge, 1991), 153–154.

32. See Hasan Hanafi. "Madha ya'ni al-yasar al-islami" (What Is the Meaning of the Islamic Left?), *al-Yasar al-islami* 1 (1981), 5–48.

33. Hasan Hanafi. "The Relevance of the Islamic Alternative in Egypt," *Arab Studies Quarterly* 4 (1982), 74.

34. Hasan Hanafi. "Athar al-imam al-shahid sayyid qutb 'ala al-harakat al-diniyya al-mu'asira" (The Influence of the Martyred Imam Sayyid Qutb on the Contemporary Religious Movement) in *al-Din wa al-thawra fi misr: al-Harakat al-diniyya al-mu'asira* (Religion and Revolution and

Egypt: The Contemporary Religious Movement) (Cairo: Madbuli Book-store, 1988), 219. For an excellent comparison of Qutb and Hanafi, see Sharough Akhavi. "The Dialectic in Contemporary Egyptian Social Thought: The Scripturalist and Modernist Discourses of Sayyid Qutb and Hasan Hanafi," *International Journal of Middle East Studies* 29 (1997), 377–401.

35. Hasan Hanafi. *al-Din wa al-thawra fi misr,* 231.
36. Hasan Hanafi. *Min al-'aqida ila al-thawra* (From Doctrine to Revolution) (Cairo: Madbuli Bookstore, 1988), 5.
37. Hasan Hanafi. *Muqaddima fi 'ilm al-istighrab* (Introduction to the Science of Occidentalism) (Cairo: al-Dar al-fanniyya, 1981), 152–153.
38. Anwar Abdel-Malek. *Rih al-sharq* (Wind of the East) (Cairo: Dar al-mustaqbal al-'arabi, 1983).
39. Anwar Abdel-Malek. "While We Were Sleeping," *al-Ahram Weekly* (November 13, 2003).
40. Zubaida. "Islam, Cultural Nationalism and the Left," 7.
41. Robert D. Lee. *Overcoming Tradition and Modernity: The Search for Islamic Authenticity* (Oxford: Westview, 1997), 191.
42. Jacques Waardenburg. "Reflections on the West" in Suha Taji-Farouki and Basheer M. Nafi (eds.), *Islamic Thought in the Twentieth Century* (London: I. B. Tauris, 2004), 268.
43. Amando Salvatore. "The Rational Authentication of *Turath* in Contemporary Arab Thought: Muhammad al-Jabri and Hasan Hanafi," *Muslim World* 85 (1995), 191–214.
44. Muhammad 'Abid al-Jabri, interview with author, Rabat, Morocco (November 1996). See also Muhammad 'Abid al-Jabri. *Ishkaliyyat al-fikr al-'arabi al-mu'asir* (Problematics of Contemporary Arab Thought) (Beirut: Center for Arab Unity Studies, 1989).
45. Aziz al-Azmeh. *al-Turath wa al-sulta* (Heritage and Power) (Beirut: Dar al-tali'a, 1990), 53.
46. Muhammad 'Abid al-Jabri. *Masala al-huwiyya: al-'uruba wa al-Islam ... wa al-gharb* (The Question of Identity: Arabism, Islam ... and the West) (Beirut: Center for Arab Studies, 1995), 10.
47. Schooled jurisprudence in Najaf, the center of Shi'i learning, Muruwwa later joined the Lebanese Communist Party, where he remained a member of its central committee until his assassination in 1987.
48. Husayn Muruwa. *al-Naza'at al-maddiyya fi al-falsafa al-'arabiyya al-islamiyya* (Materialist Tendencies in Arab-Islamic Philosophy) (Beirut: Dar al-Farabi, 1975), 5–6.
49. Muhammad 'Abid al-Jabri. *Nahnu wa al-turath* (The Heritage and Us) (Beirut: Dar al-tiba'a lil-tanwir wa al-nashr, 1980), 51.
50. Muhammad 'Abid al-Jabri. *al-Din wa al-dawla wa tatbiq al-shari'a* (Religion, the State and the Application of Islamic Law) (Beirut: Center for Arab Unity Studies, 1996), 113. These lines are also found in his "Badal al-'almaniyya: al-dimuqratiyya wa al-'aqlaniyya" (The Alternative of Secularism: Democracy and Rationalism), *al-Yawm al-sabi'* 224 (August 22, 1988); and "Al-'almaniyya wa al-Islam: islam laysat kanisa likay nufasilahu 'an al-dawla" (Secularism and Islam: Islam is not a Church that we can separate

from the State) in Muhammad 'Abid al-Jabri and Hasan Hanafi, *Hiwar al-mashriq al-maghrib: talih silsila al-rudud wa al-munaqashat* (East–West Dialog: Followed by a Series of Replies and Debates) (Casablanca: Dar al-tubqal, 1990), 46.

51. Jabri in *Hiwar*, 46. It is notable that in the famous 1989 debate (*hiwar al-maghrib al-mshriq*) that pitted Jabri against Hanafi, despite the two thinkers' many differences, both affirmed the notion that there is no church in Islam that requires separation from the state.

52. Jabri in *Hiwar*, 45.

53. Jabri in *Hiwar*, 45–46.

54. Jabri. *Masala al-huwiyya.*

55. Abdelwahab Elmessiri. "Secularism, Immanence and Deconstruction" in John L. Esposito and Azzam Tamimi (eds.), *Islam and Secularism in the Middle East* (New York University Press, 2000), 67.

56. Elmessiri. "Secularism, Immanence and Deconstruction," 68.

57. Ahmad Sidqi al-Dajani, *Madha ba'da harb Ramadan? Filistin wa al-watan al-'arabi fi al-'alim al-ghad* (What is after the Ramadan War? [October 1973 War] Palestine and the Arab Nation in the World of Tomorrow) (Beirut: Arab Center for Studies and Publishing, 1974).

58. Ahmad Sidqi al-Dajani. "The PLO and the Euro-Arab Dialogue," *Journal of Palestine Studies* 9 (1980), 82.

59. Ahmad Sidqi al-Dajani. *'Uruba wa islam wa mu'asara* (Europe, Islam and the Future) (Beirut: Manshurat filastin al-muhtalla, 1982).

60. Ahmad Sidqi al-Dajani. *Wahdat al-tanawwu' wa hadarah 'arabiyya islami-yya fi 'alam mutarabit* (The Unity of Diversity and the Arab-Islamic Civilization in a Destitute World) (Cairo: Dar al-mustaqbal al-'arabi, 1990).

61. Ahmad Sidqi al-Dajani et al, *Tajdid al-fikr al-siyasi fi itar al-dimuqratiyya wa huquq al-insan: al-tayyar al-islami wa al-marsi wa al-qawmi* (The Renewal of Political Thought in the Framework of Democracy and Human Rights: Islamic, Marxist and Nationalist Trends) (Cairo Center for Human Rights Studies, 1997).

62. Ahmad Sidqi al-Dajani. *al-Quds wa intifada al-aqsa wa harb al-'awlama* (Jerusalem, the al-Aqsa Intifida and the War of Globalization) (Giza: Markaz al-i'lam al-'arabi, 2002).

63. Tariq al-Bishri. *al-Haraka al-siyasiyya fi misr, 1945–1951* (The Political Movement in Egypt, 1945–1951), 1st edn (Cairo: al-Hay'a al-misriyya al-'amma lil-kitab, 1972).

64. See Tariq al-Bishri. "Bayn al-'uruba wa al-islam: al-mawqif min 'ghayr al-muslimin' wa min al-'ilmaniyya" (Between Arabism and Islam: The Position of Non-Muslims and Secularism), *al-Sha'b* (May 27, 1986).

65. Tariq al-Bishri. *al-Haraka al-siyasiyya fi misr, 1945–1951* (The Political Movement in Egypt, 1945–1951), 2nd edn (Cairo: Dar al-shuruq, 1983), 42. All subsequent references are to this edition of the work. My translation of this passage was completed with reference to that provided by Roel Meijer. "History, Authenticity and Politics: Tariq al-Bishri's Interpretation of Modern Egyptian History," *Occasional Paper* 4 (Amsterdam: Middle East Research Associates, September 1989), 19.

66. Bishri. *al-Haraka al-siyasiyya*, 359. See also the first chapter of Tariq al-Bishri. *Ma hiyya al-mu'asira* (What is Modernity?) (Cairo: Dar al-Shuruq, 1996), which was originally written and presented the same year (1983), esp. 7.
67. Bishri. *al-Haraka al-siyasiyya*, 17–18.
68. Bishri. *Ma hiyya al-mu'asira*, 12–13.
69. Bishri. *Ma hiyya al-mu'asira*, 8.
70. Bishri. *Ma hiyya al-mu'asira*, 11.
71. Tariq al-Bishri (ed.). *Bayna al-islam wa al-'uruba* (Between Islam and Arabism) (Cairo: Dar al-shuruq, 1988).
72. *Sa'd Zaghlul yufawidhu al-isti'mar: dirasa fi al-mufawadhat al-misriyya al-britaniyya, 1920–1924* (Sa'd Zaghlul Negotiates the Colonization: A Study of Egyptian-British Negotiations, 1920–1924) (Cairo: al-Hay'a al-misriyya al-'amma lil-kitab, 1977). The title was changed slightly for the reissued edition: *Sa'd Zaghlul mufawadhan: dirasa fi al-mufawadhat al-misriyya al-britaniyya, 1920–1924* (Sa'd Zaghlul Negotiating: A Study of Egyptian-British Negotiations, 1920–1924) (Cairo: Dar al-Hilal, 1998), 5.
73. Leonard Binder. *Islamic Liberalism: A Critique of Development Ideologies* (University of Chicago Press, 1988), 292.
74. Bishri. *Ma hiyya al-mu'asira*, 12.
75. Nelly Lahoud. *Political Thought in Islam: A Study in Intellectual Boundaries* (New York: Routledge-Curzon, 2005), 23. Lahoud distinguishes three competing currents in Islamic political thought: Islamists, Apologists, and Intellectuals.
76. Binder. *Islamic Liberalism*, 161.
77. Zubaida. "Islam, Cultural Nationalism and the Left," 2.
78. Roel Meijer. "History, Authenticity and Politics," 41.
79. Radwan al-Sayyid. "Islamic Movements and Authenticity" in Roel Meijer (ed.), *Cosmopolitanism, Authenticity, and Identity in the Middle East* (London: Routledge, 1999), 103–114.
80. The debate is recounted in *al-Jadid: A Review and Record of Arab Culture and Arts* 3:17 (1997).
81. 'Azm. *Naqd al-fikr al-dini*.
82. George Tarabishi. *Madhbaha al-turath fi al-thaqafa al-'arabiyya al-mu'assira* (The Massacre of the Heritage in Contemporary Arab Culture) (London: Dar al-Saqi, 1993).
83. Sadik Jalal al-'Azim. "Orientalism and Orientalism in Reverse," *Khamsin* 8 (1981), 5–26.

2   A more inclusive Islamism?
The *wasatiyya* trend

Just as the failure of Arab nationalist regimes in the Arab–Israeli wars accounts for some of the transformations among leftist and Arab nationalist intellectuals, so too one might identify an historic event that lent particular urgency to the development of a moderate trend in Islam: the assassination of Egyptian president Anwar Sadat by the Islamic Jihad group in October 1981. Many of the leading theorists of the Islamic revival (*al-sahwa al-islamiyya*) sought to distinguish their position from the political turmoil engulfing the country and from the extremist forces that contributed to its emergence. In doing so, they began articulating principles that have been characterized as moderate or centrist (*wasatiyya*). Other scholars have called these individuals "the new Islamists" and emphasize their focus on intellectual activity rather than on political organizing.[1] The Islamist movement has been criticized for the dearth and lack of specificity of political thought coming out of their movement. In many ways, these individuals fill that intellectual vacuum in Islamist discourse.

The individuals associated with this trend consist primarily of Egyptian Islamists – such as Muhammad al-Ghazali (1917–1996), Yusuf al-Qaradawi (b. 1926), Fahmi Huwaydi (b. 1936), Kamal Abu al-Majd (b. 1930), Muhammad al-'Imara (b. 1931), and Muhammad Salim al-'Awa (b. 1942). However, at least one Egyptian Copt, Rafiq Habib (b. 1959), espouses similar ideas and has aligned himself politically with ideas and thinkers characterized as *wasatiyya*, and the influence of many of these figures extends far beyond Egypt. Certainly this is the case with Qaradawi, whose numerous books and essays circulate widely throughout the region in print, audio, and electronic form and whose full use of satellite television has made him one of the most well-known and influential Islamic scholars in the Middle East.[2] Articles written by 'Awa, 'Imara, and Huwaydi regularly appear in newspapers published from Beirut to Rabat. To the list of Egyptian intellectuals, one must add a number of Islamists from other countries often rightly linked with the *wasatiyya* trend, including Rashid al-Ghannushi (Tunisia/England,

b. 1941) and Hasan al-Turabi (Sudan, b. 1932). Many of these figures offered early iterations of their visions in speeches given to youth groups and carrying such titles as "the priorities of the Islamic movement in the coming phase" (Qaradawi) or "the priorities of the Islamic trend in the coming three decades" (Turabi). The main components of this intellectual trend were outlined in a 1991 pamphlet, entitled *A Contemporary Islamic Vision: A Declaration of Principles* and penned by Kamal Abu al-Majd, a professor of law at Cairo University.[3] These principles were the basis for the platform of the Wasat Party that a number of former Brotherhood members and others, including several women and a number of Copts, first sought to establish in 1996.[4] Other groups of individuals in Jordan, Bahrain, and Kuwait have attempted to create political parties and groups explicitly based on *wasatiyya* principles.

The "moderate" label here is not to be either confused or conflated with the many definitions offered by Western social scientists who examine the "inclusion-moderation thesis" or by journalists seeking to distinguish some more palatable group from the radicals, extremists, militants, terrorists, or "enemies of the West." While Schwedler's working definition of moderation as "movement from a relatively closed and rigid worldview to one more open and tolerant of alternative perspectives"[5] is relevant here, in the sense that it captures the distinctive focus on dialog with others that characterizes this post-1981 trend, many will find lots of the ideas and individuals associated with this trend to be immoderate and illiberal, as all *wasatiyya* intellectuals are deeply critical of policies and practices associated with the West, and some advocate violence in particular circumstances. Part of the aim in this chapter and those that follow is to clarify aspects of *wasatiyya* thinking that demonstrate openness, inclusiveness, and tolerance – and those that fall short of these values.

Rather, moderate here is a translation of the self-appellation of *"wasatiyya,"* which is meant to refer to Qur'an 2:143: "We have made of you an *umma wasata*, that ye may be witness against mankind, and the Messenger a witness over you." The phrase *"umma wasata"* has been translated in many ways, from a "middle nation," to "a community justly balanced," to a "moderate community."

Thus, moderation involves the situating of one's self both *as a member of a community* and *as an intermediate* between existing positions deemed extreme in some manner. Both Muslims and analysts of Islamic history attribute considerable political and social significance to the notion of community, or *umma*, in Islam. Sir Hamilton Gibb rather categorically maintained that:

the key word for everything that has to do with Islamic culture is *Umma*, Community. It is in the historical development of this concept and its modalities that the true significance of Islamic history and culture must be sought ... The first political pronouncement of the Prophet Muhammad to the infant community at Madina was "Ye are one *umma* over against mankind," one single society, that is to say, welded together by community of religious purpose and the resulting social relationships and obligations.[6]

Most interpretations of *umma* render it a *Gemeinschaft*-type of relationship, that is, a notion of community in which individuals are regulated by common beliefs about the appropriate behavior and responsibility of members of the community, to each other and to the community at large. The unity of this form of community constitutes a "unity of will."[7]

Islam has existed across such a vast expanse of geographical space – and amidst all the differences those spaces provide: linguistic, ethnic, and sectarian. Is it an *umma* of equality and inclusion, or is its existence dependent upon distinctions among its members (for example, distinctions between men and women, or Arab and non-Arab) and differentiation from other non-members in their midst? The existence of non-Muslims (predominantly religious minorities, such as Christians and Jews, but also various "heretics," and, at times, Shi'is) in the Middle East has particularly challenged notions of an *umma* based on adherence to Islam. Are Jews and Christians part of the *umma*; or do they constitute a separate *umma* alongside the Muslim *umma*? If Jews and Muslims are allowed to practice their own religions within one *umma*, this suggests that the *umma* is no longer a religious community in an exclusive Islamic sense. What sort of *umma* exists when a single religion (or even religiosity) ceases to form a basis of unity, perhaps in the face of the decline in religious practices or with the growth in secular beliefs and forms of social and political organization?

The way the community has been imagined in the Middle East – the basic foundation of unity for this diverse region – has changed throughout history. Certainly in its first century or so, Islam was the religion of the Arab nation; but as Islam spread, so did its borders, such that Islam became the bond that superseded ethnicity and nationality.[8] Under the Ottoman system, "socially and culturally each [religious] community (*millet*) formed a separate entity, each kept apart from the other. There was not attempt to create uniformity. Consequently, no intercommunal solidarity or social integration evolved in Ottoman society."[9] However, by 1918 the doctrine that the Arabs constituted a nation had come to be accepted by a considerable majority of Arab intellectuals and political elite. Arab nationalism permitted fuller recognition and incorporation of the religious diversity that constitutes the Arab region. At the same time, as Abdullah al-Ahsan has pointed out, European nationalism and its appropriation by elites in Muslim majority countries created a crisis in the Muslim *umma*: "This crisis stems from the question of who commands the supreme loyalty of an individual in society. This conflict ... is primarily one between the religious *ummah* and secular nationalism."[10] When the world witnessed a "return to religion" in the latter part of the twentieth century, in the Arab region this was expressed as an "Islamic awakening," which reasserted a distinctly and exclusively Islamic *umma* against failing political regimes and an ideological understanding of Islam (as Islamism) for the Islamic *umma* to wield against secular ideologies.

What is most significant about the *wasatiyya* intellectuals – particularly in regard to recent cross-ideological activity – is the way in which they have articulated a concept of community that is increasingly less tied to notions of the *umma* as a religious community in an exclusively Islamic sense. This is significant because it not only represents a development in thought that has facilitated (and been facilitated by) dialog with non-Islamist groups, but it has also created a space for accommodation of liberal notions such as democracy, pluralism, freedom of thought, and the rights of women and minorities within the thought of perhaps the most influential strand of political Islam in the contemporary Middle East.

The priorities of the Islamic movement rearticulated

Raymond William Baker rightly notes that the moderate Islamist trend emerged out of the Muslim Brotherhood "as an independent critical force, shaped as much by reaction to the shortcomings and failures as by the successes of the Muslim Brothers."[11] The Qur'anic *sura* noted above opens Qaradawi's widely circulated and translated book, entitled *Islamic Awakening, Between Rejection and Extremism*, first published shortly after Sadat's assassination. Qaradawi understands it to affirm that "the Muslim Ummah is a nation of justice and moderation ... Islamic texts call upon Muslims to exercise moderation and to reject and oppose all kinds of extremism: *ghuluw* (excessiveness), *tanattu* (transgressing; meticulous religiosity) and *tashdid* (strictness; austerity)."[12] This book, like another equally influential essay published a decade later, *Priorities of the Islamic Movement in the Coming Phase*, is aimed at identifying the causes of – and remedies to – extremism and laying out a path forward "between rejection and extremism."[13]

However, differences between the two works are also apparent. The 1991 work is not only concerned with distinguishing a moderate Islamic perspective from the excesses of radical groups, but also addresses a perceived waning of the Islamic movement. There is a shift in audience between the two works as well. Qaradawi tells us in the introduction to the earlier work that it began as "a two-part article on the Muslim youth" and his final chapter, "Advice to Muslim Youth," makes it clear that he is most concerned with the type of thinking that contributes to the "serious and bloody confrontation between the youth and the authorities" in that period.[14] The later work is said to have started as an invitation from the director of Islamist organization "Center for the Studies on the Islamic Future," who first approached Qaradawi at the annual meeting of the Arab Muslim Youth Association in North America in December 1989 about presenting a paper at the Center that would lay out the aims of the Islamic movement. However, the essay addresses Islamic movements generally, with specific concern with communicating moderate ideas and strategies to the leadership of these movements.[15] In 1981, Qaradawi sought to distinguish a moderate Islamic path from the actions of Islamic extremists. In 1991, he sought to revive and expand a movement he feared – if rigid in thinking – would be left behind by the political forces of democratization and the economic and technological forces of globalization, by charting a pragmatic, flexible, far-sighted course for the Islamic movement.[16]

Perhaps most striking for our purposes here is Qaradawi's shift from confrontation and defensiveness toward a tone of rapprochement between these works. In Qaradawi's 1981 work one finds chastisements of "excessive and unnecessary talk about growing a beard, wearing clothes below the ankle, moving of the finger during reading the *tashahhud* in prayer, acquisition of photographs and so on." Qaradawi regrets the time wasted on these "side issues" when more important matters, such as "the unrelenting hostility – and infiltration – of secularism, communism, Zionism, and Christianity, as well as deviationist groups in the Muslim world" remain to be addressed.[17] Recognition of the need for dialog with competing groups had clearly taken root among moderate Islamists by the mid to late 1980s. Abu al-Majd who, like Qaradawi, has offered a strong Islamic voice in rejecting extremism and terrorism, argued in his 1988 book, *Dialog, Not Confrontation*, for Islamic organizations to abandon terrorism and violence and to focus efforts on dialog with both government and secularists.[18] In his outline of *Priorities of the Islamic Movement in the Coming Phase*, Qaradawi underscores the "importance of dialogue with others" at multiple levels and with distinct but related aims: rulers of Muslim majority nations who do not stand against Islam, with the aim of influencing them; dialog with rational foreigners to "make Westerners understand what we want for ourselves and for others;" as well as religious dialog with Christians aimed at improving distorted views on Islam; intellectual dialogs with

"Orientalists" and Westerners interested in Islam, to improve their scholarship; and political dialog with decision-makers in the West, to convince them "that we have a right to live by our Islam, led by its *aqeedah*, governed by its *shariʿah* and guided by its values in morals, without harbouring any ill-intention towards the West or doing it any harm."[19] In fact, in this work, written two years before Samuel Huntington proclaimed a "clash of civilizations," Qaradawi proclaimed: let there "be 'dialogue of civilizations' ... not a 'conflict of civilizations'."[20]

Qaradawi also reveals that, in the context of the Middle East, he already sought dialog with non-Islamists – and with success. By way of illustration, he recounts an exchange he had while attending a symposium in Amman, Jordan:

I will never forget what one of the participants, a nationalist Christian, said to me at the lunch table. He said: "We have changed our opinion about you completely." I asked: "And what was your opinion?" He replied: "that you are a hardliner and a fanatic." I said: "Where did you get this idea about me?" He answered: "I don't know, but frankly, that was our impression about you." I asked: "And now?" He said: "Now we have learnt through seeing, hearing, discussing and direct contact which has changed this unfair idea about you completely. We now see you as a man who respects logic, refers to the intellect and knows how to listen to the other opinions, as a man who is not stubborn or adamant, but extremely flexible and tolerant."[21]

Qaradawi maintains that there is much to be gained in such dialogs, even going so far as to suggest that "welcome to dialogue with others" should be the motto of the Islamic movement in the coming phase.

An ideology of moderation

Qaradawi identifies his moderate view as an "ideology" based on the understanding of Islam as a comprehensive way of life. Clearly *wasatiyya* Islamism is not compatible with secularism in this sense.[22] Qaradawi denies that one can treat Islam as akin to Christianity, as many secularists do, by suggesting it can agree "to the division of man and the splitting of life between God and Caesar." Even worse, from Qaradawi's perspective, are those who claim to be Muslim – performing religious duties, such as prayer and pilgrimage – while they "advocate nationalist secular thought, preferring nationalist ties to Islamist ties and adopting a purely Western line of thinking."[23] He mocks those who think it possible to be a "Muslim Marxist," which he finds as nonsensical as the idea one could be a "Muslim Christian:" "I do not know how the two could be present in one person!"[24] Qaradawi argues that Marxism is akin to a religion in requiring absolute devotion that denies compatibility with any other belief. In relations with others, Qaradawi advocates a combination of a "curative" approach based on dialog that corrects false beliefs and a preventative approach based on the proliferation of Islamic ideas, so that they crowd out – or, in Qaradawi's phrasing, vaccinate against – non-Islamic ideas. But cure is only possible in the cases of those who do not already subscribe to one of the competing ideologies and both approaches he deems most suitable in dealing with youth. Qaradawi seems to harbor little hope of converting his non-Islamists interlocutors over to his worldview. Dialog in such cases seems aimed at convincing non-Islamists to permit Islamists space to operate.

Qaradawi further characterizes his ideology as both "*salafi*" or "traditionalist" and "revivalist." But he distinguishes his view of *Salafiyya* (following in the way of the righteous *salaf* [ancestors]) both from those who claim the term while confining it to formalities and polemics and from critics who describe *Salafiyya* as backward or fanatical. *Salafiyya*, for Qaradawi, comprises moderation and adaptability: "An ideology that believes in *ijtihad* and adopts creativity, as it rejects imitation and subordination and views stagnation as death itself."[25] In short, he considers true traditionalism to be revivalist in nature, such that the principles of Islam are realized anew in the contemporary. Qaradawi identifies as his "worst fear for the Islamic movement" the dangers of rigidity and the intolerance of "free thinkers," a movement that confines its ranks to one viewpoint and fails to adapt to changing conditions.[26]

Adaptation is to be undertaken by a method of *fiqh*, which Qaradawi clarifies should not be understood as limited to "jurisprudence," as is commonly thought, but a *fiqh* in the sense of "understanding (and learning) the signs of Allah and His *Sunna* in the universe, life and society."[27] The *wasatiyya* view of Islam is based less on interpretation of traditional texts (one conventional understanding of *ijtihad*) than on a pragmatic balancing of various Islamist goals. As such, it requires not only (and perhaps not even primarily) traditional learning, but a form of practical reasoning that is able to apply religious values in particular and variable circumstances. A modern *fiqh*, Qaradawi argues, must encompass an understanding of priorities (*fiqh al-awlawiyyat*), an understanding of balances (*fiqh al-muwazanat*), and an understanding of reality (*fiqh al-waqi'*). Qaradawi's method relies upon a form of strategic thinking that balances interests and evils (or harms) with an eye toward what is possible in light of current reality and moves one toward long-term goals. Balancing interests means giving priority to higher over lower interests, public over private interests, long-term over short-term interests, and primary over secondary interests. Balancing evils means choosing lesser evils and smaller harms. So too, interests are balanced against evils "in terms of size, effect, and duration," such that slight and temporary evils are acceptable for achieving major and long-term interests, and even a great evil can be permitted if it avoids an even greater harm. In general, however, Qaradawi shows some conservatism in maintaining that "the avoidance of evil should come before the realizing of interest."[28] The foundation of the balancing is provided by study of Islamic texts and goals and a careful examination of contemporary realities. Understanding priorities requires determining which issues, aims, and foes are most worthy of attention, time, and effort – and which can be dealt with at a later time.[29] A lack of balanced understanding of reality and priorities, Qaradawi warns, will likely result in lost opportunities, isolation, and inactivity.[30]

Qaradawi sees this method as not merely some sort of strategic rationality, but as means of formulating a "balanced" political ideology and a "mature" legal foundation. The *wasatiyya* vision is a balance (*muwazin*) between those who limit themselves to only one *madhhab* (school of Islamic jurisprudence) and those who would reject all Islamic schools of thought, between those who open the doors to *ijtihad* without limits and those who close the doors completely, between those who give the heritage (*turath*) sacred status even where it shows human frailties and those who disregard the heritage even when it shows divine inspiration, between those who support *tasawwuf* (spirituality, sufism) even when it deviates and those who oppose it even when it accords with Islamic law, and between those who advocate reason (*'aql*) even when it contradicts text and those who do not use reason in understanding text.[31] The ideology of the middle course and balanced approach, Qaradawi tells his reader, looks to the future and paves the way for that future. Quoting various statements from the Qur'an and *hadith* that affirm the command to make things easy, not difficult, Qaradawi affirms the approach of the Islamic movement should be one of facilitation, rather than restriction and complication.[32]

A politics of moderation

Islamists envision a state in which Islamic law is the basis of the constitution, to which all are accountable, and where governance is conducted through a process of consultation (*shura*). However, while many early Islamists were quick to resist equations of *shura* with democracy, the *wasatiyya* intellectuals have sought to reconcile Islamic thought with democratic elections, rotation of power, party pluralism, and a respect for the basic rights of citizens. Opposition to democracy was most fully articulated by two ideologues of the Islamist movement, Sayyid Qutb

(1903 and 1966) and Sayyid Abul A'la Mawdudi (India/Pakistan, 1903–1979), who argued that democracy is a *jahiliyya* form of government, since it is based on popular sovereignty rather than God's sovereignty (*hakimiyya*).[33] However, Islamic moderates have maintained that a democratic system best codifies and preserves rights and duties that can curtail arbitrariness and authoritarianism on the part of the state.

Wasatiyya intellectuals emphasize a piecemeal approach to politics: "The realization of [the Islamic state]," Qaradawi argues, "is conditional upon a number of imperatives, some of the most important of which are: to unite all efforts, to remove all obstacles, to convince the suspecting minds of the nobility of the cause, to bring up Islamically-oriented youngsters, and to prepare local as well as international public opinion to accept their ideology and their state."[34] In this sense, the *wasatiyya* ideology distinguishes itself from the thought of more violent or revolutionary Islamist strands aimed at seizing the state through a frontal assault. Qaradawi criticizes Qutb specifically for his wholesale approach, which regarded all of society as *jahiliyya* and "advocated the idea of cutting off relations with non-Muslims and called for launching an offensive *jihad* against all people."[35] Qaradawi attributes such approaches to periods of political crisis, which inspire Muslims to undertake excessive measures. Such an approach to political change is not only extreme, but also has proven ineffective, even counterproductive. "Whenever the Prophet (SA'AS) had to choose between options," Qaradawi asserts, "he always chose the easiest, unless it was a sin."[36] Thus, he advises Islamic movements to adopt a more balanced, moderate strategy, based on dialog and facilitation.

Islamic moderates affirm that the greatest obstacle to realization of an Islamic state of both strands remains existing un-Islamic states. Qaradawi, for example, asserts that "it is the duty of the movement in the coming phase to stand firm against totalitarian and dictatorial rule, political despotism and usurpation of people's rights" and that "the most serious danger threatening the Muslim Ummah and the Islamic Movement is the rule of the Pharaohs."[37] There is no doubt that he refers to contemporary leaders of Arab states – and the reference to Pharaohs draws particular attention to Egypt's head of state. However, in this context, Qaradawi does not call for violence or revolution.

Like many Islamic thinkers, Qaradawi distinguishes between offensive and defensive *jihad*. He cites Mawdudi and Qutb as advocates of the offensive view of *jihad* and lists among advocates of defensive *jihad* Rashid Rida (Syria/Egypt, 1865–1935), Mahmud Shaltut (Egypt, 1893–1963), Muhammad Abu Zahra (Egypt, 1898–1974), Muhammad al-Ghazali, and 'Abdullah Ibn Zad al-Mahmud (Qatar). Qaradawi argues that defensive *jihad* is compulsory and should be the priority of the Islamic movement: "it is the duty to defend every land invaded by the *kuffar*" (literally, non-believers; here: non-Muslims).[38] In this regard, Qaradawi affirms the priority given to Palestine in the letters of the founder of the Muslim Brotherhood, Hasan al-Banna (1906–1949): "Palestine is the first and foremost Islamic Cause, and its liberation is the first and foremost duty."[39] While Qaradawi may seem to be suggesting that offensive *jihad* can only be undertaken once defensive *jihad* has been achieved, other passages clarify that this is not the case. Rather than restricting offensive *jihad*, Qaradawi's understanding of balancing, priorities, and reality, leads him to conclude that it is best fought through the written and spoken word to "convey our *daw'ah* [call] to the whole world" and that mastery of the latest innovations and technologies in mass media for this purpose must also be a priority of the Islamic movement.[40] Among the considerations Qaradawi discusses are the fact that the development of new communication technologies facilitates this form of *jihad* and the fact that fighting non-Muslims in an offensive military *jihad* risks considerable harm, including the loss of the weapons these countries supply Muslims for their defensive *jihad*.[41] Thus, Qaradawi concludes, in the present, military *jihad* is best pursued in defensive form and that offensive *jihad* is best undertaken through non-military means. Qaradawi and other moderate Islamists have been outspoken opponents of offensive *jihadi* actions, such as those undertaken by al-Qa'ida in the United States and Europe.

On the one hand, the *wasatiyya* approach to politics focuses on the revitalization of Islam at the grassroots, particularly at the cultural level and in the day-to-day life of the people. In this sense, the *wasatiyya* draw from the outlook articulated by Hasan al-Banna. Following the example of the Prophet, they maintain, preaching must retain priority over the establishment of an Islamic state. Qaradawi identifies three components to his method of revival, each of which involves primarily education and communication: formulation of an Islamic vanguard to lead society, development of a broad base of support among the Muslim public, and "preparation of an international public climate that will accept the existence of the Islamic Nation."[42]

On the other hand, *wasatiyya* thinkers demonstrate a faith in democracy. Qaradawi emphatically states: "I cannot imagine that the Islamic movement would support anything other than political freedom and democracy."[43] However, he clarifies that Muslims must support "a true, not false democracy." True democracy, according to Qaradawi, entails the freedom for Muslims to perpetuate their message and compete fairly in majoritarian elections. The Islamic movement "has never flourished

or born fruit unless in an atmosphere of democracy and freedom, and
have withered and become barren only at times of oppression and
tyranny that trod over the will of the people which clung to Islam."[44]
Qaradawi claims that oppressive regimes in the Middle East have
allowed secularism, socialism, and everything else but Islam to carry
on in political spheres. All *wasatiyya* intellectuals consider democracy
as the only acceptable political choice of the available alternatives.

At the same time Qaradawi resists equating Islam and democracy.
Islam is a comprehensive system of values and codes of life, whereas
democracy can never be more than a tool for realizing Islamic political principles, which he identifies as "*shura, nasiha* (advice), enjoining
the good and forbidding the evil, disobeying illegal orders, resisting
unbelief and changing wrong by force when possible."[45] In response to
fears about democracy conflicting with the Islamic notion of *hakimiyya*,
in placing human sovereignty over God's, Qaradawi clarifies that he is
speaking specifically about a population that is Muslim majority, which
would not legislate in a way that contradicts Islamic law. To insure the
Islamic basis of democratic rule, Qaradawi argues that only one constitutional provision is required: "stipulating that any legislation con-
tradicting the incontestable provisions of Islam shall be null and void."
This will not conflict with democracy, in his view, since the binding
texts are few and the texts themselves are so flexible that the scope of
legislation and democratic activity would remain wide.[46]

Absent democracy and political freedoms, Qaradawi advises Islamic
movements to seek alliances and political participation through whatever channels are available to them. He cites "[Hasan] Turabi and
his brothers," who through joining the Socialist Union and accepting
appointments under Numairi's government succeeded in establishing Islamic law in the Sudan, as a positive example of what can be
achieved by allying with non-Islamic forces and participating in non-
Islamic rule.[47] Similarly, the leader of Tunisia's Nahda Party (in exile
in London), Rashid Ghannushi, has argued that in light of the fact
that Islamic government exists only as an idea, as yet unrealized in
contemporary circumstances, Islamic movements must participate in
those areas that remain available to them in existing states.[48] Ghannushi encourages Muslims to participate and share power in existing
non-Islamic governments as a non-violent means of laying the foundation for a truly Islamic social order. Ghannushi defends this strategy as
necessitated by the "exceptional" circumstances of the present, where
Muslims are unable to establish Islamic rule directly and where the
choice is not between Islamic and non-Islamic rule, but between dictatorship and democracy. Ghannushi justifies this approach through

reference to the Islamic principle of *maslaha*: Muslims must actively pursue the implementation of Islamic laws and values, even if only in part, to serve the necessities and interests of mankind. In those countries in which Muslims form the majority, Islamic movements will benefit from working with other groups to topple dictatorships that stand in the way of the realization of respect for human rights, security, and freedom of expression, essential bases for preparing the way for the longer-term goal of establishing an Islamic government. In those countries where Muslims are minorities, they should work to transform the values of their society so that their freedom of worship and belief are secure. Like Qaradawi, Ghannushi advocates a grassroots, mass-based approach to politics. Qaradawi clarifies that the most important aspect of participation in non-Islamic rule is not "official work, such as the establishment of boards and higher councils or associations and unions of Islamic affairs, not work for government bodies, such as ministries of *awqaf*" (literally, endowments; but in most states encompassing a larger gambit of "Islamic affairs").[49] While official work has its role, Qaradawi argues, the more important work is undertaken at the level of the masses. The expressed aim is of Islamist moderates to create public pressure for Islamic reforms and policies, and public support for the election of Islamic candidates – in short, to win political battles through democratic processes. Islamic governance can only be achieved through the creation of spaces for an active, educated Islamic *umma* to develop, grow, and organize its will.

Women in Islamic society

One commonplace of Islamic discourse – though by no means exclusive to this trend – is the notion that the family is the bedrock of the *umma* and that women play a particular role in maintaining this sphere. While this is often asserted to highlight the importance of women in Islamic society, this perspective also provides justification for a conservative approach to gender roles that restricts Muslim women's participation in public spheres. On the issue of women's status in contemporary society, one of the earliest statements by an Islamist in the name of moderation came from the Sudanese thinker Hasan al-Turabi. Educated at the Khartoum University School of Law and the Sorbonne, Turabi was a leading figure in Sudan's Muslim Brotherhood in the early 1960s and in the National Islamic Front, which took power with the aim of creating an Islamic state in 1989. In 1991, Turabi founded the Popular Arab and Islamic Congress, which brought together Islamist leaders from throughout the world on an annual basis. Over the course of his career Turabi has served as Sudan's speaker of parliament, attorney general, minister of justice, minister of foreign affairs, and deputy prime minister. He has also been arrested and imprisoned, most recently in 2004–2005, by president Omar al-Bashir, his one-time political ally. Since 2000, he has led the opposition Popular National Congress Party. Turabi continues to be an outspoken and controversial figure in Islamic contexts, with his views on women's rights in Islam drawing particular attention.

The introduction to Turabi's widely circulated pamphlet, *The Emancipation of Women: An Islamic Perspective*, is penned by Abdelwahab El-Affendi, senior research fellow at the University of Westminister's Centre for the Study of Democracy. El-Affendi reveals that this writing "appeared first in 1973 as a semi-anonymous document for internal circulation within the Islamic movement" and was only officially published under Turabi's name after being "subjected to extensive discussions within the ranks of the movement, and among Ulama and Islamists outside Sudan" and receiving "endorsement of such prominent Ulama as Sheikh Mohammed al-Ghazali of Egypt."[50] According to El-Affendi, the main impetus for the work was the lack of support for – as well as outright hostility toward – Islamists by women and women's groups, who often supported communists against the Islamists. El-Affendi notes that prior to Turabi's booklet, Islamist responses to criticisms of their views "lacked coherence and clear theoretical foundations." In contrast, Turabi's perspective manages to "sweep away completely the apologetics and ... half-solutions" by taking "a radical view which unequivocally endorsed a prominent role for women in Muslim societies." Turabi characterizes his view as a progressive Islamic perspective that is distinct from both the "anti-feminist" positions of conservative and traditional Muslim perspectives and the "western liberal tendencies" that many women in Muslim societies have sought as an alternative, but which lead them to realize their femininity at the expense of their humanity.[51] In Turabi's view, the question for this Islamist movement has moved beyond that of whether or not to endorse women's liberation toward the issue of how to incorporate women's liberation within the framework of Islam and, in turn, to "turn women into a dedicated corps in support of Islamicization."[52] El-Affendi credits women's support for the movement with bolstering the Islamic transformation of Sudan in the early 1980s.

Turabi's pamphlet opens with the assertion that "in the religion of Islam, a woman is an independent entity and thus a fully responsible human being."[53] Turabi recounts numerous classical examples of women who embraced Islam against unbelieving male relatives and spouses, who maintained their faith despite hardship and torture, and who worked to propagate Islam. Further evidence is provided by the fact that the religion addresses women directly, rather than through men, and confirms that it is on the basis of each woman's own action that she is accountable to God. Turabi maintains that Islamic law does not provide different regulations or moral codes for women, though it does distinguish between the sexes in regard to a "few limited secondary regulations."[54] As Turabi analyzes the various distinctions made, he asserts principles of necessity and exceptionality: there are certain public tasks that are always obligatory for men while only voluntary for women in normal circumstances. These are "special obligations" like "maintenance of the family, attendance of group prayers and the levy or general construction for war." Turabi clarifies that women should not be barred from such collective duties, but only that women cannot be held responsible for their undertaking unless there is a shortage of men or men fall short of their completion. Turabi attempts to maintain the difficult position that a Muslim woman at once "enjoys the same capacity and freedom enjoyed by a man" and is only "duty-bound" to participate in "collective duties and obligations of public life" in cases of absolute necessity.[55]

Turabi provides numerous other examples of difference asserted between the sexes while denying that such differences stand in the way of women's full equality or emancipation. Potential tensions between claims to equality and difference are perhaps most apparent as Turabi discusses women leaving the house. They may do so "for any need." Yet their doing so is also termed an "inconvenience" and the boundaries of what is deemed necessary and by whom. Turabi claims that women will have a voice in making such determinations, but he qualifies that voice to the "full freedom of expression of their *proper* views."[56] In light of various statements about the effects of menstruation on women's "proper conduct and judgment," the reiteration of the *hadith* that women outnumber men in hell, question whether expressions are weighted according to the gender of the one who utters them.[57] Further, Turabi affirms several principles from Islamic law which seem to provide men with the final authority over matters that involve women. For example, women can propose to, choose, or reject suitors, as well as seek a divorce, yet only a male relative can formalize a marriage contract and only a (male?) judge can grant a divorce.[58] Women are required to breastfeed children for two full years, "if a father desires that the term be completed."[59]

Nonetheless, it is clear that Turabi's aim is to expand the extent and sphere of women's participation in contemporary life. Most of his critical remarks are aimed at those who would constrict those spheres out of fear of potential wrongdoing. "The greatest injustice visited upon women," he asserts, "is [women's] segregation and isolation from the general society."[60] The benefits of participation in communal life – both for women and for the community as a whole – "more than outweigh any preventative considers in the segregation of the sexes" not specifically ordained in Islamic law. Turabi argues that not only are the number of restrictions based on gender in the Qur'an few, but most are aimed at men, not women. It is not religion, but men's weak commitment to religion, that Turabi identifies as the cause of unjust treatment of women. "Masculine capricious tendencies" (such as insecurity, jealousness, vanity, and arrogance) from which "only Godly men are immune" and persistent "pre-Islamic values and prejudices" are the main problems Turabi identifies. Turabi further argues that these weaknesses have been given justification through mistaken "judicial rules and strategems," such as comparing provisions in Islamic law, "not to give relative effect to all, but to claim the abrogation of provisions introduced to extend rights immunities or liberties to women." Another "tricky approach" that Turabi criticizes consists of reading "liberally" and expanding the scope of "rules granting authority to men, while reading literally and strictly those imposing limitations on women." In addition, restrictions in the Qur'an and sunna "meant to apply exclusively to the Prophet or his wives due to their unique position" are generalized as restrictions on all women. But the main basis of the problem with "anti-feminist" readings of Islamic law lies in their subordination of means to ends, such that prohibitions are maximized and taken to extremes in order to avoid bad consequences.[61] The proper juridical principle should be one of balance, where "risks of temptation" are weighted against "the positive merits of the integration of men and women in Muslim society." Turabi argues that concern for the decline of Islamic values has led Muslims to become "unduly conservative" where they should aim for "positive" and "progressive" application of Islamic law.[62]

Here Turabi seems in tension with Qaradawi's general rule that "the avoidance of evil should come before the realizing of interest," which could preclude the realization of women's rights in the interests of avoiding harm to traditional domestic, civil, and political institutions. Certainly his views are too liberal for many Muslims. In April 2006, Turabi's views on women were heard at lectures presented to the Umma Party and in interviews with al-'Arabiyya television and al-Sharq al-awsat newspaper. He called on women to play a greater role in public life and argued that Islam permits women to serve as imams and marry Christians and Jews, while not requiring women to cover their hair (only their chest) or the killing of apostates. His remarks were met with charges of apostasy by conservative clerics.

Nonetheless, Turabi is not alone in arguing for the advancement of women's status and role in contemporary society. Many *wasatiyya* thinkers, including Qaradawi, have lamented the fact that women remain underutilized in the Islamic movement.[63] After Islamist deputies led a successful drive in Kuwait's parliament to defeat a bill that would have restored women's right to vote in that country, Fahmi Huwaydi wrote a newspaper column noting that what was a gain for Kuwait's democratic experiment entailed a great loss for Islamists who will go down in history as standing in the way of women's rights: "Islamic authority was used to deprive women of their political rights," which Huwaydi deems a "defamation of the Islam's position."[64] Huwaydi drew from the Qur'an and sunna to argue that men and women are equal in Islam and to refute the idea that there is a religious basis for their actions.

Muhammad al-'Imara, who has previously edited and commented on the Egyptian modernists Muhammad 'Abduh and Qasim Amin's writings on women,[65] has written a defense of Islam's views on women against "doubts raised by extremists," both "Islamist extremists" and "secular extremists."[66] 'Imara deals with many of the same issues of concern and draws from many of the same examples of women's participation in public matters in the early years of Islam as Turabi, as he stakes out a "moderate" Islamic position against these two extremes. However, unlike Turabi, 'Imara reaffirms a *hadith* that attributes difference to women as the more emotional of the sexes. While Imara argues that this does not mean women are less competent than men, it does offer a distinction (*tamayuz*) that points to different but equally important duties assigned to men and women. 'Imara relates this *hadith* to Qur'an 4:34, which states that "men are the managers of the affairs of women because God has preferred in bounty the one over the other and because they send their money to maintain them," thus affirming the notion that men possess the duty of guardianship (*qiwama*) over women. For 'Imara, as for so many Islamists, this translates into a particular role for men as political leaders, while women maintain a distinctive responsibility for overseeing the rearing of children and management of the household.[67] While more progressive than views that interpret *qiwama* as justification for not educating or consulting women, who are relegated to largely reproductive roles, 'Imara's view does not seem to move much beyond the view of Qasim Amin who argued that "the family is the foundation of a country. Consequently, since the mother is the foundation of the family, her intellectual development or underdevelopment becomes the primary factor in determining the development or underdevelopment of the country."[68] Women's status should be improved, but the achievement of equality is based on distinctions that continue to render women's full participation a permissible exception, rather than a general rule.

Non-Muslims in the Muslim state

More than debates over the significance of gender distinctions, differences of religion offer the greatest challenge to Islamist political thought, since it challenges the basis of an *umma* constituted by Islam as a comprehensive basis of life. Much of classical Islamic thought treats non-Muslims as political subjects with limited rights as "protected peoples" (*ahl al-dhimma*). While the concept of protected peoples was progressive from the perspective of the society of Madina in the seventh century, such protected status hardly meets contemporary standards of full citizenship. Modern Islamic thinkers have similarly recognized the citizenship rights of non-Muslims in an Islamic state, but most, like Abul A'la al-Mawdudi, also acknowledged the practical limitations to their full realization of equality, since "only those who share that official ideology can fully participate."[69] Mawdudi did not even permit non-Muslims an advisory role in formal political processes, arguing that the prophet Muhammad did not consult religious minorities at Madina. While other thinkers, such as Banna, Sa'id Ramadan, and Muhammad al-Ghazzali, had stressed that non-Muslims shared equal rights and duties with Muslims,[70] more recently, Islamic moderates have attempted to rethink and clarify Islam's approach to religious minorities in creative ways with the aim of extending their citizenship even in an Islamic state.[71]

The *wasatiyya* intellectuals go beyond traditional formulations in seeking to articulate a notion of citizenship that maintains an Islamic frame of reference in terms of values and in accordance with their demand for Islamic rule, while at the same time offering a reinterpretation that draws at least some of its conceptual makeup from modern, non-Islamic sources. Based on the prophet Muhammad's ruling in the compact of Madina regarding *ahl al-kitab* (people of the book), they affirm that Christians, Jews, and Zorastrians are citizens, not protected subjects. This view is affirmed in Qaradawi's statement that "in modern terminology, *dhimmis* are 'citizens' [*muwatinun*] of the Islamic state. From the earliest period of Islam to the present day, they enjoy the same rights and carry the same responsibilities as Muslims themselves, while being free to practice their own faiths."[72] Ghannushi similarly argues that the rights of non-Muslims and Muslims alike are the common rights of citizens in comtemporary Islamic societies.[73] In his statement of principles guiding the new Islamist vision, Abu al-Majd maintains that the *dhimma* concept offered an historical expression of rights and duties in a community of Muslims and non-Muslims, but the conditions that necessitated that formulation are no longer present and it is now up to contemporary Muslims to formulate a modern constitution that gives full freedoms and rights to all, regardless of faith.[74] A 1985 work by Fahmi Huwaydi offers one of the earliest and fullest justifications of this interpretation.[75] Huwaydi explains that the Islamic principles of equality require equal citizenship. Yet, based on principles of democratic majority, Huwaydi arrives at conclusions not much better than Mawdudi's: he states that an Islamic majority will seek to institute an Islamic state and minorities cannot be permitted to undermine "the legitimate rights of the majority under the guise of equality."[76]

This perspective has been reiterated by a number of other Islamic moderates. Qaradawi's entire political ideology is premised on the existence of a Muslim majority that desires Islamic rule. According to "the logic of democracy," Qaradawi argues, "the right of the majority should be given precedence over that of the minority."[77] Qaradawi's justification does not stop here, however. He also asserts the superiority of Islamic governance by pointing to Islam's history of protection of non-Muslims, since it has never forced them "to abandon anything they regard as necessary under their religion nor has it required them to do anything they regard as forbidden in their creed, not has it forced them to believe in anything against their religion."[78] In matters of religion, Qaradawi argues, the rights of non-Muslims are even more secure in an Islamic state than they would be under secular governance. Christians, he argues, should appreciate a rule free from the anti-religiosity and materialism of secular rule.[79] Clearly, Qaradawi's analysis not only relies upon the existence of an Islamist majority, but also upon the existence of high levels of religiosity on the part of non-Muslims. These writings as well as a 2004 fatwa given by Qaradawi, argued for Sunni–Shi'i dialog concentrated on points of agreement, affirming the importance of uniting all aspects of a religious *umma*. Qaradawi seemed to backtrack on his desire for inter-Islamic rapprochement with statements published in *al-Masri al-yawm* in September 2008 that warned of Shi'i proselytizing in Egypt. Bishri, 'Awa and Huwaydi quickly published responses to Qaradwi, arguing that Shi'is do not represent a threat to Sunnis and that their activities in Egypt should not be exaggerated. After Abu al-Majd published an open letter in *al-Dustur*, attempting to calm the debate, calling for Muslim unity, and asking for all sides to put an end to this issue in the spirit of reconciliation, Qaradawi offered only a slight clarification of his position. He noted that Sunni-Shi'i rapprochement is important, but does not mean that it is permissible for Sunnis to become Shi'i and that Sunni's must be on guard against any such attempts.[80] However, Qaradawi's writings do not seem to account for atheists or agnostics; and it is unlikely that polytheists would be able to freely exercise their religion in an Islamic state, in light of Qaradawi's restrictions on public performance of practices deemed reprehensible to Muslims.

In general, Islamic moderates are dismissive of the fears of secularists and non-Muslims regarding the concept of majority rule and the impact this will have on the full realizations of non-Islamists' rights and freedoms as citizens. Abu al-Majd suggests that the fears expressed by Christians are based on a false assumption that religion is the primary dividing line in society when, in fact, under democratic governance and the rule of law, other differences will likely prove more important.[81] Others argue that Islamic principles provide the necessary protections for non-Muslims. For example, Muhammad al-'Imara argues that Islamic law provides the basis of both majority rule and minority rights.[82] Salim al-'Awa stresses the importance of absolute equality for non-Muslims before the law – albeit, Islamic law.[83] According to Qaradawi, Islam has outlined relations between Muslims and non-Muslims based on such unparalleled relations of tolerance, justice, and mercy, such as have never been seen before, and not found in existing states. At the same time, although Qaradawi also speaks of the non-Muslims as citizens, not protected religious minorities, he does not suggest they form a part of an Islamic *umma*.[84] 'Imara clarifies that the constitution of Madina distinguished between a religious *umma* and a political *umma*. Islam, then, joins together different religious communities into one political community.[85] In the latter, he argues, there are equal rights and duties. This is a view that *wasatiyya* intellectuals have had to defend against many in the Muslim Brotherhood, who hold a different view. For example, when, in 1997, Mustafa Mashhur, then the Muslim Brotherhood's spiritual guide, asserted that Egypt's Christians are excluded from military service and must pay the *jizya* as protected subjects (*dhimmiyyun*), the response from *wasatiyya* intellectuals was immediate and clearly contradicted this. Christians, they asserted, are citizens with full national rights and notions of *dhimma* and *jizya* belong, as Salim al-'Awa put it, "in the realm of history."[86]

The notion of equal rights and duties in the thought of moderate Islamists does not seem to extend to the possibility that a non-Muslim could lead the state, though *wasatiyya* thinkers have developed this prohibition based on practical rather than categorical (religious) grounds. Most accounts specify that governmental posts with a religious content cannot be open to non-Muslims under Islamic rule. But the idea of a

Christian prime minister or president tends to be neglected as a topic of discussion as much as it is prohibited outright in many contemporary writings on religious minorities – leaving one to wonder whether it too is closed according to the same principle. Many *wasatiyya* thinkers, such as Qaradawi, tend to dismiss the scenario offhand: the Muslims will not elect a ruler who is not a believer. However, Bishri and 'Awa seem to go part of the way in rendering such a scenario permissible, even if not feasible. In both cases these thinkers formulate their arguments based on reasoning from Islamic texts – although interestingly, Bishri prioritizes national unity where 'Awa merely assumes a national context for realizing Islamic principles. Bishri asserts that Islamic scholars (*'ulama*) must engage in *ijtihad* (independent reasoning) to find a formula in the Islamic heritage (*turath*), for granting full and equal rights to Copts in order to remove any religious obstacles that stand in the way of the realization of national unity.[87] While affirming that a Coptic head of state is not feasible demographically, Bishri also maintains that depriving Copts of this right (even if it cannot be realized) would threaten national unity.[88] 'Awa asserts that the general principle of the Qur'an and sunna is that Muslims deal in a fair manner with those who respond in kind, regardless of religion. He also interprets those passages in the Qur'an that call for *jihad* against non-believers to apply only in particular circumstances necessitating a defensive *jihad*. Thus, contemporary Muslims must use *ijtihad* that follows these precedents and are justified in ignoring earlier opinions in the *shari'a* and *turath* that contradict a policy of just and kind treatment.[89] In a similar spirit, 'Awa responded to an inquiry as to what is the Islamic opinion on nominating and voting for Copts and women in an election by stating that qualifications such as honesty, absence of corruption, and courage in facing evils are the proper criterion for selecting candidates: "according to these criteria, Muslism and Copts are equal, as are men and women."[90] In a national context, Bishri and 'Awa maintain that the *umma* both binds and transcends differences of gender, religion, and ideology.

A Christian Islamist?

While certainly Christians cannot be Muslims, as Qaradawi confirms, the gestures that Islamists have made toward non-Muslims leads one to raise the question of whether a Christian could sign on to the moderate Islamist political project. One effort to draw from Islam's intellectual legacy in providing a model of contemporary governance has been presented by Rafiq Habib (b. 1956), a Protestant sociologist, son of Egypt's Anglican bishop, co-founder of Egypt's Wasat Party, and a staunch believer in political solutions rooted in Islamic civilization. In a 2001 work, Habib looks, from a national perspective, at the salience of developing a socio-political model which does not ignore people's cultural and religious sensitivities – a neglect of which Habib believes many Western models are guilty. Habib also asks the important question: why have Arabs and Muslims lagged in evolving a modern Islamic political model? Development and progress at the turn of the century, wrote Habib, only meant one thing: adopting a Western perspective, "so that it was a process of transferring a certain model to our land rather than a process of learning."[91] Instead, people should look to their own, indigenous traditions in developing modes of governance. For Habib, this means looking to Islam, and provides his justification for joining with former and present members of the Muslim Brothers in the creation of a political party.

The Coptic presence in particular signals the party's commitment to national unity that extends beyond Islam. In the context of the nascent Wasat the understanding of "Islam as a civilization" (*islam ka-hadara*) that encompasses both Muslims and non-Muslims is carried further to encompass full civic equality for all members of the *umma*, as citizens of state, regardless of faith. Habib maintains that: "Our Islamic identity is both religious and cultural. When we speak about al-Wasat, we refer to a cultural identity which all people, whether in Egypt or any other Arab country, have in common, be they Christians or Muslims."[92] "As an Arab Christian," Habib explains, "I identify with the value system of the Arab and Islamic civilization which expresses my feelings and my preferences."

Habib understands the party to encompass what he takes to be Islamic values of *hadarat al-wasat* (the culture of the center) and in this sense to provide a common ground between Muslims and non-Muslims, and one that draws not just from Islam, but also from Christianity.[93] Thus, at the same time that members underscore what they take to be the Islamic character of the Wasat Party, Habib and other members also insist upon the party's "civic character." While this is in part of concession to Egyptian law which forbids parties based on religion, it also reflects something more profound. According to the views expressed by Salah 'Abd al-Karim, the author of al-Wasat's second party platform, Christian contributions to the Arab-Islamic heritage, including their role in defending the homeland against outside invasion, constitutes the basis for their full equality and citizenship. By virtue of this shared history of struggle, Christians become co-partners (*shuraka*), rather than being conscribed to the traditional status of "protected peoples" (*dhimmi*s).[94] According to the Wasat platform, the basis of the Arab-Islamic civilization that is shared by Muslims and non-Muslims alike lies in the values placed on public freedoms, human rights, and national unity, and a common opposition to tyranny and terrorism.[95] Further, according to this platform, the institution of *jizya* (the poll-tax or tribute paid by *dhimmi*s living under Islamic rule in exchange for public services, such as defense) is said not to apply to contemporary Egypt. In the modern world, Christians are full members of the Islamic *umma* (and Egyptian *umma*), even to the extent that a Christian could presumably lead a Muslim-majority nation. The justification is that Muslims and Christians (at least those who inhabit Muslim contexts) share the same values.

The fact remains that neither the views of the nascent Wasat Party, nor those of *wasatiyya* intellectuals are shared by the leadership, let alone rank and file, of Islamist organizations such as the Muslim Brotherhood. In Egypt, former spiritual guide Mustafa Mashhour maintained that Copts should not be allowed to serve in the military[96] and no leader of the Muslim Brotherhood holds that a non-Muslim could head an Islamic state. Muhammad Habib, the first deputy of the Brotherhood's supreme guide, recently reiterated the prohibition of non-Muslim leadership more broadly: "If we are to apply the Islamic rule which says that non-Muslims have no guardianship over Muslims, then a Christian may not be president," while noting that this rule formed the "only exception" to equal citizenship of non-Muslims under an Islamic state.[97] Bishri replied to Habib's comment by constitutions and laws, not individuals, rule in modern states and thus, from a legal standpoint, "it doesn't matter if the president is Muslim or Christian."[98] Despite the boldness of Bishri's reply, moderates seem to be staking a position that assures Muslims that they will not be ruled by non-Muslims, while also assuring non-Muslims (and secularists) that they do not view a formal litmus test that would legally bar them from political office as necessary.

Community and dialog

According to Riaz Hasan, "*umma*" denotes "a transnational community which encompasses all Muslims and whose cohesiveness and social integration is inspired by, and based on, the commonly shared faith of Islam."[99] Nonetheless, as he points out, the ambiguity of the term has allowed "Muslim leaders and ideologues to manipulate its meaning and usage in order to conduct their affairs and the affairs of the society according to the appropriate political and social milieu of the time."[100] A growing number of works are focusing on the question of whether transnational *jihadi* movements, online fatwas, satellite broadcast of Friday sermons and Islamic talk shows, and so forth, are contributing to a global *umma*. These global processes are clearly important for accounting for reformatted notions of an Islamic community. However, less attention is often paid to the interaction of these transnational trends with equally important but more localized processes: re-articulations of the notion of the *umma* in response to cross-ideological and cross-religious differences within a given context.[101] Where the former posits a homogenizing force, the latter draws attention to the ways in which this concept is being transformed in order to account for – and create unity across – diversity in the context of shared spaces.

Such formulations of an *umma* contain a concession to existing nation states, even assuming a national context in their approach to politics. Certainly earlier Islamists also understood the importance of nationalism, even Arab nationalism. Hasan al-Banna understood nationalism to be a basis for the renaissance of Islam and Islamic unity: "The Brotherhood respect their particular nationality, considering it the basic foundation of their cherished renaissance. They do not consider it wrong that a person works for his country over other countries. But after this, the Brotherhood supports Arab unity as the next step toward renaissance. They then strive for Pan-Islamism."[102] Yet Banna was also clear that he took loyalty to Islam and "the tie of belief" to be supreme and the more important demarcation to be that between believers and non-believers, regardless of nationality.[103] *Wasatiyya* intellectuals would not disagree, but seem not only more willing to build bridges with non-Islamist groups and non-Muslims, but also view that bridge-building as not just a step to an Islamic unity, but as an enduring facet of the hoped-for Islamic state.

In a 1998 interview Rashid al-Ghannushi maintains that diverse ideologies can work together as members of a single *umma*, without a loss of purpose for either one: "Cooperation with moderate nationalists is an important strategic achievement for the *Ummah* regardless of the gain or loss for this tendency or the other ... When it was achieved, none of the two tendencies abandoned the essence of its mission, but just liberated itself from some of the concepts that it came to be identified with, while it is not really part of it."[104] Despite the fact that Arab nationalists and leftists, on the one hand, and Islamic moderates, on the other, seem to be embracing larger and overlapping Arab-Islamic spheres, these discussions also reveal a measure of political pragmatism when it comes to the nation state and its centrality as a locale for the settling of political claims. In Ghannushi's words:

today the choice is not between an Islamic state ruled by *Shari'a* and a secular Arab nationalist state, but rather the choice proposed to our *Ummah* is between resistance in order to preserve the minimum of what we possess including the independence of our states and in addition demand greater freedom, openness and cooperation between them, or else using us against each other and our decline towards further partition as prelude to what some call the Israeli era.[105]

The understanding of Islam as a cultural heritage shared by Muslims and non-Muslims would seem to mitigate assertions that Islam provides a blueprint for politics for the state, or even a judicial code, since the political community that is the basis for political life contains Islamic and non-Islamic members, religious and secular ideas and ideologies. However, questions still remain as to the status of religious minorities and whether freedom of expression is protected for agnostics, atheists, or Muslims who hold unorthodox (heretical) views. So too, even to the extent that moderate Islamists have addressed these issues in a progressive way, equal status for women, non-Muslims, and other minorities (whether of ethnicity or perspective), remain a marginal issue, rather than a central pillar in the political platforms of those groups and parties inspired by their thought.

NOTES

1. The secularist literary critic, George Tarabishi (Syria, b. 1939), prefers the phrasing, "enlightened salafi trend" (*al-tayyar al-salafi al-mutanawwur*), citing the willingness of individuals like Muhammad al-'Imara to compromise Islamic orthodoxy for liberal or progressive principles. Interestingly, he places Rashid Ghannushi in the "pure salafi trend" (*al-tayyar al-salafi al-khalis*), wrongly in my view. *al-Muthaqafun al-'arab wa al-turath* (Arab Intellectuals and the Heritage) (London: Riyad al-rayyis, 1992).

2. Qaradawi is founder of the Shari'a faculty at the University of Qatar and currently the head of the European Council for Fatwa and Research. He regularly appears on a weekly *al-Jazeera* program that attracts millions of viewers, *Shari'a and Life*. His opinions and rulings are also featured on Islamonline.net, one of the most visited Arabic-English web portals issuing fatwas, hosting discussion forums on religious topics, and linking to writings on topics reflecting a wide array of issues of interest to Muslims throughout the world.

3. Ahmad Kamal Abu al-Majd. *Ruya islamiyya mu'asira* (Cairo: Dar al-shuruq, 1991).

4. The party has sought and been denied state licensing as an official party multiple times. The members that remain vow to continue to seek for party status. In the meantime, the group successfully petitioned in 2000 for a permit to establish a cultural association aimed at promoting cross-ideological dialog. The organization, called *Misr, lil-thaqafa wa al-hiwar* (Egypt, for Culture and Dialog) is led by Muhammad Salim al-'Awa.

5. Jillian Schwedler. *Faith in Moderation: Islamist Parties in Jordan and Yemen* (Cambridge University Press, 2006), 3.

6. H. A. R. Gibb. *Studies on the Civilization of Islam* (London: Routledge & Kegan Paul, 1962), 173.

7. Ferdinand Tönnies. *Community and Society*, tr. Charles P. Loomis (Michigan State University Press, 1957).

8. Muslim thinkers refer continually to the early days of Islam, which are believed to have contained greater continuity of the *umma* than the present. For example, Mawdudi argued that although "differences on the basis of nationality, race and tribal conflicts did crop up now and again … the idea that the Muslims of the world constitute one *Ummah* remained intact … Islamic history is replete with instances where a Muslim went out of his country and lived in other Muslim lands for decades. He might have studied in one country, engaged in business in another, become a minister or commander-in-chief of the army in a third one and, then he might go over to yet another, settle there and get married. A well-known example is Ibn Batuta's who traveled through different Muslim countries for twenty-seven years. He did not need a passport or a visa to go to any of these countries. Nowhere was he questioned about his nationality." *Unity of the Muslim World*, tr. Khurshid Ahmad (Lahore: Islamic Publications, 1967), 14–15. In contrast, Gibb argues that the question of community – how to establish and maintain it – was one Islam faced from its very beginning, and was especially pressing with the death of Muhammad: "there were plenty of obstacles: fanatics who vindicated their conviction of being the only true heirs of Muhammad by rebellion and slaughter, partisans of rival claimants to the government of the community, disputes over principles and details of legal development." "But," Gibb continues, "it is precisely through these experiences that the concept of *ummah* gained in clarity and significance." *Studies on the Civilization of Islam*, 173.

9. Butrus Abu-Manneh. "The Christians between Ottomanism and Syrian Nationalism: The Ideas of Butrus al-Bustani," *International Journal of Middle East Studies* 11 (1980), 287.

10. Abdullah al-Ahsan. *Ummah or Nation? Identity Crisis in Contemporary Muslim Society* (Leicester: The Islamic Foundation, 1992), 3.

11. Raymond William Baker. *Islam Without Fear: Egypt and the New Islamists* (Harvard University Press, 2003), 3.

12. Yusuf al-Qaradawi. *Islamic Awakening Between Rejection and Extremism* (Herndon, VA: International Institute of Islamic Thought, 1990), 21–23. First published as *Sahwah al-Islamiyya bayna al-juhud wa al-tatarruf* (Qatar: Ri'asa al-mahakim al-shar'iyya wa al-shu'un al-diniyya, 1981).

13. Yusuf al-Qaradawi. *Priorities of the Islamic Movement in the Coming Phase* (Swansea: Awakening Publications, 2000), revised translation of the original 1992 translation of *Awlawiyyat al-haraka al-islamiyya fi al-marhala al-qadima* (Cairo: Maktaba wahba, 1991).

14. Qaradawi. *Islamic Awakening*, 11.

15. *Priorities*, 19, 21. The original paper was presented in Algeria; the published version represents a revised and extended version of what he presented there.

16. The editor of the revised translation of Qaradawi's work affirms the context of the work as a "stage of stagnation, a period that we are currently

experiencing among Islamic movements" (11). In his introduction to this same edition, Ghannushi credits Qaradawi with filling the need for a modern and moderate understanding of Islam brought about by the "winds of extremism and waves of disputes (*fitan*) and the poisons of takfeer (charge of unbelief) and rigidity" (13).

17. Qaradawi. *Islamic Awakening*, 56.
18. Kamal Abu al-Majd. *Hiwar la muwajaha* (Dialog, Not Confrontation) (Cairo: Dar al-shuruq, 1988).
19. Qaradawi. *Priorities*, 205–207, 212–213, 219.
20. Qaradawi credits Roger Garaudy (b. 1913), a French convert to Islam, with coining the phrase "dialogue of civilizations." *Priorities*, 209.
21. Qaradawi. *Priorities*, 199–200. The symposium to which Qaradawi refers was organized by Saad Eddin Ibrahim and Ahmad Sidqi al-Dajani at the Arab Thought Forum in March 1987. The proceedings have been published as Ibrahim and Dajani (eds.). *al-Sahwah al-Islamiyya wa humum al-watan al-'arabi* (Amman: Arab Thought Forum, 1988).
22. S. M. Hasan al-Banna notes in the editor's introduction to Qaradawi's *Priorities* that the understanding of "Islam as a complete code of life" remains an "ideological obstacle" common among many Muslims who consider "Islam completely compatible with secularism" (10).
23. Qaradawi. *Priorities*, 70–71.
24. While one may not be able to be a "Muslim Christian," Qaradawi's own claims about the benefits of Islamic governance for devoted Christians, as well as Rafiq Habib's championing of the Islamist cause, suggest that one can be an Islamist Christian.
25. Qaradawi. *Priorities*, 129.
26. Qaradawi. *Priorities*, 133.
27. Qaradawi. *Priorities*, 45.
28. Qaradawi. *Priorities*, 48–49.
29. Qaradawi. *Priorities*, 60.
30. Qaradawi. *Priorities*, 54.
31. Qaradawi. *Priorities*, 135–136.
32. Qaradawi. *Priorities*, 140.
33. See Sayyid Qutb. *Social Justice in Islam*, tr. John B. Hardie and Hamid Algar (New York: Octagon Books, 2000) and S. Abul A'la Maududi (Mawdudi). *Political Theory of Islam*, tr. Khurshid Ahmad (Lahore: Islamic Publications, 1968).
34. Qaradawi. *Islamic Awakening*, 163.
35. Qaradawi. *al-Ijtihad al-mu 'asir bayna al-indibat wa al-infirat* (Contemporary Independent Reasoning between Discipline and Dissolution) (Cairo: Dar al-tawzi' wa al-nashr al-islamiyya), 110–111.
36. Qaradawi. *Islamic Awakening*, 156.
37. Qaradawi. *Islamic Awakening*, 186, 189.
38. Qaradawi. *Islamic Awakening*, 163.
39. Qaradawi. *Islamic Awakening*, 164–165.
40. Qaradwai. *Islamic Awakening*, 121.
41. Qaradwai. *Islamic Awakening*, 122.
42. Qaradawi. *Islamic Awakening*, 31–32.

43. Qaradawi. *Islamic Awakening*, 187.
44. Qaradawi. *Islamic Awakening*, 187
45. Qaradawi. *Islamic Awakening*, 188.
46. Qaradawi. *Islamic Awakening*, 188–189. See also *al-Islam wa al-'almaniyya, wajhan li-wajh: radd 'ilmi 'ala duktur fu'ad zakariyya wa jama'at al-'almaniyya* (Islam and Secularism, Face to Face: A Scientific Reply to Dr. Fu'ad Zakariyya and the Group of Secularists) (Cairo: Dar al-sahwa, 1987), 128–129.
47. Qaradawi. *Islamic Awakening*, 50–51.
48. Rashid Ghannouchi. "The Participation of Islamists in a Non-Islamic Government" in Azzam Tamimi (ed.), *Power Sharing Islam?* (London: Liberty Publications, 1993), 51–63.
49. Qaradawi. *Islamic Awakening*, 26.
50. Hasan Turabi. *Emancipation of Women: An Islamic Perspective*, 2nd edn (London: Muslim Information Centre, 2000), v. The first edition, published 1991 under the title, *Women in Islam and Modern Society*, is a translation of *al-Ittija al-islami yuqddimu al-mara bayna ta'alim al-din wa taqalid al-mujtama'* (The Islamic Trend on Women, Between the Teachings of Religion and the Traditions of Society) (Jeddah: al-Dar al-sa'udiyya, 1984).
51. Turabi. *Emancipation of Women*, 47, 52.
52. El-Affendi. "Introduction," in Turabi, *Emancipation of Women*, vi–vii.
53. Turabi. *Emancipation of Women*, 1.
54. Turabi. *Emancipation of Women*, 9.
55. Turabi. *Emancipation of Women*, 15.
56. Turabi. *Emancipation of Women*, 18, my emphasis.
57. Turabi. *Emancipation of Women*, 24.
58. Turabi. *Emancipation of Women*, 17.
59. Turabi. *Emancipation of Women*, 20.
60. Turabi. *Emancipation of Women*, 49.
61. Turabi. *Emancipation of Women*, 45–47.
62. Turabi. *Emancipation of Women*, 47–48.
63. Qaradawi. *Priorities*, 90–91.
64. Fahmi Huwaydi. "Rabihat al-dimuqratiyya wa khasira al-Islamiyyun!" (Democracy Won and the Islamists Lost), *al-Ahram* (December 7, 1999), 11. An informative linguistic analysis of the column is provided in Michele Durocher Dunne. *Democracy in Contemporary Egyptian Political Discourse* (Amsterdam: John Benjamins Publishing Company, 2003), 122–124.
65. Muhammad al-'Imara. *al-Islam wa al-mara fi ray al-imam muhammad 'abduh* (Islam and Women in the View of Imam Muhammad 'Abduh) (Cairo: al-Qahirah lil-Thaqafah al-'arabiyya, 1975) and *Qasim Amin: tahrir al-mara wa al-tamaddun al-islami* (Qasim Amin: The Liberation of Women and Islamic Civilization) (Beirut: Dar al-wahda, 1985).
66. Muhammad al-'Imara. *al-Tahrir al-islami lil-mara: al-rad 'ala shubhat al-ghula* (The Islamic Liberation of Women: A Reply to Doubts Raised by Extremists) (Cairo: Dar al-shuruq, 2002), 23.
67. 'Imara. *al-Tahrir al-islami lil-mara*, 122.

68. Qasim Amin. *The Liberation of Women and the New Woman: Two Documents in the History of Egyptian Feminism*, tr. Samiha Sidhom Peterson (Cairo: The American University in Cairo Press, 2000), 72

69. See S. Abul A'la Maududi (Mawdudi). *Rights of Non-Muslims in Islamic State*, tr. Khurshid Ahmad (Lahore: Islamic Publications, 1961).

70. Hasan al-Banna. *Ila al-shabab wa ila al-talaba khassa* (To the Youth and Especially the Students) (Cairo: Dar al-da'wa, n.d.), 15; Sa'id Ramadan. *Ma'alim al-tariq* (Signposts of the Way) (Damascus: n.p., 1955); and Muhammad al-Ghazzali. *Our Beginning in Wisdom*, tr. Ismail al-Faruqi (Washington, DC: American Council of Learned Societies, 1953), 80.

71. See Tariq al-Bishri. *al-Muslimun wa al-aqbat fi itar al-jama'a al-wataniyya* (Muslims and Copts in the Framework of a National Society) (Cairo: al-Haya al-misriyya lil-kitab, 1980); Muhammad al-'Imara, *al-Islam wa al-sulta al-diniyya* (Islam and Religious Authority) (Cairo: Dar al-thaqafa al-jadida, 1979).

72. Yusuf al-Qaradawi. *The Lawful and the Prohibited in Islam* (Kuala Lumpur: Islamic Book Trust, 2001), 338. Translated from *al-Halal wa al-haram fi al-Islam* (Cairo: 'Isa al-babi al-halabi, 1960).

73. Rashid al-Ghannushi. *Huquq al-muwatana: huquq ghayr al-muslim fi al-mujtama' al-islami* (The Rights of Citizens: The Rights of Non-Muslims in Islamic Society) (Herndon, VA: International Institute of Islamic Thought, 1993), 65–75.

74. Abu al-Majd. *Ruya islamiyya mu'asira*, 15–18.

75. Fahmi Huwaydi. *Muwatinun la dhimmiyyun* (Citizens not Protected Peoples) (Beirut: Dar al-shuruq, 1985).

76. Huwaydi. *Muwatinun la dhimmiyun*, 148.

77. Qaradawi. *Priorities*, 192.

78. Qaradawi. *Priorities*, 196.

79. Qaradawi. *Priorities*, 194.

80. This and other statements by Qaradawi on Sunni–Shi'i relations can be found at www.islamonline.net. Qaradawi also endorsed what has come to be known as "The Amman Message," a sermon delivered by Jordan's Chief Justice Shaykh Iz al-Din al-Tamimi and which called for tolerance and acknowledged the diversity within Islam, affirmed the validity of all eight traditional schools of Islam (including Shi'is, Ibadis, and Thahiris) and forbade declarations of apostasy (*takfir*) against adherents to any of the schools. The text of the Message and a list of its signatories is available online at www.ammanmessage.com.

81. Abu al-Majd. *Ruya islamiyya mu'asira*, 18.

82. See also Muhammad al-'Imara. *Hal al-islam huwa al-hal? limadha wa-kayfa?* (Is Islam the Solution? Why and How?) (Cairo: Dar al-shuruq, 1995), 173.

83. Muhammad Salim al-'Awa. *On the Political System of the Islamic State* (Indianapolis: American Trust Publications, 1980), a translation of *Fi al-nizam al-siyasi lil-dawla al-islamiya* (Alexandria: al-Maktab al-misri al-hadith, 1975).

84. Yusuf al-Qaradawi. *Ghayr muslimin fi al-mujtama' al-islami* (Non-Muslims in Islamic Society) (Cairo: 1975), 7, 82.

85. 'Imara. *Hal al-islam al-hal*, 170–173.
86. Muhammad Salim al-'Awa. "Bal al-jizya fi dhimat al-tarikh" (But Jizya is in the Realm of History), *al-Wafd* (April 18, 1997). The Brotherhood's current spiritual guide, Muhammad Mahdi 'Akif (b. 1928), expresses a view closer to the *wasatiyya* intellectuals, as will be discussed in Chapter 4.
87. Tariq al-Bishri. *al-Muslimun wa al-aqbat fi itar al-jama'a al-wataniyya* (Muslims and Copts in the Framework of a National Society) (Cairo: al-Hay'a al-misriyya lil-kitab, 1980), 685ff.
88. Bishri. *al-Muslimun wa al-aqbat*, 712–713. Bishri bases his argument on the principle of taking the easier route – the principle of facilitation emphasized by Qaradawi.
89. 'Awa. *On the Political System*, 112–113, 119.
90. Muhammad Salim al-'Awa. Column in *al-Sha'b* newspaper, published by the 'Amal Party (November 21, 1995).
91. Rafiq Habib. *al-Umma wa al-dawla: bayan tahrir al-umma* (Nation and State: Manifesto on the Liberation of the Umma) (Cairo: Dar al-shuruq, 2001).
92. Karim al-Gawhary. "'We are a Civil Party with an Islamic Identity': An Interview with Abu 'Ila Madi Abu 'Ila and Rafiq Habib," *Middle East Report* 199 (1996), 30.
93. Rafiq Habib. *Hadara al-wasat* (The Culture of the Center) (Cairo: Dar al-shuruq, 2001).
94. Salah 'Abd al-Karim. *Awraq hizb al-wasat al-misri* (Papers of the Egyptian Wasat Party) (Cairo: n.p., 1998), 21.
95. Rafiq Habib. *Awraq hizb al-wasat al-misri* (Papers of the Egyptian Wasat Party) (Cairo: n.p., 1996), 16.
96. *al-Ahram Weekly* (April 3, 1997).
97. Amira Howeidy. "Muslim Brotherhood Flexes Muscles," www.aljazeera.net (December 5, 2005).
98. Ibid.
99. Riaz Hassan. *Faithlines: Muslim Conceptions of Islam and Society* (Oxford University Press, 2002), 84.
100. Hassan. *Faithlines*, 86. Hassan notes that "the term ummah appears sixty-four times in the Qur'an with multiple and diverse meanings ranging from followers of a prophet, of a divine plan of salvation, a religious group, a small group within a larger community of believers, misguided people and, an order of beings" (85–86).
101. Peter Mandaville. *Global Political Islam* (London: Routledge, 2007), nicely captures the interplay between local instances of Islamic politics and broader global trends.
102. Hassan al-Banna. *Risala al-mu'tamar al-khamis* (Cairo: Dar al-kitab al-'arabi, nd), 49.
103. Banna. *Risa'il al-thalatha* (Three Letters) (Cairo: Dar al-tiba'a wa al-nashr al-islamiyya, 1977), 25.
104. Rashid Ghannushi. "IntraView with Tunisian Sheikh Rached Ghannoushi" (February 10, 1998). Online at www.msanews.mynet.net/intra2.html.
105. Ghannushi. "IntraView."

3 Framing a cross-ideological alliance

Much of the intellectual basis for development of cross-ideological alliances in the region has been provided by the works of Arab nationalist and leftist intellectuals who have increasingly looked to Islamic sources in their accounts of the Arab nation and the writings of various Islamists who have sought to present a more moderate and inclusive vision of Islam. In many respects, the members of these ideological groupings have been brought together by the imperatives of politics and history. Arab nationalists and leftists have sought to tap into the popular appeal Islamism seems to hold. Islamists have looked to Arab nationalists and leftists as allies in resisting the harassment and imprisonment of their members and in bypassing various restrictions on their political activity. Cooperation has been encouraged not only by domestic issues (such as closed political systems), but also regional issues (such as lack of progress in Palestine and increased US intervention in Iraq and other parts of the Gulf) and global issues (such as globalization and international anti-globalization activism). As noted in the previous chapter, "moderate" in the context of these political trends should not be mistaken for non-confrontational or pro-Western.

Interactions among the intellectuals discussed in the first two chapters have both contributed to – and been facilitated by – a series of forums, conferences, and dialogs that have enabled members of a wide variety of groups to develop personal relationships and mutual understandings, and which have proven pivotal in coordinating political activities in a number of contexts. The various forums are different in significant ways, revealing varying scopes (global, regional, and local) and distinct agendas and purposes. Some of the forums seem to have their origins in intellectual projects. For example, in 1998, Dar al-Fikr, a publishing house based in Damascus, Syria began publishing a series entitled "Dialogues for a New Century," which pits ideologically opposed intellectuals against one another other in the context of a single volume. Two Syrians, the Marxist philosopher, Tayyib Tizini, and the popular Islamic preacher, Muhammad Sa'id al-Buti, started off the series with a discussion of "Islam and the Age, Challenges and Horizons."[1] The secular writer and Damascus Spring activist, 'Abd al-Razzaq 'Id, and the Islamist activist, Muhammad 'Abd al-Jabbar, faced off on the theme of "Democracy, Between Secularism and Islam."[2] A female Islamist activist, Heba Raouf Ezzat, and the secular feminist, Nawal Sa'dawi, take on the issues of "Women, Religion and Ethics."[3] Secular scientist, Hani Rizq, and the religious Saudi doctor, Khalis Jalabi, address the topic of "Faith and the Scientific Progress."[4] Despite the series' promising title, these books fall far short of "dialog," since each author addresses the topic independently and only later reads the writing of their foil and offers a short commentary. The aim of this exercise seems more to contrast two opposing views on a topic rather than to put them in conversation, let alone attempt to reconcile them.

Other forums trace their origins to foreign sources aimed at democratization, development and cross-cultural dialog. In this regard, the Center for the Study of Islam and Democracy (CSID), a non-profit organization established in Washington, DC in 1999, largely funded by US taxpayers (through the US Institute of Peace), and "dedicated to studying Islamic and democratic political thought and merging them into a modern Islamic democratic discourse"[5] has convened a number of conferences aimed at bringing together an ideologically broad range of political actors in various Arab countries. Whereas most previous CSID activities had taken place in the United States, in 2002 the center began organizing a series of workshops in Morocco, Egypt, and Yemen, aimed at bringing Islamist and secular forces together in order to discuss the questions of democracy and its relationship to Islam. A second series of workshops were held in Turkey, Algeria, and Jordan in 2004. No workshops have been held since, perhaps indicating waning support for "democracy promotion" in the US and an increased focus on a lagging domestic economy, though the CSID continues to bring Islamic thinkers, academics, and policy-makers together through their annual conference in Washington, DC.

A third type of forum can be attributed, at least in part, to local, negative reactions to Israeli actions and foreign intervention in the region. As the threat of a US military incursion aimed at regime change in Iraq loomed, other conferences were born, perhaps less focused on dialog than on direct action, such as the Cairo Anti-War Conferences, which have been held almost annually in Egypt since December 2002, with the last one taking place in March and April 2007. Each of the Cairo conferences have been followed either by a demonstration or the publication of a declaration against imperialism, globalization, and Zionism.

While many of these forums will be discussed at greater length in the chapters that follow, I focus here on one of the earliest and most sustained forums aimed at developing relations across ideological divides. The National-Islamic Conferences (NIC) were instigated by the Center for Arab Unity Studies (*markaz dirasat al-wahda al-'arabi*, hereafter "CAUS") in Beirut, a think-tank and publishing house mainly concerned with research on political issues of concern to the Arab region. The CAUS is well-known and its publications are widely distributed throughout the Arab region. As indicated by its name, the CAUS was established in 1975 by intellectuals sympathetic to the pan-Arab movement. Although the Arab nationalist ideology that formed the Center's founding principles tends to be associated with a socialist orientation, in the context of this organization, that ideological coupling was loose at its founding, and only seems to have become more so over time. Further, the Center's conferences and congresses today aim to include "the largest possible number of intellectuals and specialists from all Arab countries and in all fields." According to the organization's pamphlet:

the identity of contributors to the Centre's activities is subject to no preconditions apart from the requirement that they believe firmly in Arab unity, whatever other beliefs and opinions they may hold. The Centre represents a forum for free dialogue in which there is room for a full range of opinions.[6]

Similarly, the "firm belief" in Arab unity stated above no longer involves the early pan-Arabist vision of a single Arab state, so much as it advocates a federated political unity that acknowledges the plurality of national and other identities in the Arab world.[7] As the CAUS has attempted to bring a wider range of perspectives into its conferences – not least of which includes an Islamic perspective – it has developed a nationalist framework that increasingly enables convergences with liberal and Islamist forces. The formation of strategic alliances with the aim of facilitating mobilization has, in turn, had an impact on the ideological character of the organization. While one might be tempted to view these convergences as evidence of the resiliency of Arab nationalism as a distinct ideology, what the evidence reveals is a growing number of individuals from diverse political ideologies who are increasingly framing their collaboration in ways that reveal the quasi-contingency of the Arab nationalist ideal.

In contrast to some neo-liberal and leftist forces in the region, who prefer to ally themselves with the state in order to curb the tide of political Islam, as the opening speeches of the first NIC attest, a number of left-leaning Arab nationalists believe that (at least some) Islamists can be nationalized (Arabized) and rationalized (if not secularized). There are many trends in Islam and the intellectuals who run the CAUS find that if they are willing to shelve the question of secularism they are able to find plenty of meeting points with at least some of the Islamists. Basheer Nafi traces the origins of this Arab nationalist–Islamist engagement to the Arab defeat in the 1967 war:

> In the root of the [CAUS National-Islamic Conference's] founding were some of the fundamental changes that the Arab state and politics experienced after the third Arab-Israeli war of 1967. The 1967 defeat was not only seen as the ultimate failure of the Arab state but also signaled the beginning of the end for the alliance between the ruling clique and the Arab nationalist intellectual. For the great majority of Arab intellectuals, disengagement from the state's bankrupt project looked now as the only way for survival ... While the Arab nationalist intellectual joined the forces of opposition, the state entered the postnationalist age in which ideological authoritarianism was replaced with self-serving policies of limited political openness ... [A]s the distance between the Arab intellectual and the state evidently increased, the intellectuals discourse grew more and more to resemble that of the Islamist.[8]

However, both the timing and reference points provided by the conference organizers and participants suggest that it was the 1979 Islamic revolution in Iran that propelled this project. Arab nationalists clearly have some political and strategic interests in allying themselves more closely with the predominant oppositional force in the region. At the same time, taken together, the dialogs reveal that the trajectory of this alliance since the first CAUS conference seeking to theorize the nationalist–religious ideology relation (held in 1989) is more complex than merely a shift toward Islamism on the part of Arab nationalists.

A number of intellectuals associated with CAUS first demonstrated interest in political Islam after the Islamic revolution in Iran. At the end of 1979, the Arab Society for Sociology held a conference in Cairo on the topic of "Arab Nationalism and Islam" to address the relationship between Arab nationalism and Islam and to understand the strength of the latter.[9] In April of 1988, the Arab Society for Sociology in Cairo held a conference on "Religion in Arab Society."[10] The CAUS published the proceedings of this and the 1979 conference. In September 1988, a "National-Religious Dialogue" was held in Cairo, which, unlike the earlier meetings, included a number of prominent and moderate members of the Islamist trend, such as Rashid Ghannushi, Muhammad al-'Imara, Muhammad al-Ghazzali, 'Issam al-'Ariyan, and Fahmi Huwaydi.[11] Shortly thereafter, the matter of establishing a regular meeting of representatives from a wide range of Arab nationalist and Islamist organizations was proposed at the CAUS fourth annual Arab Nationalist conference in 1993 and an organizing committee made up

of members of groups representing both trends was set up for this purpose. The first such conference was held the next year in Beirut.

To some extent, the effect of the idea of reaching out to political
Islam is apparent by the sixth annual conference the following year.
The question "Is the *umma* Arab?" – that is, how do we understand
the relationship of Arab and Islamic notions of unity? – formed the
topic of the first round of talks that year. Beginning with the seventh
annual conference and continuing through the eleventh, that question
becomes the preface to the title of the published proceedings.[12] According to CAUS executive director, Khayr al-Din Hasib, the impetus for
this overture to Islamists was the realization that various oppositional
forces would be stronger allied than fighting amongst themselves. The
Islamists brought some of the popular appeal that the Arab nationalists
had lost and the Arab nationalists brought access to channels of power
and official institutions that had been closed off to many Islamists.[13] The
first "National-Islamic Conference" was held the next year in Beirut,
October 10–12, 1994, and four additional conferences have been held
since, with the last large conference taking place in December 2004.[14]
Nonetheless, this series of forums stands out not only for the ideological
breadth of individuals and groups it has brought together, but also for
the fact that it has been sustained for over a decade. The conferences
have succeeded in bringing together members of a wide variety of intellectuals, ideologues, and officials from a number of groups and institutions – from Hizbullah to the Lebanese Communist Party, from Hamas
to the PLO and PFLP, and from the heads of writers' and lawyers'
syndicates to university professors from various Arab countries.

The controversial nature of these conferences is attested to in the
correspondence among the participants between the first and second
conference that Dajani published, by his own account, in order to demonstrate that the dialog continued outside of the regular meetings.[15]
The letters reveal the problems the organizers have had financing and
with finding a country to host the meeting (on each occasion, Beirut
proved to be their only option), as well as in negotiating visas and other
official barriers to various members' attendance at the event. While the
proceedings of the first NIC were published shortly after the conference, the 1997 proceedings did not appear until 2000 and the third
and fourth NIC proceedings were published simultaneously, four and
two years after they were held, and only after the NIC received funding
from the Yemeni Shaykh 'Abdullah Bin Husayn al-Ahmar, whose contribution is acknowledged in both volumes. The conference organizers
attempted to hold the third conference in Morocco under the slogan of
"Unity of the *Umma* in Defense of Jerusalem and the Occupied Arab

Lands," since Morocco heads a special delegation for the defense of Jerusalem. The fifth conference was scheduled to be held in Sudan but (like all the other meetings) was delayed and then shifted to Beirut.

In some respects, the "National-Islamic Conferences" (hereafter, NIC) share the shortcomings of the Dar al-Fikr "debates." Rather than indicating a broader ideological convergence, in reading the published papers from the conference it is quite clear that the 1988 "National-Religious Dialogue" that preceded the formation of the NIC was much more dialogic in character, with papers presented and then discussed by all participants – in fact, the bulk of the published proceedings (241 of the book's 363 pages) are given over to discussion as opposed to pre-pared remarks. In contrast, the published proceedings of NIC reveal long lists of prepared remarks, absent the sort of give-and-take that characterized the earlier dialog. So too, the two chapters, each enti-tled "View (ru'aya) of the State of the Umma," that open the 1994 and 1997 National-Islamic Conferences are presented first by the "Islamic view" and then by the "Nationalist view," with no attempt to debate, let alone reconcile, the two statements. The concluding statement is singular, but was published by the conference founding commit-tee. Further, although the first such meeting in September 1989 was entitled "National-Religious Dialogue" (al-Hiwar al-qawmi al-dini), the five later conferences were specified as dialog between nationalist and Islamic thinkers (al-Mu'tamar al-qawmi al-islami). Despite some continuity among the participants, less effort was exerted at the later conferences to account for the plurality of religions in the region, while the central importance of Islam as a regional political force is duly acknowledged.

Nonetheless, in the recorded comments one finds responses, reac-tions, and re-articulations – as well as, on occasion, misunderstandings – spurred by the process of confronting and being confronted by the comments of one's ideological rivals. What analysis of the published pro-ceedings of the first four conferences convened between 1994 and 2004 reveals is that, while Arab nationalists, Islamists, and some leftists and liberals have managed to forge commonalities among their perspectives that enable cooperation in mobilizing support and in confronting vari-ous critical issues they face in contemporary politics, there also remain many points of disagreement that continue to divide the two trends, as well as a number of issues that have proven difficult to broach in the context of the course of their dialogs.[16] That is, I am interested not only in analyzing ways in which these two trends have succeeding in align-ing their discursive frames, but also in drawing attention to their less successful attempt to articulate common perspectives and stances, as well as to those topics introduced by interlocutors on both sides of the ideological divide, but which fail to resonate with, or even appear antithetical to, extant interpretive frames. These three processes – successful, partially successful, and failed attempts at building bridges – are related. The thinness in the concepts of democracy and human rights articulated and the weaknesses of the proposals for political reform put forth in the conference is in part a result of the character of those negative issues that ground the alliance. So too, these less successfully articulated aspects of their coordination disable their attempts to construct a comprehensive and substantive unity by further marginalizing many forces – women, non-Muslims, committed secularists, and youth. More precisely, it is the prevalence of the focus on foreign enemies that both detracts from and complicates attempts to focus on domestic reform and contributes to the perpetuation of illiberal values.

Forging unity to confront the Western assault

Participation of these two traditionally opposed trends in the meetings organized by the CAUS remains contingent, in part, upon their ability to successfully align their interpretive frames, to find meeting points in their respective agendas and to articulate their aims and understandings in ways that resonate with the broadest strata of members from the diverse ideological trends in attendance. The discursive format of the conference proceedings provides much of the necessary material for analysis of the "micromobilization," that is, "the various interactive and communicative processes that affect frame alignment."[17] These meetings reveal several related, but distinct, processes of frame alignment.

The most important bridge constructed between Islamism and Arabism relies upon the revival and reconceptualization of the notion of an "Islamic civilizational circle" as an alternative to the notion of the "Islamic world." The Islamic civilizational circle idea relies at least in part on the amplification of the sphere of "unity" (*wahda*) inherent in Islamist notions of *tawhid* (oneness) and Arab nationalist notions of *qawmiyya* (nationalism), while at the same time downplaying the religious specificity of the Islamic notion of an *umma* (community). This notion was articulated by a number of thinkers discussed in the first two chapters of this volume. For example, according to Dajani, the concept of "Islamic circle" first became popularized when it appeared in the letter of Gamal 'Abd al-Nasir, entitled "The Philosophy of the Revolution," which sought to articulate a civilizational collectivity "that binds the people of Islam despite different races and sects."[18] Dajani maintains that he "added the word '*umran*" (civilizational architecture)

and "began to speak about the Islamic civilizational ('*umran*) circle."
Arab nationalists and leftists assert this to, in part, recognize Islam's
central place in Arab society while mitigating the religion's social, economic, and political force – that is, while maintaining a secular stance.
The notion of an Islamic civilization is also promoted by those who
wish to incorporate non-Muslim Arabs into a greater *umma*.

One detects a similar strategy on the part of Islamists. For example,
the Shi'i scholar from Lebanon, Shaykh Muhammad Husayn Fadlallah
(b. 1935), claims that "even the Christians living in the Arab world
unconsciously think with an Islamic mentality; although they do not
have an Islamic affiliation, they take in Islamic civilization as they do
the air they breathe, like the fragrance of a rose."[19] Similarly, in responding to claims that adding "Islamness" to the description of Jerusalem
alongside "Arabness" might offend Christian Palestinians, Ramadan
'Abdallah Shallah, the secretary-general of the Palestinian Movement
of Islamic Jihad retorts with the question:

Since when has the name of Islam in our homeland offended the feelings of
Christians who have lived for centuries in this land[s] and who have a Muslim
culture and civilization? ... We know many Christian brothers who put forth
the formula "civilizational Islam" as the point on which all currents meet and
as a vessel encompassing all, based on an understanding of and respect for the
history of the nation and its civilizational and national parts.[20]

While this approach to merging national and Islamic notions of unity is
not unique to the NIC, it is expanded and promoted in this forum, as
well as given great significance in enabling the alliances.

A second series of meeting points between the various trends are
constructed in opposition to external or irredentist forces that threaten
the Arab-Islamic civilizational circle. A common struggle is conceived
as one against foreign foes and, in this context, those with more imme-
diacy, such as the conflict with Israel and, more recently, US intervention in Iraq, place a central role, though more abstract notions, such
as anti-imperialism, anti-neo-colonialism and (to a lesser extent) anti-
globalization, can also form rallying points. One seldom sees earlier,
more cultural characterizations of the struggle, such as the struggle
to assert an authentic cultural identity against the forces of modernity, which might reassert a secular–religious divide. The anti-Zion-
ist/anti-US frame reveals diagnostic and motivational aspects, which
center on the issues of justice and liberation: the imbalance of power in
international relations and the injustice of the fate of Palestinians and
Iraqis calls for a movement of liberation for Arab and Islamic peoples
and lands. According to the liberal Islamic thinker Radhwan al-Sayyid

(Lebanon, b. 1949), the raison d'être for the conference is that the Arab nationalists and Islamists, under attack from both Arab regimes and the Americans "decided to come together so as not to fight against each other, but instead to fight against neocolonialism."[21] Layla Sharaf, an Arab nationalist on the NIC organizing committee and member of Jordan's Senate, maintains that the continued collaboration depends on this common oppositional frame: "should peace come about in Palestine, the Arab nationalists and Islamists would not have much in common."[22]

Shaykh Fadlallah makes use of both the Arab-Islamic unity frame and the oppositional frame as he finds support in the Qur'an for working with others of different ideological, as well as religious, persuasions, when their aims are the same:

Christians and Jews differ with Muslims over the interpretation of the unity of God and the personality of God. Despite that, the Qur'an commands: Turn to the principle of unity – the unity of God and the unity of mankind. We interpret this to mean that we can meet with Marxists on the common ground of standing up to the forces of international arrogance; we can meet nationalists, even secular nationalists, on the common ground of Arab causes, which are also Islamic causes.[23]

According to Gudrun Krämer, Islamists make alliances with other parties out of "tactical considerations."[24] When Islamist groups are weak, for example after suffering government crackdowns on their operations, they are perhaps most willing to cooperate with representatives of different ideological outlooks. These concerns about the lack of representation and voice in official and recognized forums have been repeated by a number of the Islamist participants in the conference in other forums. For example, Shaykh Fadlallah notes that "it is true at this stage that in most places Islam lacks political clout ... From the political point of view, the Islamic people and the Islamic *umma* (nation) are dominated and kept in the wings by their rulers."[25]

The polemics against this mobilizing "other" do not always perfectly align. Arab nationalists have historically articulated their opposition to foreign intervention entirely in terms of Western imperialism, focusing primarily on the West's political, economic, and military threat to the region. The Islamist assault on the West usually takes the form of a deeper, religio-cultural antagonism, especially to Western modernity and its accompanying secularism, materialism, and atheism, as classically summed up by Sayyid Qutb's notion of *jahiliyya* or the new age of ignorance (of Islam). Nonetheless, each side demonstrates that they can speak the same language and share a common agenda in regard to confronting the West. This aspect of their alliance is successful to the extent that the CAUS general director, Khayr al-Din Hasib, refers to "the Arab nationalist and Islamist trends" as "two wings that only fly together."[26] Revealing no small measure of the notion that "the enemy of my enemy is my friend," this shared oppositional stance, like the notion of an Arab-Islamic civilizational circle, requires minimal frame realignment on the part of either of the two movements, though some of the longer term goals – such as the nature of the political order to be constructed in a post-Zionist, post-imperialist world – are not addressed.

Toward a program of political reform

"We never discuss religion with them"

The role of religion in the political order in general is seldom discussed with any precision in this forum. As Layla Sharaf succinctly put it, "we never discuss religion with them."[27] Silence on this issue, in turn, hinders the elaboration of notions of democracy and political form, issues that might provide a third substantive base of unity for these opposition groups. Development of a common platform for reform gains some strength to the extent that it is constructed based on common opposition to existing authoritarian regimes. According to Ahmad Sidqi al-Dajani, the first secretary-general of the NIC, tyranny must be confronted through the establishment of "shura, participation and pluralism and rotation of power."[28] Some version of this notion of democracy has existed in Arab political discourse, albeit in fragile form, since the modernist period. For example, the Islamic modernist Sadek J. Sulaiman (Oman, b. 1933) articulates a sentiment that has been reasserted by both Islamists and non-Islamist Muslim thinkers in the region today: "as a concept and as a principle, *shura* in Islam does not differ from democracy;" and, "the relationship between democracy and *shura* touches the essence of our national existence (*qawmiyya*). It determines the quality of our civic experience and the world we would like to leave for future generations. For this reason the subject merits our full attention."[29] Although the secretary-general of the second, third, fourth, and fifth conferences, Muhammad 'Abd al-Malik al-Mutawakkil, a liberal-Islamic professor of political science in Yemen, affirms that "one of the most important basic issues of agreement arrived at in the first founding conference was the nationalist and Islamist trends' choice of democracy, understood as a method of rule and as a tool of peaceful rotation of power," to be applied as an organizing principle for the conference and asserted as a value guiding contemporary Arab political reform,[30] throughout the proceedings of the conferences, democracy never receives full articulation.

Most participants harness the notion of democracy as a bulwark against the authoritarianism in the region and define it as the "rotation of power," with the clearly articulated aim of removing from power some of the corrupt rulers in the region. Jamal al-Atassi argues that the "reaction, quiescence and pacifism" which many tyrannical and authoritarian governments and systems "imposed on us" are best countered through "work to strengthen the values of democracy, *shura*, human rights and pluralism in its society."[31] In addition to the peaceful rotation of power, issues like free and fair elections and the strengthening of civil society are often mentioned as institutions necessary to sustain a democratic political process. On occasion, conference participants assert the necessity of an independent judiciary and the separation of political and military authority.

One of the most commonly heard criticisms of nationalists, socialists, and Islamists in the region is one that doubles as an explanation as to why they have been able to cross ideological divides. Liberal critics, in particular, argue that all of these ideologies share in authoritarian ways of thinking and acceptance of authoritarian routes to political reform and development. In the context of Egypt, Roel Meijer has argued that the state for many nationalist, socialist, and communist intellectuals in Egypt stood for modernity and rationality and, thus, all of these tendencies have focused on the state as the main harbinger of change.[32] Some critics have even charged these groups with a form of populism bordering on fascism, in the sense that the Arab nationalists will work with anyone who adopts the cause of Arab unity, even dictators and tyrants, just as Islamists will support anyone who takes up their cause of Islamicizing state and society.

However, there is another explanation for the failure to articulate a substantive notion of democracy that all sides can agree upon: the different points of reference that each draws from. More specifically, many Islamist groups, such as the Muslim Brotherhood, continue to distinguish between the religion of Islam and its divine message, which offers principles for organizing people's behaviors and dealings, on the one hand, and democracy as a mechanism for rule. That many Islamists view this mechanism as useful and positive in many aspects and contexts is clear, but all values – including social and political values – must come from Islam, not democracy, which is a product of Western civilization. As a result, throughout its history, the Muslim Brotherhood in Egypt, for example, has varied its stance toward democratic systems, rejecting it as foreign in the 1930s and 1940s and in favor of more revolutionary actions in the 1950s and 1960s, while accepting democratic rules and processes in the 1980s and 1990s.

Thus, the relationship between political and religious power is one issue that is seldom taken up. Islamist participants in the NIC, who in other contexts are commonly known to assert the comprehensiveness and unity of Islam as a way of life – *Islam din wa dawla* (Islam is a religion and a state) – and even to maintain that the Qur'an provides the constitution for any Islamic state, are relatively muted in addressing the *shari'a* and its role in issues of governance and from asserting the necessity of an Islamic state at this forum. Most of the few important exceptions to this rule reveal a moderated and contingent stance.

Denial of difference: Christians and secularists

Many Islamist participants choose to distinguish between secularists and their Arab nationalist and socialist interlocutors. For example, in the first NIC's "Islamic Perspective on the State of the Umma," the official Islamist document that opens the conference affirms the necessity of distinguishing the nationalist trend from the secularist trend, even going so far as to deny the central role secularism has played in Arab nationalist thought and practice: "it is not the case intellectually or historically that there is a connection or correspondence between Arab nationalism and secularism." The Islamic statement continues to conflate the points of reference for both Arab nationalist and Islamist thought, while imaging each as tolerant and liberal. "The general referential authority for a project of Arab Renaissance," the statement asserts, "is the Islamic referential authority, though this includes respect for the religious and citizenship rights and freedoms of non-Muslims."[33]

Doubletalk and historical revisionism comes not only from the Islamist participants. CAUS director Khayr al-Din Hasib states that, in light of the confusion of the concept of secularism, especially since it comes from the West, it is important to understand what is meant by the term in the Arab context: "Islamic civilization understands secularism in the Arab framework, such that it means rationalism, democracy and a non-theocratic state. On these concepts the nationalist trend does not disagree with the Islamic trend because this is what the nationalists mean when they use the term."[34] Others, such as Wajih Kawtharani, get beyond the question of secularism by noting its multiple meanings in different traditions and contexts and suggesting that if understood in the broadest sense as "the articulation of a civil or personal opinion," rather than a religious opinion, or "as an opinion based on reason and individual human effort," then we must consider even Rashid Ghannushi to be secular.[35]

Overall, most non-Islamist participants prefer to refrain from discussing the topic of secularism (*'ilmaniyya*) entirely. As the Arab nationalist Moroccan intellectual 'Abd al-Ilah Bilqaziz explains, the question of secularism is important, but now is not the time to discuss it. It is an issue appropriate when one is in possession of the state, "but we are not at the stage of the state; rather, in the language of the nationalists, we are at the stage of the revolution, and, in the language of Islam we are at the stage of *al-daw'a* [the call or missionary activity]."[36] Shafiq al-Hut, a former member of the executive committee for the PLO and secular writer, similarly maintains that "both the current nationalist trend and the Islamic trend do not call an elaboration of their final positions in regard to secularism."[37]

Among the most notable exceptions to the rule of evasion are the interjections of the few non-Muslim participants. Father Antoine Dhaw, a Christian Arab nationalist and secretary-general to the Independent Committee for Christian-Muslim Dialogue, opens his remarks at the first NIC with parallel quotes from the Qur'an and from the second Vatican Council. He states: "I asked myself on the first day of the National-Islamic Conference: Am I a stranger here or alone? A stranger, no! Because I am in the heart of Islam and with my Arab and Muslim Brothers." He recounts how, when Christians were called to defend Islam against foreigners, they heeded the call, and notes the role of Christians in the creation of Arab civilization and the Arab Enlightenment. "We are part of this Arab nation, our destiny is tied to its destiny."[38] The Egyptian Coptic thinker William Sulayman (1924–1999), another NIC participant until his death, has argued that the crusades linked together politics and religion in an un-Christian way and, thus, Egyptian Copts rightly fought alongside Muslims against the foreign invaders. Sulayman is the former vice deputy of the Egyptian State Council, a position also held by Tariq al-Bishri, with whom (in addition to Mustafa al-Fiqi) Sulayman co-authored an important book in 1982 on Muslim–Coptic relations in Egypt, entitled *One People and One Nation*.[39] Like Dhaw, Sulayman puts forth this argument to indicate the authentic patriotism of Egypt's Coptic community and their history of good relations with Egypt's Muslims.

However, Dhaw also notes that "the problematic today is not Islam as a religion or the question of Islamic civilization, but the problematic of the Islamic state or Islamic rule." Thus, he argues, it is important to distinguish between Muslims, with whom they share a civilization and history, and Islamists who advocate a political program.[40] Dhaw even suggests that "we are not absolutely against an Islamic state or an Islamic ruler of the state, as long as this state is one of human rights, reason, democracy, freedoms, justice, development and mutual coexistence" that permits both Muslims and Christians to develop their "rational, scientific and human possibilities." "If such an Islamic state or Islamic rule was established based on pluralism, respect for the other and mutual coexistence, then we would not oppose it." But, at the same time, Dhaw also states in clear and strong language that resounds as a warning that Christians will never accept anything less than these freedoms, true equality and full citizenship: "We will never accept being treated as castes, minorities or confessional groups."[41]

The implications of the failure to systematically and substantively debate this topic are perhaps seen most clearly in regard to the matter of human rights, which many NIC participants and concluding documents assert as a component of democracy. For example, although Hut does not feel it necessary (or perhaps wise) to reach conclusions at the NIC regarding the value and applicability of secularism, he does note the relationship between secularism and freedom of thought, though in the process de-linking democracy and secularism. He argues that "it is necessary to assert that secularism is not a synonym for democracy. There is no synonym for secularism except the true practice of the principles of intellectual pluralism, political freedom, and the refusal to eliminate the other." Secularism, he argues, means that the Islamic trend should be free to work from their Islamic referential authority, while others might work from other reference points.[42] In the context of the conferences, human rights are most commonly mentioned by Islamist participants as freedom from arbitrary arrest and imprisonment of activists, a particular concern of many Islamist activists and leaders. The concerns of secular leaders over charges of heresy and apostasy, and the calls for the death of those so charged, which often result, are less commonly discussed. While a few Arab nationalists and leftists bemoan "those who claim a monopoly on truth," individuals and groups claiming to bear the mantle of "true Islam" and who employ charged religious language in delegitimizing their political opponents, are not taken to task for this at the NIC. The unwillingness or inability of the conferences to more substantially tackle central issues – such as democratization, hindrances to it, and problems with human rights (e.g. intellectuals' lack of freedom of speech) – are among the reasons Radhwan al-Sayyid gives for not attending beyond the third meeting.[43]

Equivocal differences: non-Muslims, secularists, and non-believers

The "thinness" of notions of democracy and human rights and the lack of a full articulation of programs for political and social reform significantly impact the ability of the interactions to account for issues of tolerance for difference – class, gender, ethnic, and religious differences in particular. Many of these differences are introduced sporadically by conference participants, but for the most part these differences are quickly glossed over or shelved in the debates, since they fail to resonate with – or even appear antithetical to – the notions of unity and the common points of opposition upon which the conferences are based. While the construction of a shared conception of democratic reform – as well as the expanding notion of community entailed in the idea of an "Arab-Islamic civilizational circle" – would seem to constitute an opportunity for incorporating actors marginalized both within the social movement organizations that animate these ideological groupings and within contemporary Arab politics. Krämer has noted that "Islamist moderates" often "have cooperated with political rivals of various persuasions, from nationalist to royalist, and from liberal to Arab socialist," but that the precondition of such alliances seems to be that "the latter pledge adherence to the values of religion in general and Islam in particular."[44] As noted in Chapter 2, Islamist thinkers such as Yusuf al-Qaradawi conceptualize harmonious relations between Muslims and their "non-Muslim compatriots" in the context of an Islamic society based on Qura'nic values of tolerance, justice, and mercy. However, in the context of cross-ideological dialog, the idea of a shared civilization falls short in this regard, following more closely the dictates of political unity than liberal aims of tolerance and inclusiveness. In the case of religious and ethnic minorities, the issues are quickly and unquestioningly subsumed under a category that privileges the Islamic religion and Arab ethnicity and that denies frictions between Muslims and Copts, Sunni and Shi'i, Arabs and Kurds despite the reality of such conflicts in Egypt, Lebanon, Iraq and elsewhere. In other words, according to the logic of the Arab-Islamic civilizational circle, there can be no marginalization or oppression of minority groups, because there is no religious reason for it.

Non-believers are not discussed at all and, in light of the failure to fully engage the issue of freedom of thought and conscience, their tolerance and inclusion in the unity seem doubtful. That is, the concept of the umma can include non-Arabs and may be able to include non-Muslims, but it is not clear that it can incorporate non-believers. So too, the status of individuals articulating a commitment to secularism, that is, individuals committed to various ideas – for example, that religion should not be integrated in political matters and politics should not interfere in religious matters, that society progresses as the various aspects of life (economic, political, legal, and moral) become increasingly discrete in relation to each other, or that society benefits from a decrease in religious belief – remains less clear. One would do well to recall the assassination by radical Islamists of the liberal Egyptian intellectual Farag Foda in 1992 and the use of the Islamic notion of *hisba* (bringing to account) by Islamist lawyers to divorce the Egyptian critical theologian Nasr Hamid Abu Zayd from his wife, both actions undertaken based on these individuals' supposed apostasy.[45] As Sami Zubaida has noted:

> Many of the Egyptian intellectual Islamists ... while forthright in advocating Islamization in all spheres, are liberal when it comes to non-Muslims, especially Copts, and ingenious in revising the usual *shari'a* prescriptions regarding non-Muslims as *dhimmis*. They argue that full citizenship rights for Christians is fully compatible with the *shari'a*, and cite texts and precedents to illustrate their arguments. These stances do not convince the majority of Islamists at the popular level, for whom Islamist sentiments are nourished and reinforced by communalist antagonism, as demonstrated by periodic attacks on Coptic communities in upper Egypt and elsewhere.[46]

At least part of the problem lies in the fact that although many Islamist intellectuals – such as those associated with the *wasatiyya* trend – do articulate an understanding of equal citizenship for non-Muslims, what is lacking is a recognition, publication, and critique of those enduring sources – intellectual, religious, and social – of unequal notions of citizenship, that seem to be more popularly held. The same problem is found in regard to gender – that is, the question of women's status in Arab-Islamic societies. While here the matter is raised in slightly more critical fashion, the tensions that emerge in this context are no more successfully resolved.

Whither the women?

The "women question" presents one of the most consistent points of contention – and one that continually emerges, despite attempts to avoid or shelve the issue. Both Islamists and Arab nationalists have engaged the issues of women's role and status throughout their history. Why is this issue not given more sustained attention in these debates and how is the issue handled on those rare occasions when it does come up?

Although at one level the answer to the first question might seem obvious: despite the "reform" focus of this cross-ideological engagement and the fact that lack of women's empowerment has been singled out recently as one of three areas hindering development in the region,[47] the rights and roles of women are issues on which Arab nationalists and Islamists cannot agree and which run the risk of disrupting their fragile dialog. Yet the issue of women's status is brought up on a number of occasions, and closer analysis of those points where it is discussed reveals that the issue is more complex: at these points "woman" is central to the dialog even as women are marginalized. The points of agreement and disagreement, communication and misunderstanding, or "talking past" that occur in the context of a dialog among members of ideological groupings that have most often found themselves at odds in both thought and practice reveal distinct gendered constructions that problematize women's participation, particularly in Arab nationalist and Islamist groups. At the same time, rather than patriarchy simply providing a common framework for the various ideological trends, what one finds is that the tensions that exist between each group's particular conception of women's status and role contribute to the continual foregrounding of an issue that none of the sides wish to broach.

Certainly, topics of particular concern to women are more likely to be broached if women are present. Unfortunately, this has not been the case. There was only one female participant, the Lebanese sociologist Dalal al-Bazri, at the religious–nationalist dialog that formed the precursor to the conferences.[48] The number of women present at the National-Islamic Conferences is only slightly higher. Attending the first conference were Aman Kibbara Sha'rani, a professor at the Lebanese University and president of the Lebanese Women's Council; Rinad al-Khatib 'Ayyad of Jordan; Zahiya Qaddura, an Arab nationalist professor at the Lebanese University and president of the Union of Lebanese Universities; Layla Sharaf; and Nevine 'Abd al-Khaliq Mustafa, a political scientist from Egypt. The second conference had only two female participants: Qaddura and Bayan Nuwayhid al-Hut, an Arab nationalist professor of history in Lebanon who is of Palestinian origin. The Yemeni professor of English literature, Intilaq Muhammad 'Abd al-Malik al-Mutawakkil, along with Sha'rani, Hut, and Qaddura, were present at the third conference. Qaddura was the only female who attended the fourth conference. Thus, at a series of conferences, each of which usually draws between 100–150 participants, women constituted a total of only between one and five of those participants, and the total number of women engaged in this conference overall (accounting for repeat appearances) is six, considerably less than even the non-Muslim (all various types of Christians) presence, which ranged between five and seven individuals per conference and an overall total of twelve individuals (again, accounting for repeat appearances), and less than the number of Shi'is (though the total number here is harder to gauge). Further, although both Sharaf and Hut constitute two of the twenty-five members of the organizing committee, even their participation has been intermittent.

One could speculate as to why women do not attend in larger numbers and with more regular frequency. Arab nationalists tend to use traditional political and social forms to organize women. While many political parties have women's sections, with only a few exceptions, Arab women have not achieved high levels of participation through official political parties.[49] To cite just two examples by way of elaboration, the lack of support Moroccan women initially received from the opposition political parties for their attempt to change the *mudawwana*, or personal status code;[50] and the monopoly of the Union Nationale des Femmes de Tunisie, "a satellite of the Parti Socialiste Destourien," which hinders women's independent activity in Tunisia, are not selling points for either oppositional parties or official (state) feminisms.[51] On the other hand, one might attribute the complete absence of Islamist women at the conferences to the segregation of the female members into "women's committees" in many (though certainly not all) Islamist groups (and Islamist groups are not the only political groups who do this, though it seems more prevalent there).[52]

It is not clear to me whether the dearth of women in this forum can be adequately accounted for by either of the above explanations. Neither do their numbers appear particularly low, relative to similar forums. It is a fact that CAUS conferences generally do not tend to elicit extensive participation by women.[53] Addressing a CAUS conference on "Civil Society in the Arab World and its Role in the Realization of Democracy" in 1992, the Egyptian feminist Nawal al-Sa'dawi (b. 1931) pointedly asks: "Why is there an absence of women, as researchers and thinkers, at this forum? And why was not one of the papers assigned to a woman? Is it because Arab women do not have their great intellectuals and thus are only invited as mere listeners or commentators?"[54] Of the eighty-eight participants at that conference, only seven were women, two of whom served as paper commentators, while the remainder attended as listeners. Clearly there are Arab women who are researchers, professors, and writers, and many of these women engage in intellectual congresses that address political issues, some even sponsored by the CAUS. So, too, women have a considerable presence in civil society. But they remain a small minority outside of those congresses devoted specifically to "the women's issue."[55]

Intilaq Muhammad 'Abd al-Malik al-Mutawakkil notes the lack of both women and youth at the NIC and offers an additional explanation for women's non-participation in regional academic conferences: social and economic issues that affect women on a more personal level. She reveals that her participation in the conferences would not have been achieved "without the help of her father, husband and the Women's Studies Center at Sana'a University." The participation of women and youth are essential, she argues, for the conference's development of "a progressive and comprehensive view."[56] Muhammad 'Abd al-Malik al-Mutawakkil (Intilaq's father) confirmed that the committee responsible for drawing up the list of invitees is charged with achieving breadth and balance of ideologies, organizations, and nationalities represented at the conference, as well as some diversity of age and gender. According to the senior Mutawakkil, most of the women invited do not attend, and financial constraints are the most common explanation provided.[57]

In addition to the shortage of female participants, the National-Islamic Conferences also reveal a scarcity of discussion of women. To some extent this is surprising, since "woman" presents a common theme taken up by these ideological groupings in other contexts. Lisa Taraki maintains that "one of the most striking features of Islamist movements throughout the Arab world is their preoccupation with 'the woman question'."[58] Haddad and Smith note that Islamism "has clearly placed the issue of the roles and rights of women at the center of its agenda," paying particular attention to women's outer comportment.[59] The Muslim Brotherhood has much vaunted its female membership. In a different fashion, nationalist expressions in the Arab region often comprise gendering of the nation or symbolic use of women as a stand-in for the perils afflicting the nation and the threat to her honor. The paucity of critical discussion of the gender issue is perhaps even more disappointing in a forum that speaks of democratization, renewal, modernization, and overcoming tyranny and oppression. Nonetheless, this dearth was not a complete absence and even some of the silences speak volumes. The several interventions that discussed women reveal much about the conception of gender in the discourses of Arab nationalism and Islamism, the prevalence of patriarchy in each of these movements, as well as some of the points of difference between the two.

In his report on the "State of the *Umma*" in the first NIC, the Lebanese religious scholar, Shaykh Salman al-Masri, opened by expressing outrage at the treatment of Muslim women in the West:

Before I start my intervention regarding the state of the *umma* in the papers of the Islamists and nationalist, I want to give two minutes to the other half of this world, because I have witnessed by my own eyes how the Muslim woman is portrayed in the western media. The matter compelled me to give a lecture in the city of Dallas about the role of the monotheistic Muslim woman in the past, present and future. I said: it is an honor for you that you are not a mere commodity and you are not one of the ribs of man. And you are also not a weak creature, but a human being, exactly like man: you have your own independence and your own characteristics. If you are good, the family will be good; and if the family is good, the whole nation will be good. If you are ignorant, the family becomes ignorant; and if the family is ignorant, the whole nation is ignorant.[60]

There are a number of themes expressed in this passage that are reiterated by other representatives of both trends attending the conference. First, there is concern over the treatment of Muslim women in Western contexts. CAUS general secretary Khayr al-Din Hasib repeated this trope in his report on the fourth conference. Written in the wake of the events of September 11, 2001, Hasib noted that the conference condemned the spirit of racism prevailing in the US and elsewhere "against the Arab and Muslim inhabitants, especially against Muslim women," further noting the discrimination against "Muslim female students because of their commitment to Islam expressed in the clothes they wear."[61] Other themes Masri touches upon that are echoed elsewhere in the conference include the use of the good Muslim woman as an indicator of the righteousness and modernity of Islamic society, the notion that Islam is the basis of Arab women's equality, and the organic relationship asserted between women–family–nation.

It is not only Islamists, but also Arab nationalists who echo these themes in one form or another during the course of the conferences. This is seen most commonly in the few attempts to find meeting points. One of the most significant attempts to find a common conception of women's status that cuts across ideologies comes from a female participant, Aman Kibara Sha'rani, who attributes women's unequal status to ideas and traditions that do not have a religious source. "The real religion," she argues, "does not distinguish between two humans, between women and men, poor and rich, black and white." Echoing the assessment of many Islamists, Sha'rani maintains that "many people think the backwardness of [Arab] women is from religion, but those who know religion know the great role that these religions play in emancipating humankind."[62] However, Sha'rani does take the argument further to criticize those who "imprison" Islam and "use it in a way that does not belong to it." According to Sha'rani, even if it was true in the past that "women had duties different from those of men because of her female gender, and her being mother and wife, it is the traditional social order which has obliged her to do so" and not religion. The full participation of women, she argues, has become an "economic necessity" and a requirement of development and achievement of this does not conflict with Islam in any way, but extends its true principles.[63]

No one at the conference takes issue with Sha'rani's affirmation of Islam's advancement of women. For example, at the same conference, Amin Hassan 'Umar, president of the Sudan's Directive Council of the National House of the Sciences, claims that "the Sudanese woman has rights and representation at all the levels of government that you do not find in many developed countries," again asserting the progressive and modern character of Islamic society.[64] These National-Islamic Conferences do not provide a forum in which Islam can be directly criticized without running the risk of disrupting the fragile alliance. The only individual beside Sha'rani to articulate any concern over women's status at the hands of some of the Islamist groups is Mukhlis al-Siyadi, who notes his own hesitation regarding "what is written and said about democracy by the forces and parties from the Islamists trend" regarding various limits of participation that tend to "occur in part or totally to exclude women." Siyadi affirms that women's right to participate in public life is "one of the preconditions of the Arab-Islamic awakening."[65]

However, it is also apparent from Siyadi's other statements that despite his suspicions of Islamist groups, like a number of other participants, he envisions roles and priorities for women in the development of Arab-Islamic society that draw from the same conceptual reservoir as many Islamists. Siyadi reveals a distinct prioritization of issues of Arab-Islamic identity and women's maternal role over other issues that bear on women's status, such as education. Siyadi recounts how:

in the first half of the century, one of the leaders of this nation had to face a Western incursion which aimed at the same targets as this [current] war [with the West]. The man was Shaykh Ibn Badis and the incursion aimed to take Algeria from its Arabic origins and from its religion. One day a clever journalist asked Shaykh Ibn Badis his opinion on educating Algerian women. The answer of Shakyh Ibn Badis came to become a cornerstone in this matter: "An ignorant [jahila] mother who teaches her children to love Algeria is a thousand times better than an educated woman who teaches her children to love France." The Shaykh (God protect him) knows that an educated woman who teaches her children to love Algeria is the best, but when you must choose between a French-educated woman or an ignorant Arab-Islamic woman, the choice is clear ... I am urging the nationalists to fortify themselves with Islam and for the Islamists to fortify themselves with Arabism.[66]

Siyadi is identified as an Arab nationalist thinker who works for al-Shariqa Television (UAE), but he clearly bridges the Arab nationalist–Islamist divide through his use of Qur'anic passages that open his contribution and are scattered throughout the text. Like Masri's assertion that a good woman leads to a good family which makes for a good nation, Siyadi also defines women's most important role as educators of the next generation of lovers of Arabism and Islam. Women are most often addressed, and their mobilization sought, in the context of these conferences not as *women*, but as *mothers*.

Secular Arab nationalists, modernists, and reformers, such as Qasim Amin (Egypt, 1863–1908), have long used women as markers of the modern or regressive nature of the community in political and economic senses.[67] In the context of the NIC, one sees this use of "woman" in Muhammad 'Awida's questioning "how can we have *shura* or democracy, how can we have rights, how can we build a society if half of it is forgotten and neglected."[68] With a similar aim, the Syrian economist 'Abd al-Qadir al-Niyad critically notes that "women's relative share of economic activity remains next to nothing" and that "women do not reach 5% of the labor market in some Arab countries."[69]

Islamists, on the other hand, most often have considered women bearers of cultural authenticity and central to the perpetuation of the faith or, alternatively, as symbols for the decadence and immorality (or *jahiliyya*) of the community. In this context, Islamists also use women to imagine the Islamic community as liberal. The former emphasis is apparent when women function as what the Tunisian psychologist Alya Baffoun characterizes as the "role of the lifebuoy to which one hold on in a turbulent ocean:" "the desire to confine the Arab woman in the position of a guardian of a long lost identity."[70] One sees evidence of the latter case in references to women as the "sisters of men" whose activism must be fostered so that Islamist movements are "not deprived of women's capabilities and energies,"[71] and in the various attempts to assert Islam as a champion of the rights of women.[72] Badran notes that "Islamist women provide support for the male Islamist, who in their hour of need articulate 'new' public roles for women, encouraging their activism and encouraging a notion of Islamic gender equality in the public sphere. However, the practice of public gender equality has been spliced into a masculinist order in the private sphere with its asymmetrical gender roles."[73]

Where Arab nationalist and socialists have tended to view the West as a political and economic threat, Islamists have often viewed the threat of the West as a cultural issue. As a result, the "protection of women" involves the protection of traditional roles in the face of the West. What is interesting is the way in which, in the context of the NIC, Arab nationalists (like Siyadi) incorporate cultural and religious conceptions in their discussion of women's status. Thus, the narratives over the modern Arab-Islamic mother are distinct but overlapping, with converging (in the women = family = nation equation) and diverging (over modernist vs. authentic, political/economic vs. cultural/religious) elements. But the effect of each is similar in at least one respect: feminist interests are subordinated under the ideological dictates of nationalism and Islamism in ways that reveal material forms.

Islamist feminists may engage maternal collective action framing processes based on traditional gender and family roles for women, where they embrace their elevated states as defenders of the integrity of the Islamic family and responsible for giving birth to and educating the next generation of Muslims. Margot Badran argues that the rise of Islamism has generated a new brand of "gender activism" in Egypt.[74] As Haddad and Smith point out, "in most Islamist platforms women are not understood to be passive recipients of a newly defined identity, but active participants in the new culture and society that Islamists are intent on bringing into being."[75] As Islamic activists, women play a vital role in the advancement of the Muslim state: they are "portrayed not as diminutive and second-class members of a family unity, but as assuming the exceedingly important task of educating their children ... to what it means to be informed and contributing citizens of the Islamic community."[76] Some women have used this opportunity to take on more public roles by engaging in religious and charitable activities.

It is not only Islamist feminists who have entered a gendered political context in the form of a political movement that both foregrounds women and conscribes their concerns. Mervat Hatem has argued that nationalist discourses in Arab countries have limited the possibilities of women's movements by subordinating women to the nation's needs.[77] Sherna Berger Gluck has suggested that the decision of the General Union of Palestinian Women, founded in 1965, to seek recognition as the official representative of the Palestinian people hindered its ability "to challenge the prevailing gender ideology of the nationalist movement" and "probably doomed its potential as a feminist force."[78] As Cynthia Enloe has succinctly put it, nationalist movements ask their women to "be patient," "hold their tongues," and "wait until the nationalist goal is achieved."[79] Hatem's research reveals how, in responding to the issue of women's rights by expanding educational opportunities for Egyptian women, the policies of the Nasir regime "reproduced old dichotomous definitions of masculinity and femininity in the public realm" as women were channeled into lower status "feminine professions," such as teaching and nursing, and women's wages were set to reflect the way in which "women workers and children performed tasks that were

complementary to those performed by men." "In all of these definitions," Hatem points out, of "women's subordinate public (economic
and political) roles, religion did not play any role."[80] Even 'Awida's call
for women's equal rights, noted above, is prefaced with the assertion
that "the rights of women ... represented the heart and the basis of the
family that is the first cell of society."[81] Rather, it is the dictates of the
nations and the mobilization of women in politically limited roles – as
mothers and caregivers – that hinders a more complete articulation of
women's interests and renders the interests of other women who do not
mobilize as such less visible.

This problematique is not limited to women's participation in nationalist and Islamist movements either. While many women have also
mobilized within more socialist parties and movements, feminist scholarship has cast a critical eye on the "curious courtship"[82] and "unhappy
marriage"[83] that characterizes much of that relationship. A number of
works have noted the tendency of nationalist and Islamist discourse
to subordinate women's causes to the dictates of nation or religion.[84]
The left in the Arab region (as elsewhere) has often subsumed oppression based on gender to considerations of the more pressing issue of
oppression based on class and exploitation within a capitalist framework. In the Sudan, for example, Sondra Hale found that "the patriar-
chal ideology, structure, and organization of the Marxist-Leninist SCP
[Sudanese Communist Party] may have diminished its role as a truly
dynamic force for socialist transformation, especially in regard to the
subordination of women."[85] Feminism as such is dismissed as a divisive, "bourgeois" issue. Thus, socialism is often held out as a "promis-
sory note" to women: women's concerns can only be addressed – or will
cease to be an issue – after the "real" revolution is achieved.

Certainly, maternal symbols have provided justification for mobilization both for Islamist feminists and for the feminisms that emerged in
the context of nationalisms or state feminisms, where one sees similar
notions of woman as the embodiment of the Islamic nation, reproducer
of its culture, and an indicator of its modernity.[86] Women in the Arab
region (as elsewhere) occupy a gendered political and social context
that they do not choose and in which they become a subject of debate
and mobilization for social movements, but are constrained as agents
of transformation. Women's behavior is constrained through the gendered constructions of these discourses (whether in the name of the
nation, progress, authenticity, Islam, or liberation), even through those
that imagine an emancipated status for women. "Women's projects"
or "women as projects" appear only to create or reinforce stereotypes
of what constitutes a "women's issue." Outside of these functions

(which make up the bulk of the conference proceedings) women are marginalized or rendered invisible or both.

Is the glass half empty or half full?

As the occasional inventions by Arab women – as well as a few men – attending the NIC attest, there are moments of critical questioning and interrogation of the discourses and practices of these social movements. As Foucault has famously noted, "where there is power there is also resistance." At the same time, one must inquire as to what hinders a fuller and more sustained critique. At least part of the explanation seems to lie in the character of those frames that contribute to, and sustain, this collaboration. It is possible that an additional explanation as to the lack of a strong feminist presence at these conferences may further be provided by analysis of the frames that have been constructed and that enable this collaboration. As Rita Noonan has pointed out in a study of women's mobilization in Chile, some larger cultural frames – what she and others term "master frames" – may provide space for specific ideas (e.g. feminism), while others may not. A more "elaborated" master frame "may shape the competition between movement-specific frames, as a more 'elaborated' frame [such as democratization] allows room for a variety of interests to be expressed." On the other hand, a "restricted" master frame "may cause more intense competition among movement frames since there is not sufficient 'space' for all groups to participate."[87] This interpretation of unity would seem to preclude the emergence of discussion of the status of women, as well as religious minorities and secularists – not only because Arab nationalists and Islamists might find themselves divided over these issues, but perhaps more significantly because raising the issue of difference-based oppressions would be seen as divisive to the *watan*, the *harakat*, the *umma*.

Nowhere in any of the concluding statements are women or religious or ethnic minorities mentioned in any form, which itself signals the lack of progress on this issue, as well as the difficulty of incorporating claims to difference or criticisms of inequities based on differences. Rather, the meeting points are all issues which rely upon more successful framing alignments: the struggle against Zionism, the invasion and occupation of Iraq, preservation of the *umma*, and the need to further develop relations between the Arab nationalist and Islamist groups. There is also usually a subheading devoted to economic issues that are less consistently discussed in the context of the conference proceedings, such as "development and the barriers of globalization." Finally, the concluding remarks invariably have one subheading that touches upon issues of "*shura*, democracy and human rights."

One would think that a fuller articulation of democracy would prove broad enough to accommodate women's and feminist concerns from different ideological groupings – that is, a space that could encompass competing maternalist, liberal feminist, and socialist feminist concerns – as well as the concerns of religious minorities, secular Muslims, and non-believers. The literature on social movements has noted the potential of democracy frames – as well as shifting alliances and coalitions between parties and other political entities – to form significant "political opportunity structures," that is, factors that can enable (or thwart) attempts of those outside of traditional political formations to gain access. The limited and hazardous character of such a space may be explained by the relatively weak and narrow expression of the Arab nationalist/Islamist notions of democracy and common visions for political and social reform.

It seems doubtful that secular discourse could ever have a place in this dialog, even with the further elaboration of political concepts and programs. Chapter 1 demonstrated that even historically secular groups and individuals are retreating from a strong secular position. So too, the evidence provided here points to what other analysts of women's status in the Arab and Islamic contexts have noted: discursive constraints of the imperatives of unity placed on the myriad ideological trends and in the dialogs among them. On the other hand, at least in regard to women and to non-Muslims, one might suggest that rather than seeing the glass half empty we should see it as half full. The fact that the issues of women and non-Muslims, their status in Islamic and Arab contexts, their under-representation in politics, the lack of participation, particularly of women, in regional academic conferences (except, one must certainly note, those dealing specifically and exclusively with the "woman question") is broached at all in a context where the very presence of "woman" or "Christian" threatens to halt this fragile alliance may reveal the inescapable character of the issue. The tension over these issues reveals the tangible presence, not absence of space, for confronting this issue. In this sense, women and practicing non-Muslims may fare better here than committed secularists, let alone atheists.

While it is clear that women and non-Muslim's participation in the NIC has been lacking, it has also not been absent; although discussions of the status of women and Christians has been sporadic at best, the issue itself formed a constant point of tension. Within Arab nationalist and Islamist discourse, as well as within the dialog between groups espousing both ideologies, issues of difference continue to be subsumed under other political contingencies: Arab unity, the unity of the Islamic *umma*, the struggle against authoritarianism, Zionism, or imperialism. In a 2001 interview, Hani Shukrallah lamented the lack of critical self-reflection on the part of Arab intellectuals and activists:

We've had some Marxists and Nasserists turn zealous liberals, others turn fervent Islamists. We've been able to observe a "reconciliation" between the two arch-enemies of Arab ideological and political development during the last century: pan-Arab nationalism and Islamism. Yet none of these transitions is achieved via a thorough critique of our intellectual heritage. They come about as largely unexplained "moments of enlightenment." Structures of ideas are not criticized but rejected en masse. It's a question of apostasy and belief – rejecting one religion for another.[88]

In many respects, the NIC project has failed to forge a sustainable convergence – or even to sustain itself as a place of cross-ideological engagement. Since the last NIC conference held in December 2004, the NIC has formed an organization independent of the CAUS but, to the extent that it remains active, its work focuses less on large conferences with published proceedings, and more on issuing statements and declarations.[89] After Mutawakil stepped down as secretary-general in 2005, leadership passed to the Egyptian Muslim Brotherhood activist 'Issam al-'Ariyan (b. 1953) briefly before passing in 2006 to its current secretary-general, Palestinian Hamas spokesperson Munir Shafiq (b. 1936). But the glass may still remain half full, as tensions and failures create their own opportunities. Incongruence between nationalist and Islamist conceptions of women, as well as the persistence of women both within and outside the NIC, which kept the question of women's status from being fully subsumed in the context of this now over decade-long series of discussions, are issues which have continued to be discussed more broadly among the activists and political leaders who have mobilized for political reform, and at least some progress can be detected at this level in regard to non-Muslims in Egypt and women in Yemen, as will be demonstrated in the remaining chapters.

NOTES

1. Muhammad Sa'id Ramadan Buti and Tayyib Tizini. *al-Islam wa al-'asr: tahaddiyat wa afaq* (Damascus: Dar al-fikr al-mu'asir, 2000).
2. 'Abd al-Razzaq 'Id and Muhammad 'Abd al-Jabbar. *al-Dimuqratiyya bayn al-'almaniyya wa al-islam* (Damascus: Dar al-fikr al-mu'asir, 1999).
3. Nawal Sa'dawi and Heba Raouf Ezzat. *al-Mara wa al-din wa al-akhlaq* (Woman, Religion, and Ethics) (Damascus: Dar al-fikr al-mu'asir, 2000).
4. Hani Rizq and Khalis Jalabi Kanju. *al-Iman wa al-taqaddum al-'ilmi* (Faith and Scientific Progress) (Damascus: Dar al-fikr al-mu'asir, 2000).

5. Information about the Center for the Study of Islam and Democracy can be found at www.csidonline.org.
6. This statement can be found at www.caus.org.lb/Home/contents.php?id=26.
7. See the Center for Arab Unity Studies. *The Future of the Arab Nation: Challenges and Options* (New York: Routledge, 1992).
8. Basheer M. Nafi. "The Arab Nationalists and the Arab Islamists: Shadows of the Past, Glimpses of the Future," *Middle East Affairs Journal* 6 (2000), 111–112.
9. The 1979 conference proceedings were published as Muhammad Ahmad Khalaf Allah (ed.). *al-Qawmiyya al-'arabiyya wa al-islam: buhuth wa munaqashat al-nadwa al-fikriyya* (Arab Nationalism and Islam: Intellectual Studies and Roundtable Debates) (Beirut: Center for Arab Unity Studies, 1981).
10. The April 1988 conference proceedings were published as Elbaki Hermassi (ed.). *al-Din fi al-mujtama' al-'arabi* (Religion in Arab Society) (Beirut: Center for Arab Unity Studies, 1990).
11. The September 1988 conference proceedings were published as Tariq al-Bishri (ed.). *al-Hiwar al-qawmi al-dini: awraq 'amal wa munaqashat al-nadwa al-fikriyya* (National-Religious Dialog: Working Papers and Intellectual Roundtable Debates) (Beirut: Center for Arab Unity Studies, 1989).
12. Compare *al-Mu'tamar al-qawmi al-arabi al-sadis* (Sixth Arab Nationalist Conference) (Beirut: Center for Arab Unity Studies, 1996) to *Hal al-umma al-'arabiyya?: al-mu'tamar al-qawmi al-'arabi al-sabi'* (Seventh Arab Nationalist Conference) (Beirut: Center for Arab Unity Studies, 1997).
13. Khayr al-Din Hasib, interview with author, Beirut, Lebanon (October 24, 2004). 'Abd al-Ila Bilqaziz, interview with author, Beirut, Lebanon (October 24, 2004).
14. The 1994 conference was published as *Mu'tamar al-qawmi al-islami al-awwal: watha'iq wa munaqashat wa qararat al-mu'tamar* (The First National-Islamic Conference: Documents, Debates and Decisions from the Conference) (Beirut: Center for Arab Unity Studies, 1995). The 1997 conference was published as *Mu'tamar al-qawmi al-islami al-thani: watha'iq wa munaqashat wa qararat al-mu'tamar* (The Second National-Islamic Conference: Documents, Debates and Decisions from the Conference) (Beirut: Center for Arab Unity Studies, 2000). The 2000 conference was published as *Mu'tamar al-qawmi al-islami al-thalith: watha'iq wa munaqashat wa qararat al-mu'tamar* (The Third National-Islamic Conference: Documents, Debates and Decisions from the Conference) (Beirut: Center for Arab Unity Studies, 2004). The 2002 conference was published as *Mu'tamar al-qawmi al-islami al-rabi': watha'iq wa munaqashat wa qararat al-mu'tamar* (The Fourth National-Islamic Conference: Documents, Debates and Decisions from the Conference) (Beirut: Center for Arab Unity Studies, 2004). The proceedings of the fifth conference, held in Beirut in December 2004, has not yet been released, though a few of the papers from the conference were published in the January 2005 issue of *al-Mustaqbal al-'arabi*.

15. Ahmad Sidqi al-Dajani. *Rasa'il al-mu'tamar al-qawmi al-islami bayna kharif 1994 wa rabi' 1997* (Letters of the National-Islamic Conference Between the Fall of 1994 and the Spring of 1997) (Cairo: Markaz yafa, 1997).

16. In a paper published after the present chapter was drafted, Amr Hamzawi, Marina Ottaway, and Nathan J. Brown identified the following six ambiguities in the position of Islamist movements: the application of Islamic law, violence, political pluralism, individual freedoms, minorities, and women's rights. My own work largely confirms the findings of these authors. "Islamist Movements and the Democratic Process in the Arab World: Exploring the Gray Zones," *Carnegie Paper No. 67* (March 2006).

17. David A. Snow. E. Burke Rochford, Jr., Steven K. Worden, and Robert D. Benford. "Frame Alignment Processes, Micromobilization and Movement Participation." *American Sociological Review* 51 (1986), 464. In fact, cross-ideological framing seems to require even greater efforts in an area Snow *et al.* noted in regard to the social movements they studied: "the various movement participants we have observed spend a good deal of time together accounting and recounting for their participation; they jointly develop rationales for what they are or are not doing" (467).

18. *Mu'tamar al-qawmi al-islami al-rabi'*, 301.

19. Mahmoud Soueid. "Islamic Unity and Political Change: Interview with Shaykh Muhammad Hussayn Fadlallah," *Journal of Palestine Studies* 25 (1995), 62.

20. Khalid al-'Ayid. "The Movement of Islamic Jihad and the Oslo Process: An Interview with Ramadan 'Abdallah Shallah," *Journal of Palestine Studies* 28 (1999), 72.

21. Radhwan al-Sayyid, interview with author, Beirut, Lebanon (May 30, 2004).

22. Layla Sharaf, interview with author, Amman, Jordan (June 28, 2004).

23. Soueid. "Islamic Unity and Political Change," 64.

24. Gudrun Krämer. "Cross-Links or Double Talk? Islamist Movements in the Political Process" in Laura Guazzone (ed.), *The Islamist Dilemma: The Political Role of Islamist Movements in the Contemporary World* (Reading: Ithaca Press, 1998), 56.

25. Soueid. "Islamic Unity and Political Change," 62.

26. Khayr al-Din Hasib. "al-Bayan al-khatami: dawra 'mukim al-janin' lil-mu'tamar al-qawmi al-islami, al-dawra al-rabi'a" (Concluding Declaration: The 'Camp Jenin' Round of the National-Islamic Conference, Round Four), *al-Mustaqbal al-'arabi* 281 (2002), 151–161.

27. Sharaf, interview (June 28, 2004).

28. *Mu'tamar al-qawmi al-islami al-rabi'*, 314.

29. Quoted in Charles Kurzman, *Liberal Islam: A Sourcebook* (Oxford University Press, 1998), 10.

30. *Mu'tamar al-qawmi al-islami al-rabi'*, 571.

31. *Mu'tamar al-qawmi al-islami al-awwal*, 145.

32. Roel Meijer. *Quest for Modernity: Secular Liberal and Left-Wing Political Thought in Egypt, 1945–1958* (London: Routledge, 2003). Meijer argues

that the various political forces in Egypt (with the important exception of the Islamists) underwent a process of reorientation toward the regime in the second half of the 1950s that was facilitated by the mechanistic image of society they shared with the state's authoritarian modernist strain: "The reasons why liberals socialist, and communists supported the new regime began to resemble each other over the course of the period" (201).

33. *Mu'tamar al-qawmi al-islami al-awwal*, 26.

34. *Mu'tamar al-qawmi al-islami al-awwal*, 81.

35. *Mu'tamar al-qawmi al-islami al-awwal*, 178–179.

36. *Mu'tamar al-qawmi al-islami al-awwal*, 182.

37. *Mu'tamar al-qawmi al-islami al-awwal*, 113.

38. *Mu'tamar al-qawmi al-islami al-awwal*, 271–272.

39. William Sulayman, Tariq al-Bishri and Mustafa al-Fiqi. *al-Sha'b al-wahid wa al-watan al-wahid: dirasat fi al-usul al-wahda al-wataniyya* (One People and One Nation: Studies of the Sources of National Unity) (Cairo: al-Ahram Center for Political and Strategic Studies, 1982).

40. *Mu'tamar al-qawmi al-islami al-awwal*, 273.

41. *Mu'tamar al-qawmi al-islami al-awwal*, 274.

42. *Mu'tamar al-qawmi al-islami al-awwal*, 113–114.

43. Sayyid, interview (May 30, 2004).

44. Krämer. "Cross-Links or Double Talk?," 57.

45. Muhammad al-'Imara launched a scathing critique of Abu Zayd's writings, accusing him of offering a "materialist Marxist interpretion of Islam" and asserting that "materialist philosophy denies the existence of God." At the same time, he argues here and in other works against applying the law of apostasy. *al-Tafsir al-markisi lil-Islam* (The Marxist Interpretation of Islam) (Cairo: Dar al-shuruq, 1996), 34.

46. Sami Zubaida. *Law and Power in the Islamic World* (London: I. B. Tauris, 2003), 179–180.

47. *Arab Human Development Report* (New York: United Nations Development Programme, Regional Bureau for Arab States, 2003).

48. Bishri (ed.). *al-Hiwar al-qawmi al-dini*.

49. 'Ala Abu Zayd. *al-Mar'a al-misriyya fi al-ahzab al-siyasiyya* (The Egyptian Women in Political Parties) in 'Ala Abu Zayd (ed.), *al-Mar'a al-misriyya wa al-'amal al-'am: ruya mustaqbaliyya* (The Egyptian Woman and Public Work: A Future-Oriented Perspective) (Cairo: Center for Arab Unity Studies, 1995), 47–70.

50. Amy Freeman. "Re-locating Moroccan Women's Identities in a Transnational World," *Gender, Place & Culture* 11 (2004), 17–41; Souad Eddouada, interview with author, Rabat, Morocco (May 26, 2005).

51. Laurie A. Brand. *Women, the State and Political Liberalization: Middle Eastern and North African Experiences* (Columbia University Press, 1998), 70, 177, 225.

52. See Lisa Taraki. "Islam is the Solution: Jordanian Islamists and the Dilemma of the 'Modern Woman," *British Journal of Sociology* 46 (1995), 643–661; and Janine Clark and Jillian Schwedler. "Who Opened the Window? Women's Struggle for Voice within Islamist Political Parties," *Comparative Politics* 35 (2003), 293–312.

53. The number of female participants averages between one and seven in the dozen or so CAUS conference proceedings in my library, with the exception of a conference convened on the issue of *al-Mar'a al-'arabiyya: bayn thiql al-waqi' wa tatalla'at al-taharrur* (The Arab Woman: Between the Burden of Reality and Aspirations of Emancipation) (Beirut: Center for Arab Unity Studies, 1999).

54. In Sa'id Bin Sa'id al-'Alawi (ed.). *al-Mujtama' al-madani fi al-watan al-'arabi wa dawruhu fi tahqiq al-dimuqratiyya* (Civil Society in the Arab World and Its Role in the Realization of Democracy) (Beirut: Center for Arab Unity Studies, 1992), 837.

55. Dalal al-Bazri, Hani al-Hurani, Husayn Abu Rumman. *al-Mar'a al-'arabiyya wa al-musharaka al-siyasiyya* (The Arab Women and Political Participation) (Amman: Dar Sinbad, 2000).

56. *Mu'tamar al-qawmi al-islami al-rabi'*, 234.

57. Muhammad 'Abd al-Malik al-Mutawakkil, interview with author, Sana'a, Yemen (January 3, 2006).

58. Taraki. "Islam is the Solution," 643.

59. Yvonne Yazbeck Haddad and Jane I. Smith. "Women in Islam: 'The Mother of all Battles'" in Suha Sabbagh (ed.), *Arab Women: Between Defiance and Restraint* (New York: Olive Branch Press, 1996), 137.

60. *Mu'tamar al-qawmi al-islami al-awwal*, 252.

61. Khayr al-Din Hasib. "al-Bayan al-khatami."

62. *Mu'tamar al-qawmi al-islami al-awwal*, 102.

63. *Mu'tamar al-qawmi al-islami al-awwal*, 103.

64. *Mu'tamar al-qawmi al-islami al-rabi'*, 404. 'Umar continues: "Westerners who attack Sudan cannot speak about the situation of women there because the American women still fighting for equal wages would not believe that in the heart of Africa there are women who compete with men in everything."

65. *Mu'tamar al-qawmi al-islami al-rabi'*, 670.

66. *Mu'tamar al-qawmi al-islami al-awwal*, 340.

67. Leila Ahmed offers a critical assessment of Amin's depiction of Muslim women in *Women and Gender in Islam: Roots of a Modern Debate* (Yale University Press, 1992). See, also, the translation of Amin's main writings on women: *The Liberation of Women and the New Woman: Two Documents in the History of Egyptian Feminism* (American University in Cairo Press, 2000).

68. *Mu'tamar al-qawmi al-islami al-thalith*, 34.

69. *Mu'tamar al-qawmi al-islami al-thalith*, 39.

70. *Mu'tamar al-qawmi al-islami al-awwal*, 168.

71. Muhammad al-Sayyid Habib in Bin Sa'id (ed.), *al-Mujtama' al-madani fi al-watan al-'arabi*, 334.

72. 'Issam al-'Ariyan in Bin Sa'id (ed.), *al-Mujtama' al-madani fi al-watan al-'arabi*, 724.

73. Margot Badran. "Feminisms and Islamisms," *Journal of Women's History* 10 (1999), 198.

74. Margot Badran. "Gender Activism: Feminists and Islamists in Egypt" in Valentine M. Moghadam (ed.), *Identity Politics and Women* (Boulder: Westview Press, 1994), 202–227.

75. Haddad and Smith. "Women in Islam," 139.
76. Haddad and Smith. "Women in Islam," 145.
77. Mervat Hatem. "Toward the Development of Post-Islamist and Post-Nationalist Feminist Discourses in the Middle East" in Judith E. Tucker (ed.), *Arab Women: Old Boundaries, New Frontiers* (Indiana University Press, 1993), 29–48.
78. Sherna Berger Gluck. "Palestinian Women: Gender Politics and Nationalism," *Journal of Palestine Studies* 24 (1995), 7. In contrast, Frances Hasso has found that "nationalism and feminism were largely successful as a combined project in the 10 years predating the [Palestinian] uprising that began in late 1987." "The 'Women's Front': Nationalism, Feminism and Modernity in Palestine," *Gender & Society* 12 (1998), 442. However, Hasso also finds that once the nationalist movement became more focused on military mobilization, this "happy marriage" took a turn for the worse.
79. Cynthia Enloe. *Bananas, Beaches and Bases: Making Feminist Sense of International Politics* (University of California Press, 1989), 60, 62.
80. Mervat Hatem. "Secularists and Islamist Discourses on Modernity in Egypt and the Evolution of the Postcolonial Nation-State" in Yvonne Yazbeck Haddad and John L. Esposito (eds.), *Islam, Gender and Social Change* (Oxford University Press, 1998), 88–89.
81. *Mu'tamar al-qawmi al-islami al-thalith*, 34.
82. Batya Weinbaum. *The Curious Courtship of Women's Liberation and Socialism* (Boston: South End Press, 1978).
83. Lydia Sargent. *Women and Revolution: A Discussion of the Unhappy Marriage of Marxism and Feminism* (Boston: South End Press, 1981).
84. Sondra Hale. "Activating the Gender Local: Transnational Ideologies and 'Women's Culture' in Northern Sudan," *Journal of Middle East Women's Studies* 1 (2005), 26–52; Mervat Hatem. "The Pitfalls of the Nationalist Discourses on Citizenship in Egypt" in Suad Joseph (ed.), *Gender and Citizenship in the Middle East* (Syracuse University Press, 2000); Uma Narayan. *Dislocating Cultures: Identities, Traditions and Third World Feminism* (New York: Routledge, 1997).
85. Hale. "Activating the Gender Local," 26.
86. Nadia Hijab. *Womenpower: The Arab Debate on Women at Work* (Cambridge University Press, 1988), 2.
87. Rita Noonan. "Women against the State: Political Opportunities and Collective Action Frames in Chile's Transition to Democracy," *Sociological Forum* 10 (1995), 106.
88. Hani Shukralla. "Reflections: Spots, but still a Tiger," *al-Ahram Weekly* (June 14–20, 2001).
89. The organization maintains a website at www.islamicnational.org and a small office in Beirut.

4   The Egyptian Movement for Change: Intellectual antecedents and generational conflicts[1]

On June 8, 2006, around 700 activists, lawyers, and journalists convened at the Lawyers' Syndicate in Cairo to speak out against the ongoing detention of political activists and in support of the judges who were fighting for the independence of the judiciary and the lawyers who were to be tried for publication of the "blacklist" of judges allegedly complicit in vote-rigging during the 2005 parliamentary elections. The event featured speakers from the Muslim Brotherhood, the Revolutionary Socialists, the Nasirist-leaning Karama Party, the Islamist Labor Party, the liberal Ghad Party, the Egyptian Movement for Change (better known as Kifaya), the leftist Tagammu' Party, as well as various human rights groups.[2] Muntasir al-Zayyat, an Islamist lawyer best known for his defense of the blind Shaykh 'Umar 'Abd al-Rahman and for his writing of an Ayman al-Zawahiri biography,[3] gave the first speech, welcoming all in the name of the lawyers' syndicate and calling for the various organizations represented "to be united under these circumstances." "These are," he proclaimed, "the worst of times." Zayyat thanked Kifaya and the Muslim Brotherhood in particular "for grabbing this opportunity for us" to fight for political reform and other issues of common concern. A member of the Ghad Party, speaking on behalf of his party's chairman, Ayman Nur (b. 1964), who remains in prison on charges of forging signatures to obtain a license for his party, followed Zayyat in sending "his regards and gratitude to the Muslim Brothers and Kifaya for their role in the fight." The founder of the Karama Party, Hamdin al-Sabahi (b. 1954), and 'Abd al-Ghaffar Shukr (b. 1936), a leading member of the Tagammu', each called for the release of all political prisoners, naming an ideologically broad cast of characters, from the Muslim Brother activist, 'Issam al-'Ariyan (b. 1953), to the Revolutionary Socialist leader, Kamal Khalil (b. 1949). The event's spokeswoman, a member of the Nasirist Party, noted that "the Security forces do not differ between Muslim Brothers and secularists, Copts and Muslim citizens," and affirmed that "all parties are in this together." The speakers were regularly interrupted by chants from the audience, alternating between slogans associated with Kifaya and those of the Muslim Brotherhood, and often entailing declarations of "no to Mubarak," "no to the extensions of the emergency law," and "no to succession of Gamal Mubarak."

The event was remarkable, not only for the number of what were only a few years ago "red lines" that were categorically disregarded, but also for the amalgam of traditionally and, until recently, vehemently opposed groups that had come together in the name of unity and shared struggle, and dared to speak the name of the Muslim Brotherhood in the same breath as avowedly secular and socialist groups. This rapprochement between secular and religious forces is a relatively new state of affairs. In his 1950 work, *Our Beginning in Wisdom*, the well-known Islamic preacher, Muhammad al-Ghazzali (1917–1996), articulated a view of the relationship between Islam and nationalism that has been fairly widespread among Islamists:

Nationalism has only lost for us our Islamic unity and enabled Christians and the Zionist imperialism to rob us of our most sacred rights ... The truth is that the growth of nationalism, racialism and infidel patriotism is a loss of Islamic faith as well as a loss of Islamic rule. The revival of such evil fanaticism is a plot against God's religion – a return to the first *Jahiliyya* [the age of ignorance, prior to the arrival of Islam] with all its injustice and crime.[4]

Others have documented the more systematic Islamist critiques of Arab national-socialism that followed the 1967 defeat. Raymond Baker, for example, has analyzed the "unrelenting attack on all aspects of the Nasirist legacy, including Arabism, the industrialization drive, and the socialist measures" that were widespread in Islamic publications throughout the 1970s, such as the Muslim Brotherhood's monthly magazine *al-Da'wa* (The Call), which viewed Arab nationalism as an "affront to the universalism of Islam."[5]

Today Islamist, nationalists, and socialists can be found collaborating in the fight for political reform in Egypt and articulating those demands through frequent public demonstrations. How is it that this has come about? There are many who think that the spontaneity and often haphazard protest activity in the streets of Cairo over the past decade lacks antecedents, lacks thinking, lacks constructive political programs, and lacks political (or ideological or intellectual) significance. While overall I might be inclined to agree with some aspects of such assessments, I also think such dismissals overlook dimensions of these recent activities that lend them greater significance than any particular progress they have yet to achieve in regard to political reform. The aim of this chapter is to account for the origins, analyze the character, and assess the

significance of the growing coordination among these various oppositional elements that had in many respects backed themselves into an
ideological corner by the shrill character, as well as sheer volume, of discourse aimed at criticizing, discrediting, even demonizing their political opponents. While much of the focus here is on individuals often
associated with the now well-known Egyptian Movement for Change,
or Kifaya, it is not only the existence of this ideologically diverse grouping, but the links it has created with the country's largest opposition
group, the Muslim Brotherhood, that reveal the most about the changing landscape of Egyptian politics.

Protest activity for reform since the second intifada

The protest activity of which Kifaya formed a part emerged with the
anti-Israeli and anti-American protests at the time of the second intifada, and in the protests leading up to the Iraq war. After the September
2000 killing of Muhammad al-Durra, a nine-year-old Palestinian boy,
was televised, students began to stage demonstrations throughout the
country, despite the existence of the Emergency Law, first imposed
after the assassination of President Anwar Sadat and in place ever since,
which requires prior consent for any kind of public demonstration.[6] The
Egyptian Popular Committee in Solidarity with the Palestinian Intifada (EPCSPI) was set up by various non-governmental organizations
and activists to collect donations of money and blood for the Palestinians.[7] Among the founding members of EPCSI are various seasoned
leftist activists, such as the leftist publisher Farid Zahran (b. 1957); the
engineer and member of the Egyptian Anti-Torture Association, 'Adil
al-Mashad; psychiatrist and official of the Nadim Center for the Reha-
bilitation of Victims of Violence, Suzanne Fayyad; and Aida Sayf al-
Dawla (b. 1956), a Marxist professor of psychiatry.

These efforts culminated in the formation of the "Cairo Conference Against U.S. Hegemony and War on Iraq and in Solidarity with
Palestine," later renamed the "Popular Campaign for the Support of
Resistance in Palestine and Iraq and Against Globalization," and more
generally known simply as the "Cairo Anti-war Conference" or just
the "Cairo Conference," first held in December 2002 and annually
since. The broad character of the causes taken up by the conferences –
anti-war and anti-neoliberalism – allowed local groups to create links
across ideological and social divides. It also provided an opportunity
for Egyptian activists to affiliate with the international anti-war and
anti-globalization movement. But perhaps more significantly, it opened
space in Egypt and created momentum for development of a movement

for domestic political reform – and instigated Egypt's largest opposition force, the Muslim Brotherhood, to undertake a more confrontational stance in regard to the Egyptian regime.

The move toward a focus on domestic reform was initiated in October 2003, when Sonallah Ibrahim (b. 1937) refused to accept Egypt's Novelist of the Year award from the minister of culture. In a live television broadcast of the event, Ibrahim was heard telling the audience that the repressive Egyptian government "lacks the credibility of bestowing" the award, citing the collaboration of the Egyptian regime and other Arab governments in the US occupation of Iraq, as well as Egypt's inaction in confronting Israel's repression of the Palestinians.[8]

The appearance of Kifaya on the scene in July 2004 represented a new phase in the waves of protest activity, due to the boldness of its protest activities and confrontational tone in focusing attention on Egyptian President Husni Mubarak's unwillingness to relinquish his office and the issue of succession by his son Gamal, as well as for the cross-ideological character of the group itself. According to the assessment of the semi-official al-Ahram Center for Strategic and International Studies, "before Kefaya emerged on the scene, it had been customary for demonstrations in the country to address foreign issues, such as the situation in Iraq and Palestine. As for domestic issues, these were confined to debates in the press, seminars, and party headquarters. Domestic debates had generally been banned from the street and the official media. Kefaya managed to change all that."[9] Kifaya's "Manifesto" called for political reforms that reached far beyond more measured demands put forth by Egypt's existing political parties. Their proposal, rhetoric, and political activities have served to embolden other groups and expanded the purview of what is politically possible in the country.

The organization is dominated by nationalists and leftists, but has incorporated an ideologically broad spectrum of political activists since its formation. So too, it is possible to distinguish three political generations within this organization: an old guard, the so called "middle generation" – which will be the focus of much of this chapter's analysis – and a youth generation.[10] Most of the organizers of the group are individuals from the "middle generation," who were active in the student movements in the 1970s. However, a few of the leaders are from an older generation that started its activism against the British in the 1940s and 1950s, and much of the action in the street (and its coordination and publication on the Internet) is undertaken by a new generation of activists in their thirties or younger.[11] The first meeting of Kifaya was held in the home of Abu al-'Ila Madhi (b. 1958), a former Muslim Brother and one of the founders of the Wasat Party. Thus, members of the Wasat

Party were among the organization's founders and the group has had at least one current Brother, Muhammad 'Abd al-Quddus, with it since the beginning. Other prominent members of the Muslim Brotherhood, such as 'Issam al-'Ariyan and 'Abd al-Mun'im Abu al-Futuh (b. 1951), have signed on to Kifaya documents. The group has brought public figures, like Muhammed al-Sayyid Sa'id, deputy director of the Al-Ahram Center for Political and Strategic Studies, and 'Abd al-Halim Qandil (b. 1950), editor of the Nasirist weekly, al-'Arabi, together with activists from some more radical dissident groups like the Revolutionary Socialists and the Labor Party. A Copt and retired high school teacher, George Ishaq, acted as the group's spokesperson and general coordinator until 2007. In early 2007, Abdelwahab Elmessiri – a former literature professor whose political career includes a brief stint in the Muslim Brotherhood before joining the Communist Party in the 1950s and who more recently has articulated an Islamic orientation – took over as Kifaya spokesperson. When Elmessiri passed away, a professor of medicine, 'Abd al-Jalil Mustafa, agreed to act as the group's coordinator until the end of 2008. In January 2009, 'Abd al-Halim Qandil, a figure less known for working across ideological lines than for his vociferous critiques of the Mubarak regime, was elected Kifaya coordinator.

In 2004 Kifaya set up a website, began circulating a petition, and printed large numbers of stickers bearing the group's distinctive red and yellow logo, which declares their simple message of "Kifaya!" (Enough!).[12] Kifaya's actions also contributed to development of several other groups "for change," including the 20th March Movement for Change (an offshoot of March 2003 protests against the Iraq war), Students for Change, Youth for Change, University Professors for Change, Workers for Change, and Artists for Change. Another broad front, the People's Campaign for Change (al-hamla al-sha'biyya min ajl al-taghyir), announced in September 2004, drew support from Nasirists, communists, Muslim Brothers, the Ghad Party, and independents active in human rights organizations. An organization devoted to tracking corruption, called Shayfinkum (we see you), emerged in response to the government repression of the protestors. The slogan, "kifaya", is often used to describe these myriad groups that participate in demonstrations, and the issuing of political statements.

The forces that began protesting in 2000 were given philosophical justification and confirmation by the former judge and intellectual associated with the wasatiyya trend in Egypt, Tariq al-Bishri. In October 2004 Bishri published a letter, entitled "I call upon you to disobey" (ad'ukum ila al-'isyan), urging citizens to withdraw their support for the government and to begin engaging in non-violent protests. Noting the "personalization of the state" and "narrowing circle of individuals holding the reins of state [that] has increased the harassment of political opponents and the inclination to use violence against adversaries," Bishri questions the legitimacy of the ruling regime and calls upon Egyptian citizens to follow the example of Gandhi: "cease playing the role of the governed" and "cease cooperating with the state." He maintains that the only course of action that can get beyond the present state of affairs is to "breach the dictates of the personalized state, not through demands addressed to the personalized leadership but through practice. National groupings must realize that dynamism and movement is not legitimized by personalized leadership and its decisions, but from societal organizations and constitutional provisions for liberties and human rights." The only way to confront state violence, he argued, is through its opposite: non-violent action.[13] Kifaya took Bishri's statement as an affirmation of their activities, and many other activists, including a growing number of individual members of the Muslim Brotherhood, began to heed Bishri's call. In December 2004, a coalition of Nasirists, Islamists, and socialists organized a demonstration in Cairo brandishing Kifaya slogans – "No to reelection! No to inheritance!" (la lil-tajdid wa la lil-tawrith) – sounding a cry against Mubarak's expected renewal for a fifth term in the coming presidential election and the grooming of his son Gamal to succeed him.

On February 21, 2005, Kifaya organized the largest anti-Mubarak protest in Egypt's history, attracting hundreds of demonstrators to downtown Cairo from a wide variety of ideological trends, including leftists, Islamists, and liberals.[14] The date was chosen to mark International Student's Day and the date of the 1946 general strike undertaken by the Egyptian National Committee of Students and Workers to pressure the British colonialists to get out of Egypt. Since the protestors were not allowed to enter the university, the demonstration took place in front of the university gates. Five days later Mubarak announced that he would work to amend the constitution (Article 76) so that more than one candidate would be allowed to run and the president would be elected directly by the people.[15] Kifaya and other opposition forces were emboldened by what they took to be a response to their demands, though they only partially celebrated the move. Ultimately, the group criticized the proposed amendment as insufficient, since opponents would still lack time to organize before the September elections and still faced additional hurdles, such as the requirements of party affiliation and the need to achieve the appropriate backing from institutions, which remained generally under the ruling party's control.[16]

On March 27, 2005, the Muslim Brotherhood organized a demonstration in which Kifaya and other groups joined in to call for political reforms. The event was the group's first demonstration on domestic issues since President Mubarak came to power and broke a long-standing, informal truce between the Brotherhood and the regime – an unspoken agreement that allowed the movement to practice its missionary (da'wa) activities, so long as it refrained from directly challenging the regime in the political arena. Many took the demonstration to indicate that the Muslim Brotherhood was rethinking its traditional strategy of avoiding outright confrontation with the state.[17]

The government responded to the growing Muslim Brotherhood presence in the streets by detaining hundreds of its leaders. On May 6, 2005, 'Ariyan and three other Muslim Brotherhood members were arrested at a demonstration in Giza organized by Kifaya, while tens of other Brothers were arrested the same day for demonstrating in front of a mosque in Nasir City. Kifaya issued a statement calling for their release.[18] The day of the referendum on Article 76, May 25, 2005, Kifaya staged a number of small demonstrations throughout the capital. Government forces responded by brutally cracking down on the demonstrators. Activists were beaten by plain-clothes policemen and government-hired street thugs, in many cases groping and tearing the clothes off female protestors in order to humiliate them. Even journalists were not spared the assault.[19] According to Tamir Wajih, more protests staged over the course of the days that followed "significantly intensified, carrying Kifaya to the forefront of the battle for democracy in Egypt, and moving the Muslim Brotherhood into a clear opposition with the state."[20] However, the relationship between the Brotherhood and the other political forces developed more slowly than this assessment suggests. The Brotherhood did not organize another protest for some time and showed signs of division over the group's new public forms of activism and concern over the government response. While the group continued to appear at various demonstrations in the months that followed, it opted to keep a lower profile and restricted its numbers, both to not provoke the regime and to not overwhelm the other protesting groups.[21]

In June 2005, a group of Egyptian intellectuals formed a "National Assembly for Democratic Transformation" (al-tajammu' al-watani lil-tahawwul al-dimuqrati), the main aims of which were to foster debate about a new constitution in consultation with all political forces and to work toward the formation of the national front. The group was led by a number of prominent figures, including former prime minister (1972–1973) Aziz Sidqi (b. 1920), former deputy foreign minister 'Abdullah al-Ashal, and the editor of al-Usbu' newspaper, Mustafa al-Bakri, and several well-known Islamist intellectuals, such as Tariq al-Bishri and Muhammad Salim al-'Awa. Coordination between the Muslim

Brotherhood and Kifaya picked up again in July and August 2005, as the Brotherhood rallied as part of a coalition that included Kifaya and other groups. However, differences of style, strategy, and goals were also apparent. Often prior to a protest, the various sides would reach an agreement: the Muslim Brotherhood would refrain from shouting "Islam is the solution" and raising the Qur'an and the other more secular demonstrators would limit their protest to general policies and issues and refrain from specifically criticizing Mubarak. On at least two occasions, both sides broke the agreement shortly after the demonstration began, and the Brotherhood responded by quickly dispersing and disappearing through the back streets of Cairo.[22] At the same time, it is during this period that the Muslim Brotherhood significantly increased its public criticism of the regime for their arrests of Kifaya activists. Deputy supreme guide, Muhammad Habib (b. 1943), called for the release of Kifaya activists after a July 30 protest and the Brotherhood condemned the arrests of Kifaya members after an October 1 protest.[23]

In the run-up to the presidential elections, the Muslim Brotherhood, along with other opposition groups – such as Kifaya, the Tagammu' Party, and the Nasirist Party – first agreed to a boycott, as it had boycotted the referendum on Article 76, but then reversed its decision and urged its members, as well as the Egyptian people at large, to take part in the election. The Muslim Brotherhood called on all Egyptians to participate in the election, but did not back any particular candidate. Rather, the statement noted that the Brothers "cannot support a tyrant or cooperate with corruption or despotism," which was understood to be a criticism of the regime and a discouragement from voting for Mubarak.[24] Muhammad 'Abd al-Quddus suggested that voters go to the ballot boxes but leave their ballots blank, and said that the idea had also been put forward to have voters void their ballots by writing in the name of a Brotherhood leader.[25] The organization justified their change of position by arguing that, since they remained the most significant opposition force in the country, it was their duty to ensure that the ruling party not succeed in monopolizing the election. The decision was widely criticized, both among its members, but perhaps most forcefully by other opposition groups, who saw the move as conferring legitimacy on both the regime and the election process.

The elections themselves were marred by reports of fraud, forgery, and government repression. By October 2005, the Muslim Brotherhood joined in the establishment of the United National Front for Change (al-jabha al-wataniyya al-muwwahida min ajl al-taghyir, UNFC), which brought together various opposition parties and political forces, including Kifaya and the Wasat and Karama parties, in addition to the

Brotherhood. Although the Brotherhood still ran its own candidates as independents, rather than under the UNFC, Abu al-Futuh, who serves on the Muslim Brotherhood's supreme decision-making body, the Guidance Bureau (*maktab al-irshad*), released a statement in December confirming that "the group remains in the position of opposition, not within the framework of cooperating with the government."[26] What was most significant is that the Muslim Brotherhood allied with the National Front as an organization, publicly acknowledging its role as one of a number of groups in the opposition. These other organizations took the additional step of recognizing the Muslim Brotherhood as one of their members. This is seen most clearly in January 2006, when at a conference organized by Kifaya, entitled "A State for all Egyptians," the participants released a statement calling for the government to ease restrictions on the licensing of political parties and citing in particular the need for the government to recognize the Muslim Brotherhood as a party.[27]

In April 2006, the Judges Club, which represents the country's 8,000 judges, had listed numerous conditions that needed to be met as a condition of the judicial oversight of the elections, which was stipulated by the amendment to Article 76.[28] Among the flaws in the amendment was the stipulation that the elections take place on one day. The judges insisted that they required at least three days to adequately oversee the elections.[29] The government agreed to a voting procedure that would take place in three rounds, from mid-October to mid-November. Most of the violence and irregularities took place in the second and third rounds. The Judges Club refused to endorse the election results. Two senior judges, Mahmud Makki and Hisham al-Bastawisi, were singled out for their criticism of the proceedings and called to appear before a disciplinary board to determine their "competence." The Judges Club began a sit-in in order to protest the censure of their colleagues. The judges' protest re-ignited the opposition, including the Muslim Brotherhood.

The remainder of this chapter will address developments that have taken place within some of the main groups that have contributed to this rapprochement between secular and religious opposition forces, and offer a general assessment of the transformations apparent within these groups that have both enabled and resulted from their interactions.

The Muslim Brotherhood's middle generation and the Wasat Party

Many recent studies of the Muslim Brotherhood have noted a division among political generations within the organization, comprising an old and a new guard.[30] In fact, like Kifaya, the Brotherhood is best described as encompassing three distinct political generations. Most of the Muslim Brotherhood leadership, including the current spiritual guide, Muhammad Mahdi 'Akif (b. 1928), are from the old guard of the group. The character of these individuals was largely formed through their experience of oppression and imprisonment under the regime of Gamal 'Abd al-Nasir. The old guard is generally more conservative, fervently committed to preserving the unity of the movement and suspicious of other groups, as well as of independent initiative on the part of their own members. In general, they possess a tendency to take the long view toward the Brotherhood's role in Egypt and to emphasize the group's missionary activity, or da'wa, which they understand as a process of education aimed at gradual social transformation beginning at the grassroots.[31]

While the old guard suffered considerably under the fierce repression of the Nasir government, the "middle generation" of the brotherhood has its beginnings in the openings created by Egyptian President Anwar Sadat and the Muslim Brotherhood's own reorganization.[32] They acquired their first political skills during the 1970s while working with other student activists at Egyptian universities. As such, many are contemporaries of some of the most active members of secular groups. 'Abd al-Mun'im Abu al-Futuh, for example, led Cairo University's student union between 1974 and 1977, while Abu al-'Ila Madhi headed the student union at Minya University from 1977 to 1979 and was elected deputy head of the Egyptian National Student Union from 1978 to 1979.[33] It dominated elections for university student unions throughout the 1980s and 1990s. This middle generation has played a central role in coordinating and forming alliances with other groups. In many respects, these figures represent a rather different type of Brother, acclimated to political work through the Brotherhood's involvement in the syndicates in the early 1980s and in the parliamentary elections of 1984 and 1987, when Brotherhood members won seats through alliances with the Wafd, Liberal, and Labor parties. According to Ismail, "from the mid-1980s on, an increasing number of professional syndicates have been claimed as political space for opposition activities. This new political space was a source of unease for the regime. The politicization of the syndicates has gone hand-in-hand with their 'Islamization'," as a number of candidates elected to the boards of the syndicates ran on Islamic programs and had ties to the Muslim Brotherhood, including 'Issam al-'Ariyan (doctors' syndicate) and Abu al-'Ila Madhi (engineers' syndicate). Ismail notes that in many of these syndicates, one finds two main blocs forming, with "Islamists on one side, nationalists and secularists on the other."[34]

The 1984 elections marked the first time that the Brothers coordinated with another political party, their historic rival, the Wafd. According to one explanation of this alliance, "the Wafd wanted to take advantage of the popularity the Islamist group enjoyed at the grass-roots level, and the Brotherhood sought to enter the parliament with the help of a legitimate partner."[35] In 1987, they formed the backbone of what was called the "Islamic Alliance" (*al-tahaluf al-islami*), a coalition of candidates from the Muslim Brotherhood and the Liberal Party (*hizb al-ahrar*) and the Labor Party, which won sixty seats in parliament.[36] However, Mohammed Hafez and Quintan Wiktorowicz note that it was the Brotherhood that managed "to set the terms of the alliance. For example, it was able to exclude Marxists and Nasserists from the alliance list. It also enticed the Labor Party to amend its political program to include 'applying the *shari'a*'."[37] Nonetheless, the central role of the Brothers from the middle generation in forging these early alliances illustrate the importance they assign to political work (rather than missionary activities) and their willingness to cross class and ideological lines in order to build strategic alliances with other political organizations and overcome barriers put in front of their participation by the Egyptian regime.[38]

Despite the existence of ideological and generational differences within the Brotherhood, one must note the extent to which the group has managed to maintain internal cohesion and unity. One important exception to this is the emergence of the Wasat Party, born of a group of young professionals from the middle generation who, during a "re-entrenchment" of the Muslim Brotherhood's old guard in the late 1990s, decided to branch and pursue the establishment of a political party.[39]

The Wasat Party was launched in January 1996 by a number of former Muslim Brothers in coordination with activists from other political and ideological backgrounds after seventy-four Egyptians (sixty-two of whom were Muslim Brothers) signed the application for legal party status. Among the founders of the Wasat were seven Christians as well. A "Report on the State of Religion" in Egypt, published by the semi-official al-Ahram Center, notes that the name of the group indicates that it stems from "a middle generation in the Muslim Brotherhood, as well as a middle generation within Egypt itself, that finds obstacles on the way to political leadership in political parties and institutions." The report also states that 'the name also refers to the 'middle community' (*al-umma al-wasat*) in religious discussions as a middle between two extremes, as well as the middle between the ruling opinions and society and between different ideological and political trends."[40] According to the International Crisis Group, "The project of a new political party also arose from the impatience of the ex-campus radicals of the 1970s with the Society of the Muslim Brothers." Abu al-'Ala Madhi claimed that he left the Muslim Brotherhood to found the party for two basic reasons:

The first concerns the ideas inside the Society. I felt that, on the political side, they were not suitable, and it did not develop itself. The second reason concerns the structure of the Society, and the way decisions were made. There was no freedom to express differences ... We tried to make reform in both directions. So we decided to separate and form an independent party to express our opinions without restrictions and to present in it the evolutionary ideas we aspired to.[41]

The Wasat Party breaks from the traditional rhetoric of the Muslim Brotherhood in a number of respects. The Wasat claims to be a civil political party with an Islamic frame of reference. According to Madhi, Islam must be understood as a "civilizational concept."[42] The 2004 Wasat Party program states:

The founding members believe that a general Islamic framework is inclusive of all Egyptians: Islam is not only the religion of the Muslims: it is also, for both Muslims and non-Muslims, the cultural framework within which Egypt's creative intellectuals, scientists and leaders have made their contributions, and Arabic, the language of Islam, is the language in which Egyptian religious leaders, whether Muslim or Christian, have preached. Islamic culture is the homeland of all Egyptians, Muslim and non-Muslim.[43]

The political dimension of Islam is played down as its cultural aspects are accentuated.

The Wasat program also champions popular sovereignty, separation and balance of powers, rotation of power through elections, term limits for government post, freedom of belief and speech, the right to found parties, freedom of association, "intellectual and political pluralism," and "complete equality of men and women."[44] They also maintain that religious discourse must be reformed through *ijtihad* (independent reasoning): "its contents need to be modernized and its negative concepts, apologetic language and exclusivist, isolation tendencies need to be discoursed."[45] Although the party seeks to "make the shari'a part of the very fabric of daily life," they view Islamic law not as as a fixed set of rule and guidelines to be applied, but as "an authoritative framework of values and standards" that must be articulated through "human interpretations." The task, they argue, "is to select interpretations of Islamic law which contribute towards, rather than obstruct, the development of society."[46] In addition, they display openness toward ideas emerging from non-Islamic contexts through their rejection of the notion of a "clash of civilizations." The platform asserts that there exists a "common human civilization" and calls for recognition of "the cooperation, mutual knowledge and complementarity of all cultures."[47]

The Wasat has failed in its efforts to attain status as a legal political party, with its last petition being rejected by the government in early 2006. So, too, the composition of the group has changed with each successive petition to the Political Parties Committee (PPC). Most of the former Brothers who had joined the Wasat returned to the Muslim Brotherhood. The 1998 petition under the name al-Wasat al-Misri (the Egyptian Middle) listed ninety-three founding members, including only twenty-four former Brothers and three Christians, although the number of women had increased to nineteen.[48] Before their last petition for a license, all of the Christian members of the group had resigned under pressure from security officers.[49]

While some from the middle generation left the Muslim Brotherhood to form the Wasat Party, most chose to continue working in the larger group including, perhaps most importantly, 'Issam al-'Ariyan, who acted as the secretary-general of the National-Islamic conferences in 2005–2006, and 'Abd al-Mun'im Abu al-Futuh. Mona El-Ghobashi and Carrie Rosefsky Wickham have documented the transformation in the thinking of the Muslim Brotherhood, especially since the 1990s, and reveal the central role these younger cadres have played in their organization's articulation of a more moderated and democratic stance.[50] In many respects, the views of many of the most outspoken Muslim Brothers of the middle generation seem to correspond with the views articulated in the Wasat Party platform. Abu al-Futuh has argued that Islamic thought, like any thinking that is comprehended from the reading and understanding of fallible humans, requires renewal and change in light of developments in historical circumstances and the experiences of the movement.[51] In that spirit, Abu al-Futuh and 'Ariyan have advocated political pluralism, rotation of power through elections and equal citizenship for all Egyptians regardless of religion.[52] Further, 'Ariyan began publicly voicing his desire to see the Muslim Brotherhood develop into a political party in 2004.[53] The organization itself only officially expressed such aspirations in January 2007.[54]

The centrality of this middle generation in modernizing and moderating the Muslim Brotherhood was underscored in 1995, when the regime cracked down on the group and imprisoned many of the younger and more outspoken members. According to El-Ghobashi, the group suffered a series of "reversals" as a result.[55] El-Ghobashi points in particular to then supreme guide Mashhur's controversial remarks to the effect that Egypt's Copts should not be permitted to hold high posts in the military, and his call for reinstating the *jizya*, a tax collected from non-Muslims in exchange for their protection.[56] Other senior leaders, such as Ma'mun Hudaybi (b. 1919), were left with the task of clarifying and moderating Mashhur's statement.[57] Reflecting back on this occasion and drawing parallels with more recent statements from the current supreme guide, Muhammad Mahdi 'Akif, in regard to issues such as the desire of the organization to form a political party and the role of Copts in an Islamic party and an Islamic state, Cairo bureau chief of *al-Hayat* Muhammad Salah notes a similar dynamic between 'Akif and the deputy supreme guide, Muhammad Habib, a senior member of the Brotherhood's middle generation. Salah asks whether the "glaring contradictions" between 'Akif and Habib's statements reflected real difference of personal opinions or some sort of political strategy.[58]

While the moderated stances and greater willingness to work with non-Islamist groups may reflect the longing of the Brotherhood's middle generation to play a greater role in politics, as well as perhaps the interest of the group as a whole to present itself as moderate after September 11, 2001,[59] those impulses have gone hand-in-hand with a desire on the part of the leadership to remain cautious about taking a confrontational role with the state, preferring instead to focus on Islamicizing society through its *da'wa* activities, expanding the movement and generally pushing their agenda through a piecemeal effort. Goading this conservative group to take a more oppositional stance and join into alliances with other opposition forces has required not only moderation, but politicization. It is a testament to the persistence and growing influence of the middle generation that they have managed to do so. But their efforts have been further bolstered by the activities of Kifaya and others in the street and the group's own youth generation.

As various groups on the left increasingly organized on the issue of Palestine, the youth (*shabab*) of the Muslim Brotherhood sent an open letter to the Muhammad Salah, the Cairo Bureau chief of the Lebanese daily *al-Hayat*, which was published on April 5, 2002. The letter is addressed to Mustafa Mashhur (spiritual guide from 1996–2002) and the rest of the Muslim Brotherhood leadership. The authors of the letter note that this is the first time that they have brought their concerns directly to Mashhur. They justify their breaking of protocol by claiming, first, that their voices were not reaching him and, second, that the times called for such actions, in light of the imperatives of the issue of Palestine. Frustrated by the fact that other groups were out protesting against the occupation while the Muslim Brotherhood was merely discussing the matter in a general sense, rather than engaging the issue "in the streets," the authors of the letter ask: "Did not our Brothers teach us that the issue of Palestine is our first central issue and did not our Martyred Imam Hassan Banna establish in his intellectual treatises and works that Palestine and its occupation is the beginning and the end? ... Is the issue of Palestine and the recovery of the holy places our first and central issue or not?"[60] The "youths" requested a more active engagement with this and other issues of concern to the umma through participation in forums, protests, and demonstrations. Only a few months later, in August 2002, Ma'mun al-Hudaybi (spiritual guide from 2002–2004, after Mashhur's death) called for Muslims to support the "jihad" of the Palestinians and to boycott American and Israeli goods. Hudaybi also appeared at the second Cairo conference, held at the end of 2002, with a large number of Muslim Brotherhood members.

When the EPSCI organized a public demonstration on March 20, 2003, after the first US military strike in Iraq, to condemn the invasion of Iraq and US support for Israel, many Muslim Brothers were found among the over 20,000 protesters in Cairo's Tahrir Square. The anti-war protest emboldened activists and spawned further smaller-scale rallies in the months that followed, during which the old Muslim Brother slogan of "the road to Jerusalem goes through Cairo" was revived and put to use by activists, including leftists, who added a new slogan along the same lines: "The road to Baghdad goes through Cairo." Individual Muslim Brothers had already begun to join in the demonstrations, but the Brotherhood's leadership still remained concerned about overstepping boundaries that might threaten their fragile relationship with the regime. The organization did not yet appear in protests en masse.

Nonetheless, as the protest activity continued, the old guard showed signs that it was not immune to the pressures and changes emanating from both within their own organization and from other forces protesting in the streets. On March 3, 2004, in a formal attempt to accommodate the Muslim Brotherhood's ideology to the growing calls for democratic reforms, 'Akif dramatically unveiled a new "Initiative for Reform" shortly after his accession to leadership.[61] The initiative included a section on political reform that claimed support for "a republican, parliamentary, constitutional and democratic political order, in the framework of the principles of Islam" and affirmed that "the people are the source of all powers. No individual, party, community or group can claim a right to rule, unless it is derived from a free and true popular will." The initiative also stated the Muslim Brotherhood's commitment to the principle of the alternation of power through free and fair elections open to all citizens. 'Ariyan revealed in his report on the declaration that its release was intended to refute critics who contend that the movement's belief in the inseparability of politics and religion means that the Brotherhood's true aim is to establish a theocracy, and that the group is insincere in declaring its acceptance of the principle of political pluralism and its willingness to rotate power.[62] Because the Muslim Brotherhood claims to represent Islam, these critics conclude, it must view its political rivals as Islam's rivals. The Muslim Brotherhood would never allow another free election once it won power, as an electoral defeat would mean taking government away from Islam and handing it to non-Islamic forces.

The Muslim Brotherhood has responded to such criticisms by asserting that it does not seek to set up a religious state or a religious government. Rather, it claims that its goal is to establish a civil government and a civil state in which Islam is the source of authority. Accordingly, the *shari'a* provides a supreme, divine source of authority while, at the same time, the government derives its authority from the people it rules.[63] Potential conflicts between these two sources of authority have never been fully clarified beyond various statements, similar to those found in the works of the *wasatiyya* intellects, which assert that in any Muslim-majority state truly representative of the citizenry, the people would surely take Islam as their point of reference. However, the Muslim Brotherhood took the argument one step further in April 2005, when 'Akif issued a statement declaring: "The Brotherhood seeks to create a civil party with an Islamic reference, established in harmony with Article 2 of the constitution."[64] This is the first official acknowledgment of this goal and clearly echoes the aspirations and even language of both the founders of the Wasat Party and the intellectuals associated with the *wasatiyya* trend.[65] While this declaration reveals that the Muslim Brotherhood leadership seems to have accepted the importance of forming a party, the question remains as to whether Akif and other members of the old guard generally understand such a party to be only one small part or branch of the larger movement, or whether they would consider the party a replacement for the Muslim Brotherhood's current structure, as seems to be the position held by Abu al-Futuh and 'Ariyan. An Islamic party competing with other parties in a system of political pluralism would seem to suggest a model more akin to that of the Justice and Development Parties in Turkey and Morocco. Nonetheless, many took the desire of the Muslim Brotherhood to exist as a political party to be a positive development. By the following January, participants in Kifaya's conference on "A State for all Egyptians" would be demanding that the government let them do so.

The Revolutionary Socialists

The Nasirist counterpart to the Wasat Party is the Karama (Dignity) Party, which developed out of a conflict between an older and a younger guard in the Nasirist Party. The group is led by Hamdin al-Sabahi, head of the press syndicate's cultural committee and a member of parliament from the Delta governate of Kafr al-Shaykh. But the intellectual work that has justified a left rapprochement with the Muslim Brotherhood in Egypt has come not from the Nasirists, but from a small group of Trotskyites who have become increasingly visible, especially since the second intifada, through their role in the street protests and through their growing influence in student groups in Egypt's universities: the Revolutionary Socialists. The leader of the group, Kamal al-Khalil, is a well-known political presence who was active in the 1970s student movements and one of the early leaders of the Cairo Anti-War conference. The group's presence on college campuses has grown (though admittedly from tiny to small) and they have increased their work with grassroots groups in recent years. They were also a common target of arrests at some of the earliest protests. Members of the Revolutionary Socialists group have been one of the loudest voices calling for the left to work with the Muslim Brotherhood and took the lead in forming the National Alliance, which brought the Muslim Brotherhood together with other leftist groups.

The Revolutionary Socialists created an opening for interactions with the Muslim Brotherhood through their harsh critiques of what they view as a foolhardy alliance with the state against Islamists on the part of the "old left," particularly the Egyptian Communist and Tagammu' parties.[66] The possibility of a renewal of a left–state alliance re-emerged after many leftist groups began rethinking their cooperation with the Muslim Brotherhood in light of the group's participation and success in the 2005 parliamentary elections. A young member of the Revolutionary Socialists, Samih Najib, directly addressed the atmosphere of distrust and hostility between the left and the Islamists in a book entitled *The Muslim Brotherhood: A Socialist View*, published by the Revolutionary Socialist's Center for Socialist Studies.

Najib's analysis is directed at prominent Marxist intellectuals, such as Samir Amin, and Rif'at al-Sa'id, a well-known representative of the old guard of Egypt's left. Najib begins by identifying six arguments that have been used to justify the left's battle against political Islam: that Islamist groups seek only to take over the reigns of state; that they are a tool of the capitalist class; that there is no difference between the Muslim Brotherhood and more violent groups (their goal of taking over state power is the same); that the struggle between the Muslim Brotherhood and the regime is really just a struggle within the ruling class; that political Islam and capitalist, liberal globalization are not in conflict, but complementary; and that political Islam is not anti-imperialist and those seeming exceptions (like Hamas and Hizbullah) only articulate such a position because of political geography, which pits them against Israel and, thus, US policy in the region as well.[67] In general, Najib argues, the Egyptian left has exerted considerable effort to depict the Muslim Brotherhood as a reactionary and bourgeois force that is antithetical to modernity and democracy.

Najib offers his book as an "alternative reading" of the character of the Muslim Brotherhood, "in the context of its historical and effective social and political development."[68] According to his analysis, political Islam emerged in the first half of the twentieth century as a result of the contradictions of capitalist development and came to voice the concerns of the middle and lower classes who had become alienated from the left, because of their experiences under the Nasir regime, with the 1967 defeat, and as the classes that bore the brunt of Egypt's ongoing economic crises. The left allied itself with the state to confront the rise of political Islam, which served to further associate socialism with an oppressive regime and the status quo in the minds of the masses. Najib, like other Revolutionary Socialists, considers the Islamists to be at least in part a movement of the oppressed. The task for the left today, he argues, is to "build an independent socialist alternative, not throw itself in the ditch of the system nor throw itself in the ditch of the Islamist." At the same time, independence of the movement cannot be asserted merely by adopting various oppositional positions against other social groups that place the socialists on the wrong side in existing battles: "When the battle is between the Brotherhood and the state regarding democratic demands, such as the abolition of the emergency laws or the independence of the judiciary or against corruption," they must stand with the Brotherhood.[69] This view is summed up in a common slogan of the Revolutionary Socialists: "sometimes with the Islamists, but never with the state." That is not to say that the socialists should not criticize or work against the Brotherhood on other issues. Najib clarifies that his interest is advancing socialism, not the Muslim Brotherhood, but the Revolutionary Socialists believe that the Muslim Brotherhood can be an ally in creating new spheres of class struggle. In order to truly be a mass movement, the socialists must acknowledge their role. Revolutionary Socialists are willing to take the long view of their struggle.[70] As a result, members of this group, many of whom were among the leaders of the Cairo Conferences and the most regular participants in the first protests, have been persistent in reaching out to those in the Muslim Brotherhood who have proven willing to fight on common fronts.

The Egyptian Movement for Change

The Kifaya movement has been criticized for being clearer about what their group is against than about what it supports. Abu al-'Ila Madhi maintains that the group's August 2004 founding statement was kept intentionally general in order to incorporate a wide variety of groups: "we created a political agenda only, not an economic agenda. If we discussed economics the group would split between liberal and left."[71] When first published, the statement bore 300 signatures. According to Madhi and Ishaq, the publication of the document took several months, as each of the signatories added to and revised the working document.[72] Less than a year after its release, approximately 7,000 individuals had signed the statement.[73]

As noted above, even Kifaya's critics – of which there are many – credit the group with opening up a space for a new kind of oppositional politics. According to Heba Raouf Ezzat (b. 1965), a professor of political science at Cairo University and member of Shafikum, "there was a vacuum in Egyptian politics and Kifaya filled it."[74] The sociologist and director of the Ibn Khaldun Center for Development Studies, Saad Eddin Ibrahim (b. 1936), made a similar assessment: "There was a vacuum that neither the NDP nor existing opposition parties could fill." Like others, Ibrahim attributes this sense of a vacuum to individuals from the 1970s generation of student activists, who had parted ways and were brought back together, as they witnessed the "hardening of the arteries on the part of the regime and the parties which some of them had belonged to."[75]

Not all of Kifaya's membership has been keen to enlist the Muslim Brotherhood as such in their cause, even though individual members of the group and members of the Wasat had been a part of the group since the beginning. According to Rabab El-Mahdi, a Kifaya activist and professor of political science at the American University in Cairo, many were suspicious of the Brotherhood, not only for ideological reasons, but also due to the group's unwillingness to be confrontational with the state and the demands that the group refrain from using anti-Mubarak posters and slogans. Often, she argued, the rebuff took subtle forms, such as neglecting to invite them to organizational meetings.[76]

Other Kifaya members justified their cooperation with the Islamist forces by noting their hope that they would be moderated by the interaction. George Ishaq argued that the only way to "edit their position" was to engage them; "if we leave them alone they will continue to say the same old things."[77] Muhammad al-Sayyid Sa'id, an analyst at the al-Ahram Center and a Kifaya member, sees his group's interaction with the Muslim Brotherhood as part of a process of advancing their "learning curve." As a result of their education they tend to enter politics with extremely rigid modes of thinking. "When they debate, interact and engage in politics, the learning curve rises higher."[78] Of course, which group has had more influence on the beliefs and internal politics of the others is difficult to assess. But it seems clear that there has been movement on the part of all sides in a number of respects.

The ebb and flow of protests and alliances

After Mubarak won a fifth term in the September 2005 presidential elections, critics began to suggest that the Egyptian Movement for Change had gasped its last breath and that cooperation between the Muslim Brotherhood and the opposition was over. Kifaya never put forward the name of a presidential candidate. The group had approached Tariq al-Bishri about running, but he declined the offer, citing his advanced age and the fact that he was more suited for intellectual than political work. Neither did Kifaya back the al-Ghad candidate, Ayman Nur, whom many considered the most viable opposition candidate.[79] Further, in the parliamentary elections that followed in December, none of the handful of Kifaya candidates who ran in the elections won seats, while the ruling NDP maintained its overwhelming majority. The Muslim Brotherhood succeeding in winning over 20 percent of the seats.

However, dispute over the independence of the judiciary following the elections re-energized the protestors. The Muslim Brotherhood, both in parliament and in the streets, solidly backed the judges, along with leftist, nationalist, and liberal opposition forces. Weekly protests were held in the month leading up to the hearing of the case of the two Court of Cassation judges indicted for blowing the whistle on the 2005 parliamentary elections. Around 400 activists demonstrated in solidarity with the judges on the day the two were arrested. Of the 8,000 judges in Egypt, all but 2,000 stood in solidarity with their indicted colleagues. On May 18, Judge Mahmud Makki was cleared of all charges and Judge Hisham al-Bastawisi was reprimanded.

In the garden of the lawyers' syndicate before the meeting recounted at the opening of this chapter, the seasoned secular activist Ahmed Sayf al-Islam, father of then-imprisoned blogger and Youth for Change activist Alaa Sayf al-Islam 'Abd al-Fatah and director of the Hisham Mubarak Law Center, said that he had just been to see Ahmad Sharqawi

(b. 1982), the youth activist and blogger who had reportedly been beaten and sodomized while in detention and had still not been released, and other imprisoned activists. Sayf al-Islam outlined concerns that had been expressed to him by the detainees regarding two possible routes they thought the state might take toward undermining the opposition: either the regime would continue to extend the detention of those activists already in prison and further crack down on activists in an attempt to crush the opposition completely, or the regime might begin to release all non-Muslim Brotherhood activists while continuing their crackdown on the Muslim Brotherhood with the aim of splitting the alliance and possibly convincing the Brotherhood to retreat from their confrontational stance. The greater concern was with the latter possibility: "The regime wants to divide the Muslim Brotherhood and the other political forces and this would create a dilemma. Would other political forces continue to fight for Muslim Brotherhood detainees and would Muslim Brotherhood continue to work with others?"[80]

Ahmed Sayf al-Islam arrived with 'Ali 'Abd al-Fattah,[81] an engineer and senior Muslim Brother from the group's Alexandria branch who, like 'Ariyan and Abu al-Futuh, is often called on to coordinate with groups like Kifaya. As the two sat together, 'Abd al-Fattah took Ahmed Sayf's comments as a point of departure. 'Abd al-Fattah lamented that in many ways the reform movement was "back to square one with the regime and with the judges." Many of those attending the conference expressed concern that since the Judges' Club was talking with the minister of justice about their demands and may reach a compromise, the future of the protest activity was unclear. 'Abd al-Fattah noted that the ruling party itself was confused and divided over what to do in response to the current crisis. When asked how the Brotherhood would respond to a policy aimed at dividing the opposition, he replied: "It is not in the interest of the Brothers that the streets are peaceful, while the regime comes to our homes and quietly arrest us one by one. It is better to continue to confront the regime in the streets. We must use national issues that unite everyone. We do not want either calm streets or a bloody revolution." According to 'Abd al-Fattah, "the government's interest is to divide the opposition, with the Muslim Brotherhood one side and the rest of the opposition on the other. It is in our interest that the front appears united." "Toward that aim," he argued, "we welcome all support we receive from the others political forces. Our interest is that we present a united national front against the regime." 'Abd al-Fattah specified three issues in particular that could offer points of unity: the independence of the judiciary; freedom of press, expression, and association; and the abolishing of the emergency laws. He concluded the interview by stating that "to sum up, we want to lift all obstacles in the road to the ballot box. This will only happen when the silent majority of society moves from their state of silence to movement."[82] 'Abd al-Fattah is one of the figures who has been urging the Brotherhood to take on a more consistently confrontational stance. A number of secular activists in attendance noted that the Brotherhood had the numbers to do so, but were doubtful it would come about.

There is an ebb and flow to the activism of the groups and individuals associated with Kifaya. Boosted by the controversy over the independence of the judiciary in early 2006, their activities had begun to wane by mid-summer. On my last day in Cairo, in June 2006, I met with Muhammad al-Sayyid Sa'id, a political analyst at the al-Ahram Center who has been very active in Kifaya. He expressed frustration with the group, as well as over the general level of political discourse among the opposition. Like many, Sa'id was finding the "no to Mubarak" slogan for which Kifaya is famous to be "*mish kifaya*" (not enough). He lamented the seeming inability of the group to work toward raising consciousness and mobilizing the grassroots, its failure so far to develop a more substantive program for reform, and its inattention to establishing new organizations and institutions and links with existing organizations and institutions.[83] His recent attempts – unsuccessful thus far – to gain permission to publish a newspaper called "the Alternative" with other Kifaya intellectuals aims at remedying that lack. The end of Kifaya, of the cooperation of the Muslim Brotherhood with leftist and nationalist forces, and of street protests has been claimed many times over the past few years, but as Usama al-Ghazali Harb, observed in 2006: "The very fact that activists from different ideologies and the society are united on the urgency of democratic change is one important sign that we are not back to square one."[84] Others have been less optimistic, some even expressing concern that the demonstrations in the streets would lend legitimacy to the regime by permitting it to point to the existence of protest activity as evidence of the regime's tolerance of dissent. Still others argue the opposite: that the visible example of Kifaya and related groups has legitimized and emboldened a wide range of protest activity from online blogging to the wave of labor strikes that broke out in 2006.

Transformation short of convergence: remaining tensions and illiberalisms

The intellectual transformations that provided the framework for dialog, cooperation and coordination suggest that Egypt's opposition is not back to square one. The level of ideological transformation that has occurred is significant but limited, allowing for a sort of rapprochement, but falling short of both the "end of ideology" Salem suggests and the liberal–Islamic convergence Binder hopes for. Certainly many analysts will find much to criticize as illiberal or undemocratic in the positions articulated by the various forces engaged in this movement for political reform. The Muslim Brotherhood can certainly be criticized from the perspective of practice. They do not operate democratically within their organization, and often they tend to treat masses not as sources of autonomous action, but as something to be directed, an object of reform and control. However, it is worth noting that much of the same might be said of many of the other parties that are working with the opposition. So too, many questions remain in regard to the question of the status of non-Muslims in the state that the Muslim Brotherhood envisions. Various incidents, such as the angry reaction by Christians to a film, entitled *I Love Cinema*, said to negatively depict Copts; the case of a priest's wife who reportedly converted to Islam and was then forced by the Church to convert back; charges from a church in Asyut that an NDP official was blackmailing Christians to convert to Islam, all reveal the ongoing sensitivities and conflicts that exist barely beneath the surface between Muslims and Christians in Egypt. Many Copts have no doubt that an Islamic government will further disenfranchise, and even endanger, their community.

Muhammad al-Sayyid Sa'id notes the development of the Muslim Brotherhood's discourse on Copts. "The Muslim Brotherhood," he argues, "is finally coming out of the tunnel of anti-Nasirism," noting that, in Islamist discourse, hatred of Nasir went hand-in-hand with a hatred of communists and Christians.[85] Further, Muslim Brotherhood statements on Christian–Muslim relations have found at least one champion among Christians. Rafiq Habib, director of the Evangelical Center for Social Services, son of the former leader of the Anglican Church, Bishop Samuel Habib (d. 1997), and one of the Christian founders of the Wasat Party, became closer to the Muslim Brotherhood after numerous failed attempts to legalize the Wasat. He is now a regular contributor to *ikhwanonline*. On that forum, Habib has consistently maintained that the Christian–Muslim violence that breaks out in Egypt does not come from the Muslim Brotherhood, but from deeply held social prejudices and the social and economic problems in the country that tend to exacerbate them: "The Muslim Brotherhood is too well organized to be involved in any strife between religious groups."[86] Habib has further endorsed the Brotherhood's most recent statements regarding the full and equal citizenship of all Egyptians, regardless of religion.

One sign that a form of "political correctness" might be limiting the Muslim Brotherhood's stance on its Christian compatriots emerged after the 2005 elections. The Brotherhood had gone back to using their slogan of "Islam is the Solution" during the 2005 elections, after having adopted more civil mottos in the 2000 elections. They were harshly criticized by secular and Christian groups, many of whom called them hypocritical in using such divisive slogans while maintaining that they considered Egypt's Christians to be full and equal citizens and while pointing to their support of Coptic candidates as evidence of this. In the months following the elections, Abu al-Futuh in particular undertook a considerable media campaign to clarify that the slogan not be understood to "contradict with national unity and the position of the Brotherhood on Copts,"[87] nor to assert opposition to "Christians, communists or any other ideologies or groups."[88] The slogan, Abu al-Futuh argued, symbolizes the "civilizational awaking of the umma." This *umma*, he clarified, encompasses all Egyptians, regardless of religion or ideology.[89] One finds sentiment reflected among a growing sector of Egypt's opposition that is willing to work across the secular–religious divide.

As Rafiq Habib notes, it is the committed secularists that represent the extremist element, since they are out of step with the tenor of the vast majority of Egyptians.[90] However, this sentiment further raises the questions about freedom of thought and the status of those advocating secularism in an Islamic state. Asked whether there would be a place for secularists in an Islamic state, Habib replied that there would be, since a truly Islamic state would be governed by values of justice and freedom. Commenting on the National Islamic Conferences, Habib further noted that the conferences reveal "there is still a real gap between secularist and Islamists."[91] As the previous chapters demonstrated, this remaining illiberal thread is commonly sewn among the *wasatiyya* intellectuals, in the context of the NIC discussions, and in the discourse of engaging in politics aimed at the establishment of a civil party with an Islamic reference.

NOTES

1. When available, dates are provided for those individuals discussed in the chapter in order to give the reader a sense of generational overlaps and divisions.

2. The Muslim Brotherhood (*al-ikhwan al-muslimun*) was founded by Hassan al-Banna in Egypt in 1928. The group has been outlawed for most of its history and continually since 1954. The Revolutionary Socialists (*al-ishtirakin al-thawri'in*) are an underground, Trotskyite group. The Karama (Honor) Party was founded in 1999 by former members of the Nasirist Party and still retains largely Nasirist principles. The Revolutionary Socialists are banned and their members have suffered persecution for their association with the group. The Karama Party remains unlicensed by the state. The

Labor Party (*hizb al-'amal*) was founded in 1978 as a socialist party, but eventually developed into a leftist-Islamist party. Its activities were frozen by the government in 2000. The Ghad (Tomorrow) is a liberal, secular party, founded by former members of the New Wafd Party and licensed in 2004. The National Progressive Unionist Party (*Hizb al Tagammu' al-watani al-taqadumi al-wahdawi*) was founded as coalition among Nasirists, Communists, and Arab Nationalists in 1976 under the slogan "Freedom, socialism and unity." Kifaya members refer to themselves as part of a "movement" (*haraka*) and have never sought party status.

3. Muntasir al-Zayyat. *The Road to al-Qaeda: The Story of Bin Laden's Right-Hand Man* (London: Pluto Press, 2004).

4. Muhammad al-Ghazzali. *Our Beginning in Wisdom*, tr. Ismail al-Faruqi (Washington, DC: American Council of Learned Societies, 1953), 35.

5. Raymond William Baker. *Sadat and After: Struggles for Egypt's Political Soul* (Harvard University Press, 1990), 248. One such exemplary piece of Nasir criticism was penned by Muhammad 'Abd al-Quddus under the title "'Ashara sanawat ba'd wafah taqiya misr" (10 Years after the Death of Egypt's Tyrant), *al-Da'wa* 53 (September 1980), 26–28.

6. The Emergency Law allows the government to detain indefinitely individuals without trial and the hearings of civilians by military, and prohibits gatherings of more than five people. On May 26, 2008, the Law was extended for two more years.

7. Information on ESPCPI can be found at cairomasterclass.free.fr/EN/presseng.htm.

8. S. Mehraz. "The Value of Freedom," *al-Ahram Weekly* (October 30 – November 5, 2003).

9. Hassan Abou Taleb (ed.). *The Arab Strategic Report* (Cairo: al-Ahram Center for Strategic and International Studies, 2005), 23.

10. Following Braungart and Braungart, I maintain that a political generation is formed "when an age group mobilizes to bring about or resist change." Braungard and Braungart argue that "an age group is transformed into a political generation when a bond is created among its members based on their unique growing-up experiences in society and a shared feeling that they have a mission to perform by changing the political status quo." Margaret M. Braungart and Richard G. Braungart. "The Effects of the 1960s Political Generation on Former Left-and Right-Wing Youth Activist Leaders," *Social Problems* 38 (1991), 297, 299.

11. For more on this generation and their online activity, see Khalil al-Anani. "Brotherhood Bloggers: A New Generation Voices Dissent," *Arab Insight: Emerging Social and Religious Trends* (Washington, DC: World Security Institute, 2008), vol. II, no. 1, 29–38; and Marc Lynch. "Young Brothers in Cyberspace," *Middle East Report* 245 (2007), 26–33.

12. Kifaya's website can be found at www.harakamasria.org.

13. *al-'Arabi* (October 10, 2004).

14. *al-Ahram Weekly* (February 24, 2005).

15. Article 76 stipulates that presidential candidates must obtain the backing of the People's Assembly, the Shura Council and local councils.

16. *Khaleej Times* (March 2, 2005).

17. *al-Ahram Weekly* (April 3, 2005).
18. "Kifaya tatlab bil-ifraj 'an al-'ariyan wa mu'tawali al-ikhwan" (Kifaya Demands the Release of 'Ariyan and the Brotherhood Prisoners), www.ikhwaanonline.com (May 6, 2005).
19. Human Rights Watch, www.hrw.org (May 13, 2006).
20. Tamir Wajih. "al-tahadda alathy tuwajihah kifaya" (The Challenge Facing Kifaya), *Awraq ishtiraqiyya* 9 (2005), 38.
21. Nabil 'Abd al-Fattah, interview with author, Cairo, Egypt (May 25, 2006).
22. Anthony Shadid. "Anatomy of a Protest: In Cairo, One Camp Is Soon Two," *Washington Post* (July 21, 2005); Z. Krieger. "The Rise and Fall of Egypt's Secular Opposition: A Retrospective," *The Jerusalem Report* (March 3, 2006).
23. Muhammad al-Sharif, "al-Ikhwan yistankarun qam' tathahira kifaya bil-tahrir" (The Brotherhood Condemns the Suppression of the Demonstration at Tahrir [Square]), www.ikhwanonline.com (July 31, 2005); "Jabha wataniyya wahida tadham al-ikhwan wa al-mu'aridar" (A United National Front Joins the Brotherhood and the Opposition), www.ikhwanonline.com (October 8, 2005).
24. *al-Hayat* (August 22, 2005).
25. *al-Hayat* (August 22, 2005).
26. Yasin 'Abd al-Maqsud, "Abu al-futuh: laysa fi ijnadatna al-mushtarika fi al-hukuma" (We Do Not Intend to Cooperate in the Government), www.ikhwanonline.com (December 20, 2005).
27. "al-Musharikun fi mu'tamar kifaya yatlabun bi-hizb lil-ikhwan" (Participants in the Kifaya Conference Demand a Party for the Ikhwan), www.ikhwanonline.com (January 4, 2006).
28. *Financial Times* (April 17, 2005).
29. According to the International Crisis Group, "the Egyptian Judges Club has been waging a long-term campaign to restore the independence of the judiciary, which it considers has been severely infringed by the Free Officers' regime since 1952 but especially in recent years. In 1990 it published detailed proposals for reform of the judiciary, which it has been pressing ever since." *Reforming Egypt: In Search of a Strategy* (Middle East/North Africa Report No. 46, October 4, 2005), 23, n. 131.
30. Mona El-Ghobashi. "The Metamorphosis of the Egyptian Muslim Brothers," *International Journal of Middle East Studies* 37 (2005), 373–395; Carrie Rosefsky Wickham offers a more detailed discussion of these auto-reforms in *Mobilizing Islam: Religion, Activism, and Political Change in Egypt* (Columbia University Press, 2002); Geneive Abdo. *No God But God: Egypt and the Triumph of Islam* (Oxford University Press, 2000); Israel Elad-Altman. "Democracy, Elections and the Egyptian Muslim Brotherhood," *Current Trends in Islamist Ideology* 3 (2006), 24–37.
31. Much of the characterization of the difference between these two "guards" draws from the excellent study by Elad-Altman. "Democracy, Elections and the Egyptian Muslim Brotherhood."
32. Wickham, *Mobilizing Islam*, offers a more detailed discussion of these auto-reforms.

33. Abdo. *No God But God*, 83, 110–111.
34. Salwa Ismail. "State-Society Relations in Egypt: Restructuring the Political," *Arab Studies Quarterly* 17 (1995), 37–52.
35. Nasr Mohamed Arif. "Political Parties in Egypt: The Problems of Existence, Legitimacy and Function," *Strategic Papers* 14 (January 2005), 19. One must also note the important work of 'Abd al-Ghaffar Shukr, which documents earlier interactions among various ideologically opposed forces. *al-Tahalufat al-siyasiyya wa al-'amal al-mushtarak fi misr, 1976–1993* (Political Alliances and Joint Action in Egypt, 1976–1993) (Cairo: Markaz al-buhuth al-'arabiyya, 1994).
36. Muslim Brotherhood candidates ran as independents in the 2000 and 2005 legislative elections.
37. Mohammed M. Hafez and Quintan Wiktorowicz. "Violence as Contention in the Egyptian Islamic Movement" in Quintan Wiktorowicz (ed.), *Islamic Activism: A Social Movement Theory Approach* (Indiana University Press, 2004), 74.
38. 'Abd al-Ghaffar Shukr. *al-Tahalufat al-siyasiyya*.
39. See Peter Mandaville. *Global Political Islam* (London: Routledge, 2007), 117. The continuity between the politically experienced and pragmatic middle generation of the Brotherhood and the leaders of the Wasat Party is noted by a number of scholars. See Björn Olav Utvik. "*Hizb al-Wasat* and the Potential for Change in Egyptian Islamism," *Critique: Critical Middle Eastern Studies* 14 (2005), 294; Meir Hatina. *Identity Politics in the Middle East: Liberal Thought and Islamic Challenge in Egypt* (London: Tauris Academic Studies, 2007), ch. 9; and Meir Hatina. "The 'Other Islam': The Egyptian Wasat Party," *Critique: Critical Middle Eastern Studies* 14 (2005), 171–184.
40. Nabil 'Abd al-Fattah (ed.). *Taqrir al-hala al-diniyya fi misr*, 2nd edn (Cairo: al-Ahram Center for Strategic and International Studies, 1998), vol. II, 221.
41. ICG, *Reforming Egypt*, 16.
42. Abu al-'Ila Madhi, interview with author, Cairo, Egypt (May 23, 2006).
43. *Al-Wasat Party Program, 2004* (Heliopolis: al-Azzazy Press, 2006), 3–4.
44. *Wasat Party Program*, 6–8, 43.
45. *Wasat Party Program*, 41.
46. *Wasat Party Program*, 4.
47. *Wasat Party Program*, 57.
48. Joshua A. Stacher. "Post-Islamist Rumblings in Egypt: The Emergence of the Wasat Party," *Middle East Journal* 56 (2002), 422–423.
49. Rafiq Habib, interview with author, Cairo, Egypt (May 23, 2006). This explanation for the departure of Wasat's Christian members was confirmed by a number of other individuals interviewed who requested anonymity. Asked in the same interview if he would still be a member of the Wasat had there not been pressure to resign, Habib confirmed he would. Asked whether he would join the Muslim Brotherhood if it were ever licensed as a political party, Habib replied: "I think so."
50. El-Ghobashi. "The Metamorphosis of the Egyptian Muslim Brothers;" and Wickham. *Mobilizing Islam*.

51. 'Abd al-Mun'im Abu al-Futuh, "al-Fikr yanimu bil-tajdid, la bil-taqlid" (Thinking Grows from Renewal, Not from Imitation), www.ikhwanonline. com, May 10, 2006.
52. These views are reported in various issues of *Cairo Times* (see February 10–16, 2000; March 9–22, 2000; and January 24, 2001).
53. *al-Mujtama'* (March 13, 2004) and *al-Hayat* (February 28, 2004).
54. Yasmine Saleh. "Muslim Brotherhood in Final Preparations to Establish a Political Party," *Daily Star Egypt* (January 14, 2007).
55. El-Ghobashi. "The Metamorphosis of the Egyptian Muslim Brothers," 385–386.
56. *Ruz al-Yusuf* (April 14, 1997).
57. *Ruz al-Yusuf* (April 28, 1997).
58. *al-Hayat* (July 23, 2005). Salah suggests that it is most likely a "political game."
59. Some analysts, such as Hazim Saghiya, a Lebanese Arab nationalist thinker, speculated that the impact of September 11, 2001 on Islamists would prove tantamount to fallout of 1967 for Arab nationalism. *al-Hayat* (December 2001).
60. *al-Hayat* (April 15, 2002).
61. 'Issam al-'Ariyan, "Mubadara al-ikhwan al-muslimin lil-islah fi misr" (Initiative of the Muslim Brotherhood for Reform in Egypt), www. ikhwanonline.com (March 17, 2004).
62. 'Ariyan. "Mubadara al-ikhwan al-muslimin."
63. Rafiq Habib, "al-Ikhwan harasum 'ala mumarisa al-dimuqratiyya fi kul al-mustawwiyyun" (The Brotherhood is Eager to Practice Democracy at all Levels), www.ikhwanonline.com (April 15, 2005).
64. Muhammad Mahdi 'Akif, "biyan al-ikhwan al-muslimin hawl tasrihat al-sayyid ra'is al-jumhurriyya" (Declaration of the Muslim Brother-hood Regarding the Statements of the President of the Republic), www. ikhwanonline.com (April 28, 2005).
65. The influence of *wasatiyya* intellectuals, such as Qaradawi, 'Imara, Huwaydi, and 'Awwa on members of the Wasat Party has been noted by a number of scholars. See Hatina. "The 'Other Islam'," 179; and Stacher. "Post-Islamist Rumblings," 417–418. Hatina points out instances where these individuals have defended Wasat members against criticisms by the Muslim Brotherhood. 'Awa has further acted as a lawyer for Wasat Party members who have been arrested.
66. The acrimony of the relationship between the left and the Islamists can be seen in the debate between Tagammu' leader Rifa't Sa'id and Labor leader 'Adil Husayn (1932–2001): *al-Hiwar bayn rif'at al-sa'id wa 'adil husayn* (Cairo: al-Ahli, 1995). One recent critique of the Tagammu' was presented by Yahya Fikri. "Ayyuha al-munadhilun al-yasiriyyun al-shurifa dakhil al-tajammu': irhalu 'anhu ... wa indhamu ilayna" (Attention Esteemed Left-ist Fighters in the Tagammu': Leave it Alone and Leave it to Us), *Awraq ishtiraqiyya* 9 (2005), 45–48.
67. Samih Najib. *al-Ikhwan al-muslimun: ru'aya ishtirakiyya* (The Muslim Brotherhood: A Socialist View) (Cairo: Center for Socialist Studies, March 2006), 5–6.

68. Najib. *al-Ikhwan al-muslimun*, 53.
69. Najib. *al-Ikhwan al-muslimun*, 54.
70. This long view is apparent as well in the group's "platform" published at the same time as Najib's justification for working with the Muslim Brotherhood: *al-Ishtirakiyya alati nadfa' 'anha: ru'aya al-ishtiraki li-taghyir misr* (The Socialism We Defend: The Perspective of the Revolutionary Socialist Trend for Changing Egypt) (Cairo: Center for Socialist Studies, March 2006).
71. Madhi, interview (May 23, 2006).
72. George Ishaq interview with author, Cairo, Egypt (May 23, 2006); and Madhi, interview (May 23, 2006). Interviewed independently.
73. Abou Taleb, *Arab Strategic Report*, 24.
74. Heba Raouf Ezzat, interview with author, Cairo, Egypt (May 28, 2006).
75. Saad Eddin Ibrahim, interview with author, Cairo, Egypt (June 6, 2006).
76. Rebab El-Mahdi, interview with author, Cairo, Egypt (May 16, 2006).
77. Ishaq, interview (May 23, 2006).
78. Muhammad al-Sayyid Sa'id, interview with author, Cairo, Egypt (May 18, 2006).
79. Ayman Nur received only 7.6 percent of the vote. Nu'man Guma' of the Wafd Party finished third with 2.9 percent.
80. Ahmad Sayf al-Islam, interview with author, Cairo, Egypt (June 8, 2006).
81. 'Abd al-Fattah is secretary-general of the executive council of the Egyptian Center for Sciences, Culture and Development (*al-markaz al-misri lil-'ilam wa al-thaqafa wa al-tanmiyya*).
82. 'Abd al-Fattah, interview with author, Cairo, Egypt (June 8, 2006).
83. Muhammad al-Sayyid Sa'id, interview with author, Cairo, Egypt (June 10, 2006).
84. *al-Ahram Weekly* (June 8, 2006).
85. Sa'id, interview (May 18, 2006).
86. Habib, interview (May 23, 2006).
87. Ahmad Mahmud, "Abu al-Futuh: al-islah bi-ta'awwun ma' kul al-quwa" (Reform in Cooperation with All Forces), www.ikhwanonline.com (October 3, 2005).
88. Abu al-Futuh, "al-Islam huwa al-hal yamthal nahdha hidhariyya lil-umma" (Islam is the Solution Represents a Civilizational Awakening of the Umma), www.ikhwanonline.com (November 3, 2005).
89. Ayman Sayyid, "Abu al-Futuh, 'al-Islam huwa' al-hal shi'ar al-umm, kulluha" ("Islam is the Solution" is a Slogan for all of the Umma), www.ikhwhanonline.com (November 13, 2005).
90. Rafiq, interview (May 23, 2006).
91. Habib, interview (May 23, 2006).

5   Yemen's Joint Meeting Parties: Origins and architects

In November 2005, the secretary-generals of Yemen's largest Islamist party, the Reform Gathering (*al-tajammu' al-yamani lil-islah*, hereafter, Islah); the Socialist Party (YSP) that ruled the south prior to unification; the Popular Nasirist Unity Organization; and a small party consisting largely of liberal Zaydi[1] intellectuals, the Union of Popular Forces (UPF), announced the publication of "The Program of the Joint Meeting for Political and National Reform" in a joint press conference.[2] The conservative Zaydi Party, *al-Haq*, also signed the document.[3] In July 2006, these same five parties upped the ante of their alliance by nominating Faysal bin Shamlan, a former oil minister and independent member of parliament, to oppose Yemeni president 'Ali 'Abdullah Salih's bid for re-election. The composition of the oppositional alliance that has come to be known as the Joint Meeting Parties (*ahzab al-liqa al-mushtarak* [JMP]) is particularly surprising when one considers that since unification in 1990 the ruling General People's Conference (*al-mu'tamar al-sha'bi al-'am* [GPC]) and President Salih have sought to pit the two main parties to the agreement – the YSP and Islah – against each other through a process of alliance with – or bolstering of – one at the expense of the other. As recently as 1994, these two parties were literally killing each other in Yemen's War of Succession. The JMP joins groups committed to secularism with groups committed to implementing Islamic law (*shari'a*), Zaydi Shi'is with Shafi'i Sunnis, and Islamists with socialists and Arab nationalists. How did such ideologically opposed groupings come together to stand under a common platform and behind a single presidential candidate? What is the significance of this alliance for Yemeni politics? Does the alliance signal these groups' retreat from ideology and dogmatism toward a more pragmatic, perhaps even more open and tolerant approach to politics?

This chapter attempts to account for the emergence of this oppositional alliance. While other explanations have paid attention to the historical course of events that led to a breakdown of relations between the ruling GPC and its ideological rivals, my aim here is to analyze more closely some of the intellectual and ideological transformations and personal relationships that have contributed to, and been fostered by, these historical circumstances. Jillian Schwedler analyzed the Islah Party's participation in elections and other formal political processes and concluded that this participation has not resulted in the moderation of the group – "in the sense of being relatively more open and tolerant of alternative perspectives" – as a whole.[4] In most respects, the analysis presented here confirms Schwedler's findings. However, by focusing less on political parties as a whole and more on the role of individuals within political groupings, this chapter expands upon something Schwedler's work noted: that Islah encompasses a "mixed bag of Islamists," including some who are willing to work with groups similarly excluded by the ruling party but which form their ideological rivals.[5] So, too, a shift in focus from inclusion in formal pluralist political processes to a focus on cross-ideological interaction also reveals something more in tension with the original inclusion-moderation thesis: it is often exclusion from, more than inclusion in, formal politics that puts various political actors into contact and conversation with alternative views.

The assumption of most studies of inclusion and moderation seems to be that it is in the context of political liberalization that cooperation is most likely to occur. While Yemen did experience a significant pluralization of politics with unification in 1990, after the 1994 War of Succession there was a closing rather than an opening of spaces for political participation.[6] Robert Burrowes and Catherine Kasper argue that the trend since the 1980s toward concentrating political power in the hands of tribal shaykhs, military officers, and northern businessmen was "interrupted and challenged" briefly from 1990–1994, but then "accelerated after the war of succession in 1994 eliminated or weakened politicians from former South Yemen and their Yemeni Socialist Party."[7] The forging of those interpersonal and conceptual relationships that initiated and have bound together actors in the Joint Meeting Parties has taken place in a context of constricted political space, and is undertaken by individuals who must do the work of developing and justifying news strategies for changes in structural conditions against other forces within their own parties intent on maintaining old strategies.

The analysis presented here works at three levels. I begin by looking historically at the difficult interactions among various competing parties and ideological trends in Yemen, while also drawing attention to the way in which the Salih regime's attempt to control and marginalize his opponents by playing them off one another ultimately contributes toward their cooperation and dialog and their alliance as an oppositional force. I next trace the intellectual path of, and personal relationships among, those individuals whose development accounts for the emergence of a strategy of cooperation among competing groups and for the JMP's ability to put forth a common platform and a single candidate for the 2006 presidential elections. I then move to an examination of the ideological character and limitations of the alliance through a study of various forums that have placed these political actors in conversation. Their dialogs reveal points of agreement and compromise, as well as remaining differences. The chapter ends by assessing the significance of this alliance for Yemeni politics and for our understanding of how ideational and structural factors interact in cases of cross-ideological interaction.

Yemen's struggle for unity

Prior to the formation of the unified Yemen republic in 1990, Yemen consisted of two states, each of which often formed surrogates for struggles between competing foreign powers. After an Egypt-backed army coup in North Yemen (called the Yemen Arab Republic [YAR] after the overthrow of the Imamate in 1962) the country provided the site of a struggle between Saudi Arabia and Egypt for dominance in the Arab region throughout the 1960s. Egyptian President Jamal 'Abd al-Nasir withdrew his forces in the wake of the June 1967 war and King Faysal of Saudi Arabia ended his support for the Royalist cause shortly thereafter, but central control of the country was not established until Colonel 'Ali Abdullah Salih was elected president in 1978.

After the British left Aden in 1967, South Yemen (known as the People's Democratic Republic of Yemen [PDRY] between 1970 and unity) became the site of a struggle between Saudi Arabia and the Soviet Union. The Soviet Union overtly supported the regime in South Yemen until the mid-1980s, though there were also pro-Chinese factions in the PDRY and the party tried to remain neutral in the USSR–China rivalry. As the Soviet Union began to weaken, it abandoned its pursuit of the Cold War in the PDRY and, over the course of the Gorbachev years, increasingly offered less economic and military assistance to the country.

Relations between the conservative pro-west YAR and the socialist pro-Soviet PDRY remained antagonistic throughout the 1970s and 1980s, with the two states often engaging in violent, military clashes and attempts to overthrow the other's regime. Despite ideological differences that kept the regimes at odds, the two Yemens remained committed, at least rhetorically, to unification and continued unity talks and visits to each other's capitals during this period. An internal party struggle in South Yemen culminated in a short and violent civil war in 1986 that further marginalized resistance to unification. The unity of the two ruling regimes was further facilitated by moves by both parties toward more democratic and plural political structures. The 1988 parliamentary elections in the YAR showed some pluralism. In December 1989, the YSP announced a multiparty system.

After secretly negotiating the unity agreement during 1989, in May 1990, President 'Ali 'Abdullah Salih of the YAR and President 'Ali Salim al-Bidh, president of the PDRY, officially proclaimed the unity of north and south through a coalition government, the main contention of which was that the multiparty system and elections after an interim period would constitute sufficient basis for a political unity while allowing each side to retain separate identities. In the newly formed Republic of Yemen (ROY), Salih and Bidh agreed to establish a five-member presidential council, with Salih as chairperson and Bidh as vice chairperson, in addition to two members from the GPC and one from the YSP. The two parties shared power during a transitional period that lasted three years.

Thus, unification in 1990 brought together two ideologically opposed states: a Marxist-oriented south – by most accounts the Soviet Union's most reliable satellite in the region – that was largely secular, bureaucratized, and economically planned, and a more free market-oriented but conservative north that was governed in a decentralized style by a military-dominated regime in tandem with tribal leaders. The party that ruled the south, the YSP, was established in 1978 as a union of a number of parties, organizations, and national fronts operating in both north and south, and has contained members with a militant Marxist–Leninist orientation, as well as democratic socialists. The north's ruling party, the GPC, was established in 1982 as a "conference" (mu'tamar) rather than a party (hizb). Intended as an umbrella for various political trends, the GPC ultimately developed more along party lines after unification – though it still lacks ideological coherency, and functions primarily to rally support around President Salih.

Michael Hudson notes that YSP leaders approached unification with "deep misgivings about what they saw as a closed, tribal-dominated Northern establishment."[8] A number of Islamist groupings were operating in Yemen at the time, particularly in the north, including – though neither limited to nor dominated by – the Muslim Brotherhood.[9] Former southern and then post-unification prime minister Haydar Abu Bakr al-'Attas voiced reservations to Hudson about more extreme religious elements allied with the GPC: "While stating that the YSP welcomed the Muslim Brotherhood in the new pluralist political order, [Attas] noted that the welcome depended on the Brotherhood's refraining from calling other parties (like the YSP) traitors or unbelievers (*kafirs*)."[10] Such concern was justified by 'Abd al-Majid Zindani's (b. 1938) return from Saudi Arabia to declare war on unity and *jihad* against the atheists of the PDRY, alleging that the southern leaders are afflicted by an imported culture abhorred by the Yemeni people. Zindani was one of the founders of Yemen's branch of the Muslim Brotherhood, and led the group from 1969–1978. Since 1978, the Brotherhood has been headed by Yasin 'Abd al-'Aziz al-Qubati, who has also served as minister of education. Zindani has long been a controversial figure, even within Islamist circles, due to his often radical pronouncements and the attention they garner.[11]

Much of the tension between secular and Islamist forces at unity centered on the draft constitution, which referred to the *shari'a* as the "main" source of legislation. Zindani and others insisted that the *shari'a* be affirmed as the "only" source of law. YSP leader 'Ali Salim al-Bidh cautioned against "obscurantist forces seeking to cast doubts in the minds of the people about the draft constitution, so as to hinder the process of unification."[12] 'Umar al-Jawi (1938–1997), secretary-general of the socialist Unionist Gathering Party (*hizb al-tajammu' al-wahdawi al-yamani*), denounced "certain Islamist elements which owe allegiance to foreign parties, the very ones which fought against the republican regime and the revolution in our party."[13] Unification was threatened by Islamic forces who staged demonstrations and gathered the voices of religious scholars and tribal shaykhs against the "godless communists" and by groups, such as the "Islamic Jihad" led by Tariq al-Fadli, which began undertaking assassinations of YSP leaders to avenge against oppression under the PDRY, as well as by socialist forces who threatened to resort to arms if the nation moved toward an "Islamic dictatorship."[14] A presidential decree, stating that no law can contradict *shari'a*, was intended to forge a compromise, and the constitution was approved by referendum. However, many Islamists remained unsatisfied.

A few months after unity, a coalition of conservative tribal and religious forces founded the Islah Party. The GPC supported the formation of Islah, believing that an Islamist party would put pressure on the socialists, who were considered the main threat to GPC power at the time. As an organization that articulates classical Sunni ideas, Islah also helped the state counterbalance Yemen's Zaydi forces. While Islah's members tend to be more socially conservative than members of the ruling party, throughout the 1990s Islah and the GPC were close political allies and the former is best characterized as "a party of the establishment center."[15] President Salih's respective tribal and personal ties with Islah's two most important leaders, Zindani and 'Abdullah Bin Husayn al-Ahmar (1931–2007), reinforced this alliance. Until his death, Ahmar headed both Islah and the Hashid tribal confederation, which includes President Salih's own tribe. Zindani was speaker of Islah's Shura Council (the party's central committee) until 2007. He has also acted as an advisor to Salih on educational matters since as early as the 1970s and served on the five-person Presidential Council after the 1993 elections.[16] Zindani is considered by many to represent Islah's most radical faction and the US government is currently seeking his arrest as part of its war on terrorism.[17]

Ideological conflict between Islamists and the YSP reached its height between 1990 and 1997, when Islah and the GPC were most closely aligned. Islah members commonly denounced YSP members as secularist, atheistic, and traitorous apostates. The YSP deplored Islah and other Islamist groups as reactionary forces, doing the bidding of Saudi Arabia, and considered their agenda of *shari'a* as anathema. In some respects, these differences reflected the rhetoric of the north–south rivalry. The leaders of the two Yemens have long held misgivings about each other. Northerners saw the south as irreligious and oppressive; southerners viewed their ordered and disciplined system in positive terms against what they took to be an anarchical and violent tribalism of the north.[18] North–south tensions continued post independence and many YSP members considered Islah as representative of the worst aspects of their former rival, but the Islamist–secularist opposition gave the rivalry additional force.

By the time the YOR's first elections were held in 1993 there was clear evidence of an overt political struggle that would eventually lead to the onset of war in late April 1994. The growth in influence of Islah, which touted itself as the party of reform in seeking stricter implementation of Islamic law, was the source of much tension. Often the differences between Islah and the YSP resulted in violence. For example, at the end of April 1993, supporters of one of Ahmar's sons carried out a rocket attack on YSP offices in the northern town of Hajja, killing around twenty-five people and wounding around fifty others. The YSP maintained that a "campaign of assassinations" against YSP officials by "traditionalist forces" had claimed the lives of over 150 party members. Jarallah 'Umar, a YSP member of the transitional state's Consultative Council, blamed the violence on "traditionalist forces" attempting to undermine democracy: "The battle is between democracy and modernization on one hand and keeping Yemen as it is now, or even driving it backward, on the other."[19]

After the 1993 elections gave the GPC 123 seats, followed by Islah with sixty-two and the YSP with fifty-six, the GPC announced that a tripartite government coalition would be formed.[20] The YSP was alarmed by the GPC's domination of government, by the rise of a third party that shifted the balance of power between north and south, and by the growth of a political force that was clearly benefiting at their expense. After a series of quarrels, vice president 'Ali Salim al-Bidh retreated to Aden, along with other YSP ministers and civil servants, from where he issued a list of demands to be met as a precondition for his return to Sana'a. Leaders began calling for a national dialog. In November 1993, a twenty-seven-member multiparty mediation committee began work on a document designed to restructure and reform the state so as to end the row between northern and southern political leaders. The task of forging the agreement was later picked up by the secretary-general of the Arab League and King Hussein of Jordan. In February 1994, the "Document of Pledge and Accord for the Basis of Building a Modern Yemeni State" was signed by Salih and Bidh in Amman. However, this agreement did not succeed in normalizing the political situation in Yemen. Bidh and Salih had arrived separately to the signing in Amman and, although they shook hands reluctantly after the document was signed, Bidh refused to return to Sana'a after the signing, claiming that he was unsure of his safety in the capital until the document was fully implemented. The document specified that implantation should be achieved within three months. After war broke out between north and south, Bidh would repeatedly cite the government's lack of implementation of the document as the cause. Until the JMP program was published, most opposition figures and parties cited the Document of Pledge and Accord as the basis for political reform and the construction of a unified, modern state.[21]

Conflicts between the parties were further exacerbated by the different interpretations of the document. The YSP saw the document as mandating a decentralization of power and the establishment of a federal system, something the GPC and Islah adamantly opposed. Salih viewed the proposals for unifying the northern and southern armed forces, which the YSP insisted should be accompanied by the appointment of new commanders for many of the key units, as a threat to one of the main bases of his power. Islah also viewed the restructuring of the military as an attempt to deal a blow to its tribal grassroots, since many of the military's commanders who would be retired under the document were members of the Sanhan tribe – to which Salih belonged and which was part of the Hashid tribal confederation which Ahmar led. For its part, the GPC interpreted the document as requiring Bidh and his followers to return the capital and to submit to the central authority.

Despite the agreement, the crisis escalated, with assassinations and armed confrontations finally leading to the outbreak of a full-scale civil war in May of 1994 when Aden was bombed by planes from the north. In accounting for the breakdown of relations, many analysts note that the 1990 unity accord contained within it the seeds of its own failure which eventually culminated in the 1994 civil war. In Michael Hudson's words, the unity agreement established a Yemen that was "amalgamated" but not "integrated."[22] In fact, unity was based upon a formal partnership between sovereign entities, rather than the true integration of political structures and institutions. According to 'Abd al-Rahman al-Jifri (b. 1943), vice president of the short-lived southern secessionist regime and current president of the National Opposition Front in exile, "each side remained a monopolizing power in the areas they had ruled before unification. The armies, the security forces, the currencies, the media, the administrations, the laws, and even the vice presidents remained two, although in the latter case they were called president and vice-president."[23] Ideological differences meant that the traditionalist and free-market oriented north and Marxist-oriented south found the creation of a unified political organization difficult, with neither leadership willing to be subsumed within the other. To the extent that the basis of unity was democratic, it placed the south and the YSP at a disadvantage, since the area that made up the PDRY only accounted for about one-fifth of the total population of Yemen. While initially the numerical inferiority of the south was mitigated by the YSP's over-representation in the transitional parliament and cabinet, by the 1993 elections the YSP had been relegated to a third position behind the GPC and Islah, which had emerged as a key player in Yemeni politics.

Civil war broke out in May and was widely expected to be a stalemate. However, Zindani rallied his "Afghans-Arabs" – Yemen's *mujahidin* who had returned in the early 1990s from their fight against Soviet communism in Afghanistan – to fight on behalf of the north against socialists at home. During the war, a Friday sermon by Zindani declared: "We Yemeni's are called upon by God to fight against the communists ... The YSP are communists, infidels and non-believers ... The war we are fighting is jihad and I demand that all theologians declare it so."[24] 'Abd al-Wahhab al-Daylami, an Islah member who would become minister of justice after the war, issued a fatwa declaring all socialists unbelievers and sanctioning their killing. Two months later, the YSP was decimated, with many of its leaders killed or in exile, and its offices confiscated or destroyed. While not all YSP members supported secession, the defeat of the movement was largely taken to be a defeat of the party itself.

After the north declared victory, a political coalition formed between the GPC and Islah. Islah's project to revise the constitution, initially blocked by the socialists, began to be debated, as Islah sought to make Islamic law Yemen's sole legislative basis, instead of one of its "main sources" of law.[25] It seems the party believed that their support for Salih during the war had given it a valuable bargaining chip. Zindani maintained that acceptance of Islamic law as the basis of the constitution formed a precondition for the YSP's renewed participation in government. On this point, Islah prevailed, but the group was less successful in maintaining its position of power as a ruling partner in the new government. The GPC no longer needed Islah to counterbalance the YSP and with its loss of usefulness to the ruling power came a loss of influence. Thus, Islah's political marginalization and, ultimately, its shift toward a more oppositional role vis-à-vis the GPC is directly tied to the GPC's success in its struggle for domination over the YSP.[26]

Prior to the second parliamentary elections scheduled for April 1997, Islah began a dialog with the YSP and other parties of the Higher Coordination Council for the Opposition (HCCO) to address mounting irregularities in voter registration and other violations of the electoral law. Although the precise date of the establishment of the JMP itself is unclear, even based on the recollections of the alliance's constituent members, these series of meetings mark the first time the appellation is used, here marking the coordination between the HCCO members and Islah.[27] Little reference to the JMP is found again until Islah allies with the other opposition parties following the 2001 elections, after which the name enters into common use. In this sense, the appellation seems to refer specifically to an oppositional alliance that includes Islah. These early interactions resulted in the publication of a document calling for free and fair elections and questioning the legality of the Supreme Commission for Elections and Referendums (SCER).[28] Nonetheless, Islah still entered into a pre-election agreement with the GPC in which each would refrain from opposing the other in a number of constituencies and eventually dropped its complaints against the SCER. The YSP boycotted the elections in protest over the coordination agreements, fraudulent voter registration lists, continued restrictions placed on their party, and delays in returning assets and properties confiscated after the civil war, allowing the GPC to emerge from the 1997 elections with a majority of parliamentary seats.

Immediately after the elections, Islah accused the GPC of widespread intimidation and fraud at the polls. Islah was not offered any cabinet positions in the new government and a member of the conservative Zaydi Party, al-Haq, was named minister of endowment, a position previously held by a member of Islah. Asked in 1998 why Islah still had not formally joined with the HCCO, Ahmar responded that "the HCCO includes political parties that are close to each other in terms of thought, attitude, and policy" and Islah "does not converge with them," while Islah shares more "common denominators" with the GPC.[29] Islah supported Salih in the 1999 presidential elections, while the HCCO members called for a boycott. Nonetheless, by 2001 Islah would find itself not only securely in the opposition, but also in alliance with its former arch-enemy – the YSP – and other opposition parties it had previously opposed.

Signs of Islah's increased alienation from the ruling party and growing coordination with the YSP are readily apparent by August 2000, when the then Islah secretary-general Muhammad al-Yadumi delivered a speech before the second round of the YSP's fourth general congress in which he conceded: "We see that non-participation of the YSP in the 1997 parliamentary elections led to a political imbalance which did not serve the process of democracy."[30] Prior to the 2001 local elections,[31] Islah joined the HCCO in calling for a number of guarantees to reform the political climate and electoral processes, including separation of leadership of the ruling party and president, and demanding electoral supervision by a body other than the SCER, whose legality and neutrality they questioned. An article in the UPF weekly paper, *Sawt al-shura*, announced the JMP's broader aims: the establishment of a democratic approach toward the realization of freedom, pluralism, rule of law, the peaceful rotation of power, and respect for human rights.[32] Islah went so far as to call for an electoral boycott if voter rosters were not corrected, but remained divided over whether or not to support the proposed constitutional amendments, which would increase the term of parliament from four years to six and of the president from five years to seven, thus leaving Salih eligible to remain in office until 2013.[33]

After President Salih addressed Islah members at their annual congress, the party withdrew its threat to boycott the elections. Nonetheless, for the first time neither Islah (nor the YSP) negotiated seats with the GPC in advance. The elections were marred by violent incidents and complaints of malpractice, most involving rival supporters of the ruling GPC and Islah. Ahmar accused the ruling party of using the state's power over the media, army, and government funds "to marginalise the

political parties and to turn them into a mere decoration to claim democracy."[34] 'Abd al-Wahhab al-Anisi, Islah's first secretary and current
secretary-general, claimed that "after the GPC sensed its failure [in the
election], it created a lot of problems through its associates."[35] The GPC
accused Islah of engaging in election "terrorism" and Anisi responded by
suggesting that what the GPC characterized as "terrorism" was actually
undertaken by those with resources, such as the army, on its side. This
sentiment was echoed by Yadumi, who stated in no uncertain terms that
the GPC "stopped voters exercising their democratic rights" and committed acts of "terrorism and violence against its opponents."[36]

The newly reshuffled government in Yemen went into open conflict
with Islah in May 2001 over plans to incorporate the country's religious
institutes into the state educational system. These so-called "scientific
institutes" were originally set up with funding from the Sana'a government (and Saudi assistance) in the 1970s, while Zindani was minister of
education. YAR president Ibrahim al-Hamdi appointed Zindani *mur-
shid* (guide) to lead the institutes. Although the government intended
these institutes as a bulwark against the spread in the north of Marxist
ideas and movements from the south, by the 1990s, the government
had began to regard the institutes as a menace, insofar as they were
acting as a recruitment and propaganda vehicle for the Islah Party. In
1992, following the unification of north and south, parliament passed
a law integrating the institutes into the state system. The law was never
implemented while the GPC and Islah were allied, but the ruling party
had at times used the threat of closing the religious institutes in order
to elicit Islah's cooperation. As Islah became increasingly oppositional
in character, the willingness to clamp down on the schools grew as well.
Presiding over the new government's first meeting, President Salih
announced that "There is no reasonable justification for maintaining
two educational systems in Yemen."[37] Islah responded by boycotting a
vote of confidence in the new government.

In a July 2001 interview, Ahmar reflected back on the decision to
reverse Islah's original plan to boycott the elections in response to presidential pressure. Asked if Islah would do the same in the next elections,
he noted that "a fox is not caught twice in the same trap." In the same
interview, Ahmar characterized his party's relationship with the YSP
and the other opposition parties as "coordination to prompt the government to return to the democratic path" and declared that "for the sake
of democracy, we should give our help to all the forces that are loyal to
democracy."[38] This was a clear shift from Ahmar's 1998 assertion that
Islah shared more with the GPC than the opposition.

In the run-up to the 2003 elections, Islah joined the YSP and four other opposition parties under the framework of the Joint Meeting Parties in signing an "accord of principles" to coordinate their actions to win seats in the parliament and prevent the ruling party from obtaining an overwhelming majority as it did in the 1993 and 1997 elections. Each of the parties committed "to not compete against other JMP members – either directly or indirectly – if the outcome would serve to favor another party's candidate winning the seat."[39] However, discord remained as all JMP parties wanted to retain their constituencies. Only 100 out of 301 constituencies were agreed upon by the Joint Meeting Parties.[40] Further, many political observers expressed concerns over a possible unraveling of the JMP due to Islah's reuniting with its old ally, the ruling party, GPC. The result of the 2003 elections was that President Salih's GPC increased its majority in parliament, winning 228 of the 301 parliamentary seats, up from 187 after the last elections, which, once combined with the ten independents who affiliated with the party immediately after the elections, gave the ruling party almost 80 percent of the seats in parliament. The Islah Party saw its seats reduced further, to around forty-five. The YSP added seven seats after a boycott of the 1997 elections had put them out of parliament. The Nasirist and Ba'ath parties won three and two respectively. Four candidates remained independent.[41]

In January 2004, the European Union chose Yemen as the site for an International Conference on democracy and human rights and the Joint Meeting Party used this opportunity to publish their "perspectives on major issues that are still preventing Yemen from achieving an optimum and comprehensive transformation to democracy." Among their observations were the need to abide by national constitutions and human rights laws, to conduct free, fair, and honest elections, to limit state functions and separate legislative and executive powers, to maintain the freedom and independence of civil society institutions, and to ensure freedom of expression. In September 2004, the JMP announced that they were developing an initiative to reform the political and economic situation of the country. One year later, in November 2005, "The Program of the Joint Meeting for Political and National Reform" was published. The forging of this alliance among parties who less than a decade earlier had fought each other in a civil war seems nothing less than extraordinary, and could not have been accomplished without considerable effort on the part of key individuals from each of the signatory parties, often amidst intense criticism from within their own parties.

Architects of the JMP

From party socialism to social democracy: 'Umar

Over the course of the past several decades the YSP has moved from a centralized Marxist party-state to an oppositional entity that espouses the values of party pluralism and democratic socialism. More recently, the party has engaged in another move no less dramatic: from the ideological opposite and mortal enemy of the Islamist forces in the region to an important ally of Yemen's largest Islamist party. According to former parliamentarian, Saadaldeen Ali Talib, "the real architect of the 'joint meeting' coalition," was Jarallah 'Umar: "It took great negotiation skills and generous compromises to bring together the YSP, Islah, Nasserites, Baath, and other smaller parties, around a common cause, which all agreed was the protection of the democratic life in Yemen." In Talib's view, only 'Umar possessed those skills and traits necessary to accomplish the task.[42] This sentiment is broadly shared among the JMP members I interviewed during December 2005 and January 2006.

'Umar's political awareness began when he came into contact with Yemeni students returning from study in Egypt and Syria during the 1950s with the ideas of Arab nationalism, especially in its Nasirist conception. He became a member of the Arab Nationalist Movement in 1962, but after the June 1967 defeat and Egypt's departure from Yemen, combined with a period spent in prison from 1968 to 1971, during which he was able to read the works of Marx, Gramsci, Che Guevara, and others, his party politics moved away from Arab nationalist priorities toward leftist and regional emphases.[43] While an officer in the police academy, 'Umar participated in clandestine party politics and helped found a new political entity called the Democratic Revolutionary Party, which was close politically to the radical administration in the PDRY. The different political movements in the north and the south secretly unified into one party under the leadership of the YSP and 'Umar became a member of the ruling regime in Aden while living in Sana'a. Like other northern YSP leaders, 'Umar participated secretly in decision-making in the south – often traveling to Aden in the morning and returning home to Sana'a in the evening – and engaged in armed struggle in the north, with the goal of unifying Yemen under the leadership of the YSP in the south. When a group calling itself the National Democratic Front (NDF) undertook armed insurgency against the northern regime with support of the south in 1979, 'Umar acted as field commander. The NDF was defeated, largely due to support for the government from the Islamic Front, an informal grouping of members of the Muslim Brotherhood, tribal leaders and other Islamists, many of whom would later form the core of the Islah Party, some of whom later joined the GPC.

'Umar is often credited with moving the YSP toward a social democratic vision. In the party's 1986 internal struggle for power, 'Umar sided with the more radical faction of 'Abd al-Fattah Isma'il and Bidh that eventually won the conflict.[44] However, by his own account:

Despite the victory of my faction, I had the increasing sense that we had all lost. The January events prompted me to ask why there were these constant struggles within the party. Why had such killing occurred? Why had the South stopped its support of armed struggle in the North? I concluded that the problem resulted from the absence of democracy within the party and in our society. There were simply no possibilities for criticizing the party.[45]

Some time after the 1986 purges, 'Umar wrote a report through the political office of the YSP, noting the need for a plan to realize Yemeni unity and calling for political pluralism and democracy within the party.[46] As 'Umar recounts:

The leadership first rejected this suggestion, but events in the Soviet Union, the troubled economic situation in the South, and the deleterious effects of the January events eventually worked to encourage the leadership to accept the call for political pluralism. We also began discussing with the Yemen Arab Republic the possibilities of creating a unified nation-state of Yemen. My role was to support unification but on the condition that there would be democracy, political pluralism and permission for parties to operate.[47]

After unity, 'Umar served briefly as minister of culture. When the civil war broke out in 1994, 'Umar recounts that he was unpopular with both sides of the conflict, since he opposed both aspects of the unity and the move toward succession, so he left Yemen for Egypt. 'Umar states that his primary aim when he returned in 1996 was to rebuild the YSP on the basis of social democracy: "I had become convinced that social democracy was the best way to solve people's problems because it combines both political freedom and social justice."[48]

In 1997, the YSP experienced another internal conflict in which two opposing trends emerged. One side was led by 'Umar, who maintained that the YSP should participate in the elections and continue its dialog with the two ruling coalition parties (GPC and Islah). The second side was led by the then YSP secretary-general, 'Ali Salih 'Abbad Muqbil, a member of the old guard which had taken over leadership of the party after Bidh departed for Oman during the civil war. Muqbil linked participation in the elections to resolving several issues that remained from the 1994 war, including the return of YSP assets seized during the war and the repatriation of exiled YSP leaders. Although 'Umar adhered to the decision of the majority to boycott in the interest of preserving party unity, the YSP political bureau split over the elections, and Muqbil resigned his post and suspended his activities as secretary-general of the HCCO. In a 1998 interview, 'Umar revealed that the upcoming YSP congress – the fourth in the party's history, but its first since 1985, when the party congress resulted in a bloody internal conflict – would mark "a turning point towards democracy for the YSP." 'Umar asserted: "Ideology will no longer feature prominently in our program. We will concentrate more on practical issues: democracy, human rights, general liberties, social justice, modernization and several other similar topics. There will be more openness in our party."[49] In the first round of the party congress, held in November 1998, the YSP published new documents laying out the party's commitment to political pluralism and general freedom. The second round of the congress, not held until August 2000 due to concerns about achieving the highest level of participation from the party's members in exile, resulted in the party's first democratic elections. The outcome of the elections, which included Umar's elevation to deputy secretary-general, was viewed as a success for party reformers.

In his 2002 address to the Islah Party congress, 'Umar acknowledged that relations between the YSP and Islah had passed through many phases, but affirmed that their present relationship was preferable to the past because of their predisposition toward cooperation and coordination. He praised Islah as "a party with a distinguished position as a great political power that cannot be ignored." He argued that in order to build a modern democratic country, intellectual and political pluralism, freedom of expression, and the right to protest had to be strengthened both in society and within political parties: "The consolidation of the country's political system presupposes the existence of a powerful opposition based on a society abundant in [political] movements, activism and independent civil organizations, as well as an effective free press. Without a doubt, the Joint Meeting forms a step in this direction."[50]

'Umar's intellectual transformation toward a pragmatic social democratic vision is not the only factor that accounts for his ability to play such a central role in forming a cross-ideological opposition to the Yemen's ruling authority. By virtue of his experiences and training he is able to speak the language of Islam as well. 'Umar began his education in traditional Islamic schools, first studying the Qur'anic recitation in al-Ajlub and then Islamic law in Dhamar.[51] In his speeches and writings 'Umar quotes comfortably from the Qur'an and other religious sources, while at the same time holding to a consistently secular stance based on a conviction that Islamic notions of justice, toleration, and democracy can only be realized in a secular society. 'Umar's northern roots are also of significance. According to one analyst: "Whenever an issue comes up for discussion in the party, a fault line develops between those who look at it from a strictly political viewpoint (the Northern members), and those [who] look at the issue from a Southern economic and social viewpoint (Southern members)."[52] Northern YSP leaders seem to have more readily moved beyond the question of whether or not to unify toward a more pragmatic consideration of the character of a united Yemen.

On December 28, 2002, the YSP's second-ranking official, Jarallah 'Umar, was assassinated after delivering a speech at an Islah party conference that confirmed the commitment of the two parties to join together in fighting issues of common concern. The individual accused of the murder reportedly admitted to targeting 'Umar because he had brought Islah together with "secularists." GPC newspapers accused Islah of being behind the assassination, while Islah accused the state of "politically exploiting" the incident and trying to "drive a wedge" between Islah and the YSP. The Egyptian Islamist Fahmi Huwaydi clearly suggested that the Yemeni ruling party was behind the assassination of 'Umar, asserting that Islah "was instrumental in gathering other political forces in an opposition bloc under the banner of a 'common ground'" and that "this fact, alone, suggests that a certain party has a major stake in dismantling the coalition and in provoking a rift between the Socialist Party and Al-Tajamu (Islah)."[53] Most JMP members seem to agree that it was the government that was most threatened by the coalition and most likely to benefit from a deterioration of relations among the opposition. In a comprehensive study of the assassination, entitled *Who Killed Jarallah 'Umar?*, YSP member Muhammad al-Maqalih dismisses both the notion that the act was merely the crime of a deranged individual and the idea that this was a crime of religious conviction, insisting that it was an assassination undertaken by political forces, for political aims.[54] In June 2003, an organization calling itself the "National Body for Pursuing the Matter of the Martyr Jarallah 'Umar's Assassination" (*al-hiya al-wataniyya li-mutaba'a qadhaiya igtiyal al-shahid jar allah 'umar*) formed to continue investigation into – and to pursue prosecution of – the culprits in the assassination. The body was particularly concerned that this crime not be viewed as a regular criminal action, but instead be considered a political assassination because, they argued, "ending the case without a full and inclusive investigation would only yield further similar incidents."[55]

After 'Umar's death, Yasin Sa'id Nu'man (b. 1946), an economist and prime minister of South Yemen from 1986 until unification and former speaker of parliament after unification, was viewed by many as the only remaining YSP leader with potential to appeal to all sides in the JMP. However, his assumption of the role of head the party was not seamless. Like 'Umar, Nu'man left Yemen for the United Arab Emirates during the civil war, only returning after a presidential amnesty was issued in September 2003. Shortly after his return, he faced a fatwa, attributed to some group at private and ultraconservative al-Imam University (headed by Zindani), which described him as an "infidel." The fatwa against Nu'man recalled an earlier one issued during the civil war which named all socialists as unbelievers and decreed that all actions taken against them were permitted.[56] Unlike 'Umar, Nu'man, an economist by training, lacks any religious credentials and is from the south. Nonetheless, he is generally viewed as a pragmatic political leader. In July of 2005, Nu'man was elected secretary-general of the YSP. Despite the uncertainty of the future of the YSP, the tragedy of Jarallah's assassination seems to have strengthened, rather than undermined, JMP relations.

Toward an independent Islamic opposition: Islah's modernist wing

Although the Islah Party emerged with the blessing of the GPC, the group claims to have been a party of opposition since its origins. Islah member Muhammad 'Abd al-Rahman al-Maqrami explains that Islah opposes only "programs and policies," not "personalities and parties."[57] Reflecting the traditional Sunni view of the state, which maintains that obedience to the ruler is a religious duty, in the context of Yemen this interpretation of religious duty forms an important contrast with the Zaydi principle of *khuruj*, that is, raising against an unjust ruler, a perspective retained by parties such as al-Haq, as well as by members of the UPF. Maqrami identifies the fight against the constitution drafted at unity, which specified the *shari'a* as the main, rather than sole, source of legislation, as the party's first act of opposition. Islah documents present the group as the preserver of Islamic and traditional values and its program has focused on restoring Islam as the regulator of social, economic, and political activities. Its main slogan proclaims that "the Qur'an and Sunna supersede the constitution."[58]

It was not until Islah won the second largest number of parliamentary seats in 1993, Maqrami maintains, that it formally became a part of the ruling authority (*sultan*) and, even after joining into a ruling coalition, Islah found itself at odds with the GPC on such issues as Yemen's participation in an October 1995 economic summit that included an Israeli delegation in Amman. Justifying Islah's protests over this and other decisions taken by the government they ruled with, Yadumi stated that:

We are not proficient in putting one man in power and one man in the opposition. Whenever we oppose the ruling authority, it is out of sensitivity to our national duty required by our religion and our love of our people and country. What appears as criticism against the governing coalition springs from the duty to enjoin good and forbid evil [al-amr bil-maʿruf wa al-nahiy ʿan al-munkar].[59]

One sees evidence of a slight shift in the party's position after the 1997 elections, when the GPC won a parliamentary majority and began to rule alone, without a coalition with either the YSP or Islah. After this, Maqrami argues, Islah entered into the opposition in a different sense, truly moving into "active opposition" as one of two wings of the system: "Without a ruling wing and an opposition wing, the ruling system cannot soar higher, nay it is not possible for democracy to be rightly erected, for how can the flourishing of democracy be conceived without the existence of a true and active opposition."[60] Other shifts in political thinking are apparent as well. Islah's 1993 program mentions peaceful transfer of power and "consultative democracy" (al-dimuqratiyya al-shuruwiyya) as the bases of government, but refrains from mentioning a multiparty system. The 1997 party program seems equally comfortable speaking of "consultative democracy" or just "democracy" and is more explicit about the necessity of pluralism. Party pluralism, like an active opposition, is identified as a cornerstone of democracy: "Political and party pluralism represent the firmly established basis of the rotation of power and its peaceful transfer between organized political groups and forces."[61]

Despite Maqrami's seamless history of the party, certified by the then secretary-general Yadumi's preface, Islah can hardly be described as ideologically unified. Rather, Islah consists of a broad coalition with at least three wings: tribal forces, most significantly represented by parliamentary speaker Ahmar before his death; a radical wing, represented by Zindani; and urban-based, university educated Islamists, who are often characterized as champions of conservative merchant interests. Paul Dresch has rightly noted that "although the grouping is sometimes spoken of as a 'fundamentalist' party, it is actually a party that contains fundamentalists – a rather different thing. Briefly put, tribesmen involved with Islah generally dislike the fundamentalists and the fundamentalists generally dislike the tribesmen."[62] Islah's partnership in a cross-ideological oppositional alliance could not come from the tribal values of Ahmar, and certainly not from the radical and militant Islamism of Zindani. While each wields considerable influence in Yemeni politics – Ahmar, as paramount shaykh (*shaykh mushayikh*) of the Hashid tribal confederation and long-time speaker of parliament; Zindani as a force with Islamic activists and militants and in the country's mosques and religious institutes; and both by virtue of their close ties to president Salih – it was younger, more moderate and pragmatic individuals who led the way to entering the JMP.

Muhammad Yadumi, 'Abd al-Wahhab al-Anisi, and Muhammad Qahtan represent what François Burgat has characterized as Islah's "modernist wing."[63] These moderates occupy many administrative positions in the party and, as Schwedler's analysis has adeptly demonstrated, represent the sector of the party most willing to play by the rules of the political game.[64] Unlike Zindani and Ahmar, Islah leaders Yadumi, Qahtan, and Anisi are each referred to not as "shaykh" in Islah party documents, but as "professor" (*ustaz*), signifying their status as party intellectuals rather than as religious authorities or spiritual guides.[65] The moderates bring political experience rather than religious credentials to their positions in Islah. After earning a degree in history, Yadumi graduated from a police academy in Cairo and is widely known to have worked for the state's security apparatus. He was the first editor of *al-Sahwa*, launched in 1985 with strong ties to the Muslim Brotherhood, which later became the Islah Party's newspaper.[66] Yadumi was the party's secretary-general until 2007 and remains on Islah's Shura Council. Qahtan is one of the founding members of Islah and currently heads its political office. Current Islah secretary-general, Anisi, is said to maintain good personal relations with president Salih. According to Schwedler, Anisi has "diverse credentials that cross tribal, Islamic and Leftist lines."[67] Of the JMP members I interviewed in December 2005 and January 2006, these three figures were most commonly cited for their pragmatism by both Islah and non-Islah members. In a 1992 interview, Muhammad al-Yadumi, then a member of Islah's political bureau, stated: "We are certainly not fundamentalists. Since the start of party activities we have done nothing that can be described as extremist." While the "we" in his claim seems to refer to the party as a whole, it can only refer to a part. This is apparent in Yadumi's response in the same interview to the question of whether Islah requires changing the constitution to stipulate Islamic law as the only source of legislation. Yadumi replied: "If there's a good commitment to apply it, that's all right. The practice is the most important thing."[68] His suggestion that changing the constitution was not a high priority for the party is either insincere or, more likely, demonstrates Yadumi's different priorities.

Yadumi and other moderates are not without detractors from within Islah, many of whom take them to task for overstepping various lines. For example, after Yadumi leveled sharp criticism at the GPC at the opening session of the party's sixth conference, holding it responsible for shortcomings and deterioration in all aspects of life in the country, a presidential visit to the home of Ahmar ensued. For a while in the run-up to the 2003 elections, it looked as if Islah would have three different candidate lists: one from the tribal wing led by Ahmar, a Muslim Brotherhood list led by Zindani, and a list dominated largely by intellectuals from Islah's political organizational wing led by Yadumi, Qahtan, and Anisi.[69] After the 2003 elections, Qahtan launched incisive critiques of the ruling GPC and President Salih for what he deemed their subversion of democracy. He was quoted as addressing Salih directly: "You, president, were the reason behind this problem, yet it will never be solved [the issue of real democracy] if you don't want to solve it."[70] Qahtan later issued an apology to the president, presumably under pressure, and the Islah Party also formally apologized for the offense. Qahtan again found himself under fire from within his party following a symposium on "Horizons of Peaceful Transfer of Power" sponsored by Women Journalists Without Borders. Qahtan was reported to have responded to the suggestion that only Salih could lead Yemen by asserting that "there are many women as well as men who could likely rule better than president Salih and former President Ibrahim al-Hamdi, and even Shaykh 'Abd al-Majid al-Zindani."[71] Later reports suggested Qahtan had declared women better than Zindani, and public criticisms of Qahtan were leveled by Zindani supporters at al-Iman University. Around the same time, Qahtan received a threatening letter on his doorstep. Qahtan later apologized for the comments, saying they were taken out of context and not intending to harm Zindani's image. Qahtan blamed the state's secret police, rather than Zindani's supporters, for the threatening letter. In the run-up to the 2006 presidential elections, Qahtan, along with YSP leader Yasin Sa'id Nu'man, were the two leaders whose names most commonly circulated as potential candidates representing the JMP, though that honor was to go to an individual outside both parties.

The third force: Mutawakkil

According to Muhammad 'Abd al-Malik al-Mutawakkil, a political science professor and deputy secretary-general of the Union of Popular

Forces, a small liberal Zaydi opposition power, "the ideological confrontation in our country is not a confrontation between capitalism and
Marxism or between nationalism and regionalism or between Muslims
and non-believers or between South and North. It is a confrontation
between a democratic ideology and an oppressive ideology."[72] He further clarifies that "the military and tribal institutions are ... on the
side of the oppressive regime, whereas civilian institutions are more
keen to see democratic government." Acknowledging that there are
"military and tribal people who are for a democratic government," as
well as "people in civilian institutions who stand with the oppressive
regime," Mutawakkil maintains that this classification represents the
"general orientation of these institutions." So, too, these civilian institutions must themselves be reformed since they are in many respects
"the result of a totalitarian ideology and culture which contradict the
foundations of a democratic system."[73] The same sentiment is found
in a textbook that Mutawakkil wrote for his political science courses at
Sana'a University. Again, he clarifies that "the ideological struggle in
the Yemeni today is not a struggle between Marxism and capitalism,
or between Pan-Arab nationalism [qawmiyya] and state nationalism
[wataniyya], or between Islam and unbelief [kufr], nor even a struggle between south and north or between Shafi'i and Zaydi, or between
Qahtanis [indigenous southerners] and 'Adnanis [immigrant northern-
ers]." Mutawakkil defines the struggle as one between two sets of "values:" the values of democracy and the values of domination.[74] The issue
of most importance, Mutawakkil asserts "is that we adopt one concept
of human rights, that we affirm it collectively and that we struggle collectively against its usurpation ... regardless of whether it is clothed in
Arab nationalist, Islamic or national garb."[75]

In Mutawakkil's assessment the problem with the movements for
change in Yemen lies in the lack of full comprehension of basic requirements for building a modern and democratic state. In the 1990s, he
argues, proponents of democratic change did succeed in articulating
the basis for such a state in the "Document of Pledge and Accord."
However, in his view, even the authors of that document did not man-
age to build tools sufficiently powerful to implement the necessary
changes. Specifically, they did not address the need for full and democratic development and transformation of institutions of civil society
(al-mujtama' al-madani). Mutawakkil maintains that this required
democratic practice and decentralization and respect for differences
of opinion so that civil society comes to embody these values, forms
them in the minds of the people, and contributes to a popular desire
for a democratic state that builds the foundation: "The first and basic

step for building a new society and establishing the democratic state includes the rebuilding of civil society so that it becomes a model for the desired state and it becomes an alternative to a state built on the basis of the military."[76] Mutawakkil underscores the necessity of a political and intellectual elite (*nukhba*), who work with "institutions of civil society that adhere to the democratic ideology," truly understand the meaning of democracy, and exemplify in their behavior, institutions, and leadership "all principles and values of the democratic ideology."[77]

Mutawakkil manages to communicate with all sides not only because of his personal demeanor – which comes across as scholarly and reasoned, more the professor than the ideologue – but also by the intellectual position he occupies: he is at once highly religious and consistently liberal in perspective. At the same time, Mutawakkil has proven to be sharply critical. By his own account, he comes from "a Zaydi background in which the principle of *khuruj* from a despotic ruler forms an important basis," though he denies that Zaydi doctrine advocates use of violence.[78] While his critique is most often directed at the ruling party, Mutawakkil has not refrained from criticizing the opposition as well. In this latter role, he has been significant in keeping a number of sides in the opposition. This is demonstrated after the surprise appointment of the Zaydi religious scholar and al-Haq leader, Judge Ahmad al-Shami, as minister of religious affairs, a position previously held by an Islah member. Shami took the job, even though his party declared its support for abolishing the religious affairs ministry altogether. The appointment was viewed by many as an attempt to put pressure on, and curb the influence of, Islah. Mutawakkil warned al-Haq that it was being used to settle scores for the GPC and that al-Haq could contribute more in opposition than in joining a government in which it would have no say.[79]

Mutawakkil's desire to construct an opposition truly independent of the governing power was again apparent after opposition parties failed to get the parliamentary votes necessary to nominate a presidential candidate in the 1999 elections. Mutawakkil predicted that:

After the comedy of the Presidential elections is over, the ruling parties will try to tempt the opposition parties in an attempt to deprive them of the chance of being a real opposition that people may choose someday when they think of a change. The success of the Government in this regard depends on the Coordination Council for Opposition and its reaction to such attempts. The opposition parties had to make a clear-cut decision after the rejection of its nominee.[80]

Mutawakkil called for boycotting the elections. On election day, Mutawakkil quipped: "I went to the mosque instead [of the voting] to mourn the death of democracy in Yemen." There was no need to vote, he explained, because the results were already known.[81]

Creating a bird with wings that fly together: dialogs, compromises, and silences

Though most JMP members refused to identify an author of a first draft of the JMP platform, insisting it was truly a collaborative effort without any author, according to YSP member Muhammad al-Maqalih, Muta-wakkil was key in drafting the first version of the reform document, based on previous JMP statements, though the draft was revised after considerable discussion.[82] Mutawakkil would admit to no more than having a role in the initial outline of the program.[83] Mutawakkil also claims that the idea of engaging Islah first developed through discussions he had with 'Umar at the 1994 National-Islamic Conference (NIC) convened by the Center for Arab Unity Studies in Beirut.[84] The NIC represents one of several forums that have placed these individuals in dialog. Both Mutawakkil and 'Umar have regularly attended the conference since their first meeting in 1994. Mutawakkil was the general coordinator for the second, third, and fourth conferences. 'Umar's first real relationship with Islah was with Anisi and developed in large part through their joint participation in the National-Islamic conferences in 1997 and 2000. Qahtan also attended the 1997 and 2004 meetings. Members of both parties also have been brought together by the National Democratic Institute (NDI), a non-profit organization based in the United States with offices abroad to provide assistance to civic and political leaders advancing democratic values, practices, and institutions. NDI activities, which date back to Yemen's first multiparty legislative elections in 1993, have always included consultations with individual political parties. More recently, NDI has brought together groups, including the YSP and Islah, for joint consultations and workshops. The weekly newspaper *al-Shumu‘* reported in 2001 that the Islah–YSP alliance was a direct result of meetings coordinated by the NDI.[85] According to NDI's quarterly report covering the period from April to June 2005, the institute held a consultative meeting with women's committees of the GPC, YSP, Islah, and Nasirist parties, a workshop on conflict resolution techniques for members of the same four parties, and a workshop on group facilitation techniques for members of all parties' central branches.[86] In October 2002, the Center for the Study of Islam and Democracy (CSID), a non-profit organization based in Washington, DC, organized workshops addressing the issue of the "Compatibility of Islam and Democracy." Among the participants were 'Umar, Anisi, and Qahtan, as well as leaders of the Nasirist, Ba'thist, UPF, and al-Haq parties. The second plenary session featured Qahtan and 'Umar. In response to Qahtan's statements affirming his party's commitment to democracy 'Umar stated that, if that was his party's position, the YSP had no quarrel with them, though 'Umar's statements also affirmed the necessity of secularism in order to foster an atmosphere of tolerance.[87] These various organizations and meetings provided important opportunities for dialog and facilitated development of a reform platform that could appeal to an ideologically wide range of groups frustrated by the GPC's domination of political life in Yemen.

Platform for reform

The 2005 JMP program asserts that Yemen "stands at a crossroads" and "the route it chooses to take will decide its fate: whether it chooses the path of comprehensive national and political reform ... or continues along its same path" which will inevitability lead to catastrophe. The JMP put forth a common project for reform calling for political, economic, and social reforms, by their own assessment, in order to avoid the latter fate. Among its most significant features are a call to replace the current system of "one-person rule," where power is concentrated in the president's hands and corruption is encouraged, with a parliamentary system with a separation of powers, an independent judiciary, and administrative decentralization. In regard to the economy, the document calls for development of "a national strategy for inclusive and sustainable development." Additionally, the program mentions reforms at the cultural and social levels, including legal protections for journalists, education reforms, and women's advancement.

The GPC reacted immediately and harshly to the program, alternatively criticizing it for not providing any real suggestions for reform, for targeting the president, and for fomenting national divisions prior to elections. The GPC met individually with leaders of the YSP and Islah shortly after release of the program and rumors began circulating that one or the other of the parties was planning to realign with the ruling power prior to elections. But the alliance was not rattled. In a further act of unity, the JMP succeeded in electing Mutawakkil's party, the Union of Popular Forces, as head of the JMP during the alliance's first official congress in December 2005, with the heads of the six participating parties forming the JMP executive committee and Muhammad Qahtan of Islah acting as JMP spokesperson.

Perhaps the alliance's greatest sign of unity was revealed when Faysal bin Shamlan (b. 1934) was chosen as the JMP candidate for president. He has ties to both the YSP and Islah, but has maintained independence from both. Born in the Hadramout region, Bin Shamlan was minister of public works and transport, as well as a member of the Supreme People's Council in South Yemen. Bin Shamlan also has ties to moderates in the Muslim Brotherhood in Yemen. Prior to independence, he was involved with establishing a Brotherhood branch in the south to aid with the fight for independence.[88] With the pluralization of political parties after unity, Bin Shamlan helped found a liberal Islamist party called the Free Yemeni Forum (*hizb al-minbar al-yamani al-hur*), though he returned to his independent status after a brief period.[89]

Bin Shamlan's credibility within the JMP seems to lie in his consistent stand against corruption in government. He has resigned from government positions at least twice to protest about what he saw as government misdeeds. When he resigned as oil minister in 1995 to protest about the dismissal of his proposal for reforming that ministry, it is said that he returned his ministry car before catching a taxi home. In 2003, he resigned his seat in protest against the extension of parliament, a move he deemed unconstitutional, reportedly stating that he would not serve beyond the four years for which the people had elected him.[90] Bin Shamlan's campaign slogan – "a president in service of Yemen, not Yemen at the service of the president" – reflected a similar view.

Bin Shamlan identified the circulation of the JMP reform initiative as one of the main goals of his candidacy.[91] The document represents the outcome of over a year and a half of discussions, debates, and revisions. It is a carefully crafted text and marks a significant step toward forging an effective, substantive and unified oppositional alliance. Yet it is also important to consider what is not mentioned in the document and those points where the text falls short of the actions of its members.

Silence on secularism

At the first meeting of the National Islamic Conference, 'Umar maintained that "on the issues of Palestine and confronting foreign occupation, colonialism and imperialism in its new forms, we do not differ and we can easily form a declaration now." However, on the issues of the right to *ijtihad* and freedom of expression, which he understands as an absolute and unrestricted right, 'Umar suggests differences remain.[92] Article three of Yemen's constitution, ratified in 1991, states that "Islamic law is the main source of legislation." Immediately following the civil war, the article was rewritten to specify that "Islamic law is the source of all legislation." In addition, article fifty-nine of the new constitution made the defense of religion a "sacred duty." Referring to the changes, 'Umar notes that while Islamic law provides a "general authority," "*ijtihad* [independent reasoning] is guaranteed according to the general interest and development of the community." He argues:

After the [civil] war was finished and Yemeni socialist party was defeated, representatives of the Islamic trend said that they want to remove the passage that guarantees *ijtihad*. Others were not able to oppose this demand because they feared their opposition would be against their religion ... I see that the cessation of *ijtihad* and the rigidity that overtook this *umma* is one of the reasons for the stagnation, non-development and backwardness that has overcome us.[93]

In a 1998 forum held at the Yemeni Center for Strategic Studies on "The Future of the Yemeni Socialist Party in Light of its Fourth Congress,"[94] 'Umar again questioned Islah's stance on the role of Islamic law in politics, here in response to criticism from two other members of the forum: Zayd al-Shami, head of Islah's education division, and Muhammad al-Maqalih. After diplomatically confirming his understanding that criticisms of YSP regarding its relationship to Islam "only emerge from a desire of these brothers to improve the position of the socialist party," 'Umar clarified that while there is no question about the central role of Islam as a religion and a doctrine, differences emerged when Islam is said to provide a law for the state.[95] First, various schools of law and individual jurists cannot agree on what constitutes Islamic law. Second, there are many things that Islam did not legislate because they did not exist at the time of revelation. 'Umar argued that although Islam speaks of such things as consultation and justice, the tools for addressing these issues must come from the contemporary age and religion can only offer "a general point of reference." To establish his point, 'Umar quoted from both the Qur'an and from a respected jurist: "When God said: 'Today I finished your religion for you,' he did say [he determined] every issue of life." Further, "as Shaykh al-Asfahani said: 'Issues are not finite, but the text is,' and indeed the issues of life are not finite." 'Umar maintained that the YSP "wants a civil state but this civil state need not contradict Islam." Those who say the YSP must be an Islamic party in the context of Yemen miss the crux of the problem:

Our problem is not with the sky. Our problem in on the earth, issues of the people, issues of despotism, issues of building the state, of democracy, human rights – these are what our programs include. Thus I affirm that the YSP is a party that complies with the constitution so long as it is committed to Islam as the religion of the state in a general form. However, we are clearly against the establishment of a religious state and with the establishment of a civil state.

The difference between a religious state and a civil state, 'Umar clarified, is that the leader of the religious state is accountable only to God, while the leader of a civil state can never be considered more than a mere man who is elected by those to whom he is accountable.

In a 2003 interview with Farraj Ismai'il, Yadumi responded to a question regarding whether Islah will continue to seek an Islamic state by asserting that:

> there is no longer any principled dispute between the political forces in the Yemeni arena and Islah over this issue. The dispute between us is now over programs because all these forces and organizations abide by the constitution, whose articles stem from the Islamic shari'a. Also, they abide by the parties law, which obliges every Yemeni party to reject slogans, principles, and policies that conflict with the Islamic shari'a.

He continued, "Communism has disappeared from the world and leftist parties and organizations are reviewing their situation. Nationalist organizations are doing the same. Thus, everyone is undertaking self-examination. The constitutional and legal circumstances in our country place us all in the same situation. They do not disagree over goals; they only disagree over the means."[96] One could interpret this statement as affirmation that Islah considers the matter of Islamic law resolved in its favor and sufficient for establishing Islamic rule in the country. One could also read it as an indication that Islah is willing to forgo raising the issue further, as long as the *shari'a* is upheld in the text of the constitution, even if not fully realized in practice. Neither interpretation seems to account for the lack of a single mention of Islamic law in the JMP document. The parties refrained from broaching the subject in the text, despite the ability of individuals to put forth moderate, albeit divergent, views on the topic.

Women's political participation

Historically, 'Umar and other members of the YSP have viewed their party's stance on women as one of its defining elements. Compared with northern women, women in the south enjoyed a much greater public role under the YSP. Generally, the YSP and Islah speak a different language in regard to women. In their 1993 election platform, the YSP stated "the guarantee of women's equal rights" as a centerpiece of its platform, whereas Islah stipulated: "Women should be protected from exploitation."[97] Women have been active in Islah and the party has supported their participation in elections, in some regions even providing women voters with transportation to polling stations. But the party has not supported women as candidates for political office, since this would give them authority over men.[98] Among the constitutional changes of

1994 was the specification of women's rights in accordance with Islamic law in article thirty-one: "Women are the sisters of men. They have rights and duties, which are guaranteed and assigned by the shari'a." A 1996 Islah document on women's electoral participation noted that, because democracy was "still in its infancy and required a period of maturation" and issues such as the achievement of "equality of opportunities between the rich and poor, between those with influence and power and ordinary people, and between the ruling party and the party of opposition" remain unresolved, raising the issue of women's status was premature. Only after society achieves progress in these areas would the time prove ripe for "joining opinions and values based on the shari'a," in order "to point Yemeni women toward a better tomorrow."[99]

The JMP platform identified "empowering women to enjoy their constitutional and legal rights and participation in public life" as a goal, but seems intentionally vague on the character of participation to be sought. Conversations with several JMP leaders revealed that the issue of women was one of the main points of disagreement, second only to the issue of secularism – or the status of Islamic law in the constitution. According to Mutawakkil "it was apparent that Islah preferred to discuss this issue [of women] among themselves," rather than with the other parties. It appears that Islah did continue to discuss the issue internally, and certainly women's groups continued to seek party nominations, as well as a more general quota system.

Prior to the 2003 elections, Qahtan announced that his party would again decline to nominate women candidates. However, his statement on the issue revealed that there was disagreement within Islah. Qahtan, who is well known to be in favor of women's political participation, justified his party's decision by saying that women would not be nominated primarily because they would not win:

Our society is still ignorant and there are still some social, cultural and ideological principles that women cannot stand against. Although Islah was first to nominate women to its higher committees, we reached a conclusion that it is still difficult to nominate women from Islah for the coming elections. We also found it impractical, especially if we consider the number of previous nominations of women even within our party itself.[100]

Qahtan later announced that Islah required "two years to reach a clear position on women candidates."[101] JMP members sought to maintain their alliance as the election neared through the construction of a platform that all of the relevant opposition parties could sign onto, but the *Yemen Times* reported that "the JMP could not reach an agreement on how to tackle the parliamentary elections" and that "nomination of women [candidates] is the first sticking point."[102] In 2004, Qahtan asserted that there were "absolutely no red lines for the involvement of women in the political affairs of the party," and there was "nothing to prevent Islahi women from running in the local council elections in 2005 and the parliamentary elections in 2009." But he also acknowledged that women in Islah would not be able to fully realize their rights without a struggle and called for "the women in Islah and other parties to impose their views."[103] Shortly before the publication of the JMP program, Qahtan again affirmed Islah's acceptance of female candidates. But there was concern that this only reflected his personal opinion, since no official party declaration followed his statement. Qahtan acknowledged internal divisions, revealing that older Islah members who clung to "traditional views" were holding the party back on this issue, but also claiming after a long dialog within the party they had "moved on" and would propose female candidates for local and parliamentary elections.[104] They never did.

The failure of the parties as such to achieve meaningful support for female political candidates underscores that liberalization is not something that develops merely through interaction across a plurality of parties or groups. It also requires actors within that group who are already well ahead of their parties, and willing to do the work of introducing and defending new practices. The failure also reveals the inability of Islah's moderate wing to prevail over other more conservative or radical forces within their party. It is worth noting that when measured by women's political participation, moderate and progressive forces are weak not only within Islamist groups, but more generally in Yemeni politics. Less than 1 percent of candidates in the local elections were female and, of those, most ran as independents, suggesting a general lack of party support for female candidates.[105] The weakness of moderate forces in Islah was even more evident as two of its most powerful leaders, Zindani and Ahmar, made a final hour decision to back president Salih's re-election, despite their parties' formal position as sponsors of a JMP presidential candidate. Further, although Bin Shamlan was the JMP candidate, one YSP member, Ahmad al-Majidi, and one Islah member, Fathi al-Azab, ran as independent candidates. The YSP suspended Majidi's membership in the party, but no similar action was taken against Azab.[106] In February 2007, Ahmar was re-elected party chairperson, despite attempts to replace him, and in violation of Islah bylaws that limit leadership to three terms. However, the re-election took place while Ahmar was receiving medical treatment in Saudi Arabia and Yadumi, and the leader many considered the primary rival to Ahmar in the elections was elected deputy chairperson. After Ahmar's death in December of that same year, Anisi became secretary-general of Islah. Combined with changes in Islah's Shura Council – including the replacement of Zindani as speaker in favor of deputy speaker Muhammad 'Ali Ajlan and the election of thirteen women to the 130-member body for the first time in Islah party history – developments may bode well for moderates in the long run.

The JMP is plainly dependent upon certain key political actors within the main opposition parties. These are largely individuals who have forged this cross-ideological platform for reform. It is promising that moderate individuals occupy key positions in many parties, including Islah, and are able, on occasion, to cooperate with ideologically opposed groups, even when evidence of party moderation is inconclusive. The relative ease with which JMP offices have rotated among the various parties also bodes well for the group's continuation: in early 2008, Anisi, as head of Islah, became the leader of JMP, succeeding YSP leadership, which had received the position from the UPF. YSP parliamentarian, Muhamad Salih al-Qubati took over as JMP spokesperson from a Nasirist Party member Muhammad Yahya al-Sabri.[107] The ability of JMP architects to act politically has been demonstrated by publication of the program for reform and their presidential candidate's respectable 22 percent of votes. Yet even those JMP initiatives that have been successful in demonstrating the party's independence as an oppositional force speak to the weaknesses as well as strengths of this alliance. The long-term viability of oppositional alliances, such as the JMP, depends not only upon individuals maintaining and deepening interpersonal and ideational relationships across ideological divides, but also upon successful defense of these relations and strategies and their own positions within their parties against competing strategies, particularly as the parties prepare for the parliamentary elections scheduled for 2009.

NOTES

1. Zaydism is a Shi'i sect that predominates in Yemen's north-central highlands. A Zaydi imamate ruled northern Yemen until it was overthrown by military coup in 1962.
2. The Popular Nasirist Unity Organization (al-tanzim al-wahdawi al-sha'bi al-nasiri) was founded in Ta'iz in 1965. The Union of Popular Forces (ittihad al-qiwa al-sha'biyya) was founded in 1959 by Ibrahim bin 'Ali al-Wazir, a member of a prominent family of Zaydi sayyids who led a failed constitutional movement against the imam in 1948.

3. The Haq Party (*hizb al-haq*) was established in 1990 by a group of Zaydi scholars and sayyids, primarily to defend Zaydism against the growth of the Wahhabi movement in Yemen. The National Socialist Arab Ba'th Party (*hizb al-ba'th al-'arabi al-ishtiraki*), a small Iraqi-leaning party that emerged in Yemen in the 1960s out of the Arab Nationalist Movement, was originally counted among the JMP membership and even listed among the signatories in the press when the JMP document was publicized. However, the party's secretary-general never actually signed on and eventually the party positioned itself closer to the GPC.

4. Jillian Schwedler. *Faith in Moderation: Islamist Parties in Jordan and Yemen* (Cambridge University Press, 2006), 192.

5. Schwedler. *Faith in Moderation*, 192.

6. Determining whether Yemen has become more or less democratic over a period of time is an inexact science at best. While some studies indicate marginal progress in regard to particular indicators at points, the more general assessment seems to be that democratization in Yemen stalled in the mid-1990s. See Jillian Schwedler. "Yemen's Aborted Opening," *Journal of Democracy* 13 (2002), 48–55; Sheila Carapico analyzes the curtailment of local initiatives by an increasingly centralized state following a period of democratic experimentation between 1990 and 1994. *Civil Society in Yemen: The Political Economy of Activism in Modern Arabia* (Cambridge University Press, 1998), ch. 7. Comparing the 1993 and 1997 parliamentary elections, Abdu H. Sharif notes a series of "reversals" in Yemen's progress toward democracy. "Weak Institutions and Democracy: The Case of the Yemeni Parliament, 1993–1997," *Middle East Policy* 9 (March 2002), 92. Freedom House moved Yemen from "not free" to "partly free" in 2003, but has more recently noted that "in the two years from the end of 2003 until the end of 2005, Yemen's overall performance on democratic governance weakened, with little progress to report on strengthening the rule of law, fighting corruption, and increasing transparency." Brian Katulis and David Emery. "Yemen," *Countries at the Crossroads 2006* (New York: Freedom House, 2006).

7. Robert D. Burrowes and Catherine M. Kasper. "The Salih Regime and the Need for a Credible Opposition," *Middle East Journal* 61 (2007), 264 n.6, 264.

8. Michael Hudson. "Bipolarity, Rational Calculation and War in Yemen" in Jamal S. al-Suwaidi (ed.), *The Yemeni War of 1994: Causes and Consequences* (London: Saqi Books, 1995), 22.

9. Paul Dresch and Bernard Haykel report that "the Brothers in Yemen are few, and they are not unified." "Stereotypes and Political Styles: Islamists and Tribesfolk in Yemen," *International Journal of Middle East Studies* 27 (1995), 406.

10. Hudson. "Bipolarity," 22.

11. Schwedler reports that "after more than a decade under Zindani's guidance, a number of younger Muslim Brotherhood members felt it was time for a change in leadership and mounted what several of them describe as an internal coup against Zindani. They felt that Zindani was developing his own cult of personality at the expense of the teachings of Hassan

al-Banna, the Egyptian who founded the Muslim Brotherhood in 1928."
"Islam, Democracy, and the Yemeni State," paper presented at the CSID
annual conference (Washington, DC: April 2001). Zindani was based in
Saudi Arabia in the 1980s, where he headed the Institute for Scientific
Inimitability, an organization devoted to proving the correspondence of
science and revelation.

12. British Broadcasting Corporation. Summary of World Broadcasts (April
19, 1990).

13. British Broadcasting Corporation. Summary of World Broadcasts (April
19, 1990).

14. Joseph Kostiner. *Yemen: The Tortuous Quest for Unity, 1990–1994* (London:
The Royal Institute of International Affairs, 1996), 42. Despite his violent
actions against southerners and socialists, Tariq al-Fadli was eventually
absorbed into the GPC and even appointed to the upper house of parliament by the ruling party.

15. Dresch and Haykel. "Stereotypes and Political Styles," 405.

16. The Presidential Council was altered in 1993 to include one Islah member
and then eliminated in 1994 through constitutional amendment.

17. Biographical information on both Ahmar and Zindani can be found in
Khalil Muhammad al-Surimi. *Lamhat min masira al-islah al-yamaniyya* (A
Brief View of the Journal of Yemeni Islah) (Sana'a: n.p., 2004), 103–105
and 106–108, respectively.

18. Hudson. "Bipolarity," 22.

19. Quoted in Salah Nasrawi. "Yemen in Turmoil as it Heads for Elections,"
The Associated Press (August 24, 1992).

20. Iris Glosemeyer. "The First Yemeni Parliamentary Elections in 1993,"
Orient 34 (1993), 446.

21. See, for example, this affirmed by Muhammad al-Maqalih, then with
al-Haq; 'Abd al-Rahman 'Ali al-Jifri of the Yemeni National Opposition
Front (MOWJ) and Rabitat Abna' al-Yaman (RAY); Muhammad 'Abd
al-Malik al-Mutawakkil of the Popular Forces; and Anis Hassan Yahya of
the YSP in E. G. H. Joffé, M. J. Hachemi, and E. W. Watkins (eds.). *Yemen
Today: Crisis and Solutions* (London: Caravel Press, 1997), 66, 45–46, 67,
151 respectively. At this same forum, 'Umar al-Jawi claimed that "the coalition between Islah, the GPC and the YSP stood against the opposition"
and "stood against the Document of Pledge and Accord" (84). According
to Jawi, "up to now, the opposition – and I am part of it – in our country
has not fulfilled its duties" (88).

22. Hudson. "Bipolarity," 20.

23. Abdul Rahman Ali al-Jifri. *A Paper on the Yemeni Crisis*. Department of
Politics, University of Exeter (October 29, 1997), 6.

24. *Yemen Times* (June 20, 1994).

25. Yemeni Reform Gathering. *Masira 'ata, April 1993-April 1997* (Sana'a:
al-Afaq lil-tib'a wa al-nashr, 1997).

26. This shift is well documented by Jillian Schwedler. "The Islah Party in
Yemen: Political Opportunities and Coalition Building in a Transitional
Polity" in Quintan Wiktorowicz (ed.), *Islamic Activism: A Social Movement
Theory Approach* (Indiana University Press, 2004), 205–228.

27. The first reference in print I have found to the JMP as such is in *al-Milaf al-watha'iqi lil-intikhabat, 1997: ihsa'iyyan, tahliliyyan, siyasiyyan* (Documentary Portfolio of the Yemeni Parliamentary Elections, 1997: Statistical, Analytical, Political) (Sana'a: Awan for Services and Information, 1997), 39–40. Another early reference is found in Mahmud Mansur. "al-masar al-tatbiqi lil-tajriba al-dimuqratiyya fi al-yaman wa mu'ashshirat al-mustaqbal" (The Practical Democratic Course in Yemen and Indications of the Future), *Markaz dirasat al-mustaqbal* 3 (Fall 1998), 68–80. The Higher Coordination Council for the Opposition Parties (*majlis al-tansiq al-'ala li-ihzab al-mu'arida*), founded in 1995 to ally the YSP and several small, mostly left-leaning parties, consisted of seven political parties in 1997: the YSP, the Nasirist Party, al-Haq, UPF, the Yemeni Unity Gathering (*hizb al-tajammu' al-wahdawi al-yamani*), the Ba'thist Party and the Constitutional Freedom Party (*hizb al-ahrar al-dusturi*). Bilqis Ahmad Mansur. *al-Ahzab al-siyasiyya wa al-tahawwul al-dimuqrati: dirasah tatbiqiyya 'ala al-yaman wa bilad ukhra* (Political Parties and Democratic Transformation: A Study Applied to Yemen and Other Countries) (Cairo: Maktabat Madbuli, 2004), 368. The HCCO is not to be confused with Higher Council for the Opposition, an allegedly government-sponsored alliance of "opposition" parties who seem to focus on opposing the opposition. The government's policy of creating organizations that duplicate those set up by their critics is sufficiently common to have earned its own name in popular discourse: cloning (*istinsakh*).

28. The SCER, formed in 1993 according to election law number 41, passed in 1992, is responsible for administering and regulating all aspects of the electoral process. Its status as a neutral institution has been consistently questioned by the opposition parties since its inception. However, the Committee's legitimacy was cast in doubt when, after the passage of a new election law in August 1996 which reduced the number of SCER members from eleven to seven, the actual number of members was not reduced until January 1997.

29. British Broadcasting Corporation. Summary of World Broadcasts (July 7, 1998).

30. *Yemen Times* (September 4, 2000). The YSP's fourth party congress was held in two rounds, the first in November 1998, where various party policies and programs were voted on, and a second in August 2000, when party elections were held.

31. Parliamentary elections scheduled for 2001 were postponed until 2003.

32. *Sawt al-shura* (August 26, 2001).

33. *Yemen Times* (January 29, 2001). There is much speculation in Yemen that Salih intends to remain in office until his son, Ahmad (b. 1970), is old enough to run for president.

34. *al-Ahram Weekly* (March 1, 2001).

35. *Yemen Times* (February 26, 2001).

36. *Agence France Presse* (February 26, 2001).

37. *Yemen Times* (April 23, 2001).

38. British Broadcasting Corporation. Summary of World Broadcasts (July 27, 2001).

39. The National Democratic Institute. "Parliamentary Elections in The Republic of Yemen" (April 27, 2003).

40. *Yemen Times* (March 31, 2003).

41. Ahmed Saif. *The Yemeni Parliamentary Elections: A Critical Analysis* (Dubai: Gulf Research Center, 2004).

42. Saadaldeen Ali Talib. "A Decade of Pluralist Democracy in Yemen: The Yemen Parliament after Unification, 1990–2003" in Ali Sawi (ed.), *Parliamentary Reform* (Cairo: Konrad Adenauer Stiftung, 2003), 208. A similar assessment of 'Umar's role in brokering the YSP–Islah alliance is offered by Sheila Carapico, Lisa Wedeen, and Anna Wuerth. "The Death and Life of Jarallah Omar," *Middle East Report Online* (December 31, 2002), online at www.merip.org/mero/mero123102.html.

43. Many biographical details were provided by the Fawwaz Traboulsi, a close friend of 'Umar's since the early 1970s. Traboulsi was kind enough to share a written version of the unpublished remarks he delivered at a memorial held for 'Umar at the Cultural Council for South Lebanon in Beirut.

44. 'Abd al-Fattah Isma'il was killed in the conflict.

45. Jarallah 'Umar, "A Short Autobiography," *Yemen Gateway*, online at www.al-bab.com/yemen/biog/jarallah.htm.

46. Traboulsi, unpublished remarks delivered at 'Umar's memorial in Beirut. Provided by the author.

47. 'Umar. "A Short Autobiography."

48. 'Umar. "A Short Autobiography."

49. *Yemen Times* (November 2, 1998).

50. A text of the speech is found in Sadiq Nashir. *Jar allah 'umar yatakallam: qisa hayat min shahqa al-milad ila rasasa al-mawt* (Jarallah 'Umar Speaks: The Story of a Life from the Breath of Birth to the Bullet of Death) (Sana'a: Markaz al-'abadi, 2003), 80–84.

51. Nashir. *Jar allah 'umar yatakallam*, 12–13.

52. *Mideast Mirror* 13:126 (July 5, 1999).

53. Fahmy Howeidy. "Edging towards the Abyss: There is More than Meets the Eye to Recent Events in Yemen," *al-Ahram Weekly* (January 16–22, 2003).

54. Muhammad Muhammad al-Maqalih. *Man qatala jar allah 'umar: al-jarima bayn al-din wa al-siyasa* (Who Killed Jarallah 'Umar: The Crime Between Religion and Politics) (Sana'a: Markaz al-'abadi, 2004). Maqalih has moved through a number of organizations. By his own account, he began as socialist member of the Muslim brotherhood, later joining al-Haq – drawn to Zaydi ideas of revolution – before finally settling in with the YSP. Nabil al-Sufi, editor of *News Yemen* and Islah member, explained Maqalih's move as follows: "since parties are so undemocratic, if you find you have a disagreement, then you have not choice but to leave." Nabil al-Sufi, interview with author, Sana'a, Yemen (January 11, 2006).

55. *Yemen Times* (June 23, 2003).

56. *Yemen Times* (November 17, 2003).

57. Muhammad 'Abd al-Rahman al-Maqrami. *al-Tajammu' al-yamani lil-islah: al-ru'ya wa al-masar – dirasat fi al-nash'a wa al-tatawwur* (The

Yemeni Reform Gathering: Vision and Path: A Study of the Origin and Development) (Sana'a: Yemeni Reform Gathering, 1998).

58. This slogan was also the theme of a December 1992 "Unity and Peace Conference" held by Islah in Sana'a.
59. Quoted in Maqrami. *al-Tajammu' al-yamani lil-islah*, 113.
60. Maqrami. *al-Tajammu' al-yamani lil-islah*, 164.
61. Maqrami. *al-Tajammu' al-yamani lil-islah*, 189. The passage quoted is from a party document.
62. Paul Dresch. "The Tribal Factor in the Yemeni Crisis" in Jamal S. al-Suwaidi (ed.). *The Yemeni War of 1994* (London: Saqi Books, 1995), 39.
63. François Burgat. "Yemen: On which side?" *Le Monde diplomatique* (April 9, 2003).
64. Schwedler. *Faith in Moderation*.
65. Ahmar's status as a shaykh derives from his leadership of the Hashid tribe and has different resonances than Zindani's title, which appears to stem from his status as a religious scholar. The shaykh–professor distinction may indicate a juxtaposition of "traditional" and "modern" as well.
66. Paul Dresch. *A History of Modern Yemen* (Cambridge University Press, 2000), 175, 187.
67. Schwedler. *Faith in Moderation*, 72.
68. Quoted in Brian Whitaker. "Rumblings from a Distant Outbreak of Democracy," *The Guardian* (January 4, 1992).
69. *Yemen Times* (February 24, 2003).
70. *al-Ahram Weekly* (May 8–14, 2003).
71. *Yemen Observer* (October 4, 2005).
72. Muhammad 'Abd al-Malik al-Mutawakkil. "The Gap Between the Government and the Governed" in Joffé, Hachemi, and Watkins (eds.), *Yemen Today*, 67.
73. Mutawakkil. "The Gap," 68, 69.
74. Muhammad 'Abd al-Malik al-Mutawakkil. *al-Tanmiyya al-siyasiyya* (Political Development) (Sana'a: n.p., 2004), 189–90.
75. *Mu'tamar al-qawmi al-islami al-awwal: watha'iq wa munaqashat wa qararat al-mu'tamar* (The First National-Islamic Conference: Documents, Debates and Decisions of the Conference) (Beirut: Center for Arab Unity Studies, 1995), 270.
76. Mutawakkil. *al-Tanmiyya al-siyasiyya*, 193–194.
77. Mutawakkil. *al-Tanmiyya al-siyasiyya*, 194.
78. *al-Mu'tamar al-qawmi al-dini al-awal*, 268.
79. *Mideast Mirror* (May 23, 1997).
80. *Yemen Times* (August 16, 1999).
81. Quoted in Faiza Saleh Ambah. "Low Turnout, Attacks Mar Yemen's First Direct Presidential Election," *Associated Press* (September 23, 1999).
82. Muhammad al-Maqalih, interview with author, Sana'a, Yemen (January 7, 2006).
83. Muhammad 'Abd al-Malik al-Mutawakkil, interview with author, Sana'a, Yemen (January 10, 2006).
84. Muhammad 'Abd al-Malik al-Mutawakkil, interview with author, Sana'a, Yemen (January 3, 2006).

85. *al-Shumu'* (February 3, 2001).

86. National Democratic Institute. *Yemen: Political Party Capacity Building and Women's Participation* (CEPPS/NDI Quarterly Report: April–June 2005). Online at www.idea.int

87. See Center for the Study of Islam and Democracy. *Workshops on Islam and Democracy: Morocco, Egypt, Yemen* (2002). Online at www.csidonline.org

88. *al-Hayat* (July 6, 2006).

89. *Newsyemen* (August 8, 2006).

90. Nabil Sultan. "Yemen: Breath of Principle in Presidential Race," *Inter Press Service News Agency* (July 5, 2006).

91. *Newsyemen.net* (July 5, 2006).

92. *al-Mu'tamar al-qawmi al-islami al-awal*, 168.

93. *al-Mu'tamar al-qawmi al-islami al-awal*, 168–169.

94. Though not officially linked to Islah, the Center for Strategic Studies' first and present directors – Nasr Taha Mustafa and Muhammad al-Afandi, respectively – have been members. In 2002, Mustafa left Islah to join the GPC and the CSS to become editor-in-chief of *Saba*, the Yemeni government's news agency.

95. The conference took place on December 8, 1998, and was published in the fifth volume of the serial *Nadwat al-mustaqbal*, entitled *Mustaqbal al-hizb al-ishtiraki al-yamani fi dhaw mu'tamaru al-rabi'* (The Future of the Yemeni Socialist Party in Light of Its Fourth Congress), ed. Faris al-Saqqaf (Sana'a: Markaq dirasat al-mustaqbal, 2002). 'Umar's remarks are found 120–127.

96. *al-Majalla* (June 29 – July 5, 2003), 24–25.

97. Rashad Muhammad 'Ulaymi and Ahmad 'Ali Bashari. *al-Baramij al-intikhabiyya lil-ahzab wa al-tanzimat al-siyasiyya fi al-jumhuriyya al-yamaniyya: dirasa muqarana* (Electoral Programs of Political Parties and Organizations in the Yemen Republic: A Comparative Study) (Sana'a: Majallat al-Thawabit, 1993).

98. Reference is to a *hadith* that states "Women are the full siblings of men" (*al-nisa shaqa'iq al-rijal*) and Qur'an 4:34, which asserts, "Men are the protectors of women," alternatively translated as "Men are in authority over women" (*al-rijal qawwamun 'ala al-nisa*).

99. Memo from the women's office of Islah, entitled "The Experience of Women in the Past Parliamentary Election for the Islah Party." In *Taqrir 'an al-halqa al-niqashiyya hawla taqayyum musharaka al-mar'a fi al-intikhabat al-sabiqa abril 93 wa tashji' musharakat al-nisa ka-nakhubat wa marshuhat fi al-intikhabat al-niyabiyya al-qadima abril 97* (Report on the Debate Forum on the Assessment of Women's Participation in the April 1993 Elections and the Encouragement of Women's Participation as Candidates and Representatives in the Upcoming April 1997 Parliamentary Elections) (Sana'a: National Committee for Women of the Yemeni Republic, n.d.), 21.

100. *Yemen Observer* (February 1, 2003).

101. *Yemen Times* (February 3, 2003).

102. *Yemen Times* (February 3, 2003).

103. *Yemen Observer* (September 25, 2004).

104. *Yemen Observer* (October 9, 2005).
105. European Union Election Observation Mission. "Yemen, Final Report: Presidential and Local Council Elections" (September 20, 2006).
106. A fifth candidate, Yasin 'Abd al-Sa'id, ran as the candidate for the "National Opposition Council," an alliance of a dozen smaller parties that, despite their name, are known to be close to the ruling GPC. Sa'id is head of the Nasirist Democratic Party, not to be confused with the Popular Nasirist Unity Organization, which is part of the JMP and led by Sultan al-Atwani.
107. *Yemen Observer* (January 15, 2008).

Conclusion: Ideological rapprochement, accommodation, transformation – and their limits

This book presents analysis of the intellectual and historical antecedents of contemporary cases of cross-ideological coordination among various oppositional elements that have traditionally opposed each other. As such, it responds to those who think that the spontaneity and often haphazard protest activity in the streets of Cairo and the surprising formalization of a socialist-Islamist opposition bloc in Sanaʿa lack antecedents, lack thinking, lack constructive political programs, and lack political (or ideological or intellectual) significance. The origin, character, and significance of these instances of contentious politics is only revealed through fuller examination of the individuals, trends, and groups that have instigated and justified these alliances, and undertaken the intellectual groundwork that contributed to their emergence.

1) **Origins:** what are the circumstances that have brought historical rivals together? While certainly particular political, economic, social, and other material conditions contributed to the emergence of the current wave of protest politics in Egypt and the oppositional bloc in Yemen, there is a tendency to see the actions as merely reactive: merely the result of electoral disputes, or a response to events in the Palestinian–Israeli conflict, or as a result of the Bush administration's Greater Middle East Initiative, or as a reaction to globalization. Certainly this is part of the story. However, consideration of the intellectual antecedents, of increased willingness of ideological foes to reconsider and reformulate their perspectives, of the considerable dialog and *ijtihad* undertaken that predate the particular events and policies these groups and individuals ally to address, and of the ideological and conceptual framework of the construct, are an equally essential part of the story.

2) **Character:** how have these opposing groups and individuals come together? How do they articulate and justify their coordination? Where and to what extent do they agree or disagree, what can they talk about, what can they not? What sort of opposition do such alliances create? Perhaps most importantly, what are the *limitations* to their alliances?

By limitations, I mean not only points of disagreement, but also the shortcomings, their illiberalisms, and their undemocratic aspects. The second argument of the present work is that the character of the cross-ideological intellectual activity taking place (the framings entailed and their limitations) is reflected in the character of the protest activity we are witnessing. While Islamic moderates have come a long way in providing the details and elaborations of their political projects – which their critics often accuse them of lacking – and in formulating more inclusive notions of a political community, and many Arab nationalists and leftists as well as Islamic moderates have accommodated notions of democracy, pluralism, and political rights in their thought, these ideological strands still retain reactionary elements that do not bode well for freedom of thought and improved status of marginalized groups in the region.

3) **Significance:** here I may fall a bit short for my political science colleagues, since I am not in a position to assess how important these acts of protest are in terms of political outcomes. I do not know where they are going or what they will achieve. My significance speaks to something slightly different: the impact of cross-ideological dialog and cooperation on intellectual developments in the Arab region. Has, as Tibi and others suggest, Arab nationalism and socialism been supplanted by political Islam? Or are we witnessing a form of ideological convergence taking place, whether through the formulation of Islamic liberalism (that Binder sought) or by virtue of various conversion experiences toward political Islam (as Burgat has noted)? Or has Arab political discourse reached a post-Islamism or even post-ideological age and moved toward increasingly pragmatic modes of thought, as suggested by Roy and Salem?

Previous scholarship on contemporary Arab political ideologies fails to consider the possible emergence of an ideological rapprochement among the various contending political groups in opposition – let alone their joining forces despite enduring ideological differences in order to challenge the regimes in power. Without dismissing any of these four theses, the third and overarching conclusion of this book is that the relationship among competing ideologies of opposition in the contemporary Arab region is best characterized as accomodationist, with strategic alliances forming among more pragmatic and moderate wings of otherwise opposed ideological factions of marginalized groups. *Wasatiyya* intellectuals hold out great hope for the Islamist potential of new generations, but do not expect to convert entrenched secularists, nationalists, and leftists to their cause. Some Arab nationalists and leftists may believe that they can "tame" Islamist movements through their engagement, rather than isolation, but their retreat from staunchly secular positions is clearly aimed at cultivating a nascent progressivism in Arab society, not in contributing to the success of Islamic movements.

As Salwa Ismail has demonstrated, reference to religious motifs and themes and invocation of the divine does not necessarily entail conformity to religion as a set of rules or acquiescence to Islamism.[1] Neither should the development of Islamic frames and repertoires in new forms be seen as a dilution of Islam as a referent – a view Ismail associates with Olivier Roy's conclusion that Islamism has failed as a political project and that what we are witnessing presently is the advent of post-Islamism.[2] Rather, Ismail argues that the invocation of Islamic frames offers a means of entering into political spheres that might otherwise be unavailable. While Ismail is primarily concerned with the emergence of competing Islamist discourses, the research presented here highlights the development of non-Islamists who effectively engage and employ Islamic frames – often as a means of engaging Islamists or reaching Islamist publics.

While the longevity of the street politics that falls under the heading of Kifaya and the oppositional alliance embodied in the Joint Meeting Parties remains an open question, manifestation of the cross-ideological cooperation that has taken place in Egypt and Yemen is significant in three ways, which are missed by studies that test the inclusion-moderation thesis by focusing only on inclusion in (rather than considering exclusion from) formal political process, by focusing too exclusively on official political parties (while neglecting individual and generational networks that form across or outside parties) and by focusing predominantly on material opportunity structures (without considering the way in which opportunities are created by – as well as create – intellectual transformations). First, there are discernible transformations in thinking and strategy in both contexts – perhaps most importantly the movement of the Muslim Brotherhood from a position of official opposition to a more confrontational stance and their expressed desire to interact as one party in pluralist politics, but also in Yemen where individuals from Islah have taken steps to bring about a similar role for their group. Second, these examples of coordination indicate the changing character of political opposition in the two countries. In Egypt, the opposition has formed networks that cross not only ideology, but also generations. Yemen's networks remain at the level of individuals, but these individuals are prominent, if not dominant, within their parties. Finally, in both cases one sees the emergence of a new political generation, formed through their common experiences of dialog with each other and defiance against authoritarian state institutions over the last several years.

While the main aim of this study is to account for the political, historical, and especially intellectual conditions that have contributed to dialog, cooperation, and alliances among historically opposed ideological groupings, at the end of this analysis I am led to offer two more critical assessments regarding the significance of my findings. The first involves an assessment of the character of these engagements and their limitations, intellectually and practically. The picture drawn here supports the conclusion that movements for political reform aimed at authoritarian and failing states in the region have been significant but weak. The second addresses claims that current calls for reform in the region are an outgrowth of foreign policy initiated by the United States. As I have argued elsewhere, and this study further attests, the seeds of democratic political reform in the region were well planted prior to the Bush administration's Broader Middle East Initiative, launched in 2004.[3] However, the course of Arab political thought since the war on Iraq leads me to further conclude that US policy is relevant to efforts at democratization and liberalization, but as much as a negative force – a point of opposition that has turned enemies into allies – than as a promoter of democratic values (despite the otherwise laudable efforts of such US organizations as the Center for the Study of Islam and Democracy, discussed in Chapter 3). In fact, the focus on opposing foreign intervention in the region, more often than not, distracts movements calling for political reform from more local concerns.

This conclusion has been noted by some Arab intellectuals, but its critical thrust is worth reiterating, especially in light of recent studies like Binder's and Baker's, which celebrate the emergence of liberal trends in Islamic and Islamist thought. Perhaps the keenest analyst of the shortcomings is the Lebanese writer, Ridwan al-Sayyid, who notes a threat to what he refers to as "cosmopolitanism" – what others might characterize as a threat to liberalism, democratization, or secularism in the Arab region:

The greatest threat [to the development of a cosmopolitan perspective] emanates from the Islamist revivalism movement and its adherence to particularism and authenticity, which lays great stress on symbolism and cultural differences rather than on common aspects of different cultures. Due to its influence, the concept of a Western cultural invasion (al-ghazw al-thaqafi) and conspiracy will not easily disappear from the political and cultural scene. The ideological tents of the Islamic movement have become so pervasive during the past two decades that nationalists as well have adopted the notion of cultural invasion. As a result, the atmosphere is presently not suitable for an open cultural and political debate.[4]

This work is not intended merely as a call to disaggregate political forces (focusing on individuals and groups within parties, rather than parties as a whole) or merely an affirmation of Schwedler's and Clark's efforts to shift the focus from inclusion in formal pluralist political processes to a wider range of interactions that take place across ideological divides. Rather, the focus on individuals' interactions points to shortcomings of the causal relation posited by the inclusion-moderation thesis from the outset. Formulating the question as to how structural arrangements (changes in practice) impact ideas (changes in thinking) neglects the modes of thinking and the character of individuals necessary to bring about the interactions in the first place. This is not to reverse the causal relation by suggesting that the existence of moderate ideas alone will necessarily bring about more liberal and democracy practices. In fact, the differences between the Egyptian and Yemeni cases revealed the greater significance of protest momentum in the former, and the more central role of formal dialogs to establish and repair relationships among primary actors in the latter, in developing and expanding cross-ideological cooperation. My aim is rather to underscore a premise that seems very basic to this political theorist: that structures and agents, material conditions, and ideological contexts exist within a dialectical relationship. "Moderation" in any of the senses in which it is currently used requires intellectuals who are free to interact and develop alternative frameworks for politics and society. The real challenge for the cultivation of progressive political ideologies in the Arab region is not the existence of Islamist thinkers or movements, but the dominance of particularist discourses that intellectuals try to assert as the basis of unity with the aim of responding to and opposing what is understood to be a cultural assault from the West.

NOTES

1. Salwa Ismail. *Rethinking Islamist Politics: Culture, the State and Islamism* (London: I. B. Tauris, 2003), 20–21.
2. Ismail. *Rethinking Islamist Politics*, 21; Olivier Roy, *The Failure of Political Islam*, tr. Carol Volk (Harvard University Press, 1994).
3. I argue this point at greater length in Michaelle Browers. *Democracy and Civil Society in Arab Political Thought: Transcultural Possibilities* (Syracuse University Press, 2006).
4. Ridwan al-Sayyid. "Islamic Movements and Authenticity" in Roel Meijer (ed.), *Cosmopolitanism, Authenticity and Identity in the Middle East* (London: Routledge, 1999), 113.

Bibliography

Abaza, Mona. *Debates on Islam and Knowledge in Malaysia and Egypt: Shifting Worlds* (London: Routledge, 2002).

'Abd al-Fattah, Nabil (ed.). *Taqrir al-hala al-diniyya fi misr*, 2nd edn (Cairo: al-Ahram Center for Strategic and International Studies, 1998), vol. I and II.

'Abd al-Karim, Salah. *Awraq hizb al-wasat al-misri* (Papers of the Egyptian Wasat Party) (Cairo: n.p., 1998).

'Abd al-Quddus, Muhammad. "'Ashara sanawat ba'd wafah taqiya misr" (10 Years after the Death of Egypt's Tyrant), *al-Da'wa* 53 (September 1980), 26–28.

Abdel-Malek, Anwar. *Rih al-sharq* (Wind of the East) (Cairo: Dar al-mustaqbal al-'arabi, 1983).

Abdo, Geneive. *No God But God: Egypt and the Triumph of Islam* (Oxford University Press, 2000).

Abu al-Majd, Ahmad Kamal. *Hiwar la muwajaha* (Dialog, Not Confrontation) (Cairo: Dar al-shuruq, 1988).

  Ruya islamiyya mu'asira (A Contemporary Islamic Vision: A Declaration of Principles) (Cairo: Dar al-shuruq, 1991).

Abu-Lughod, Ibrahim. "Retreat from the Secular Path: Islamic Dilemmas of Arab Politics," *Review of Politics* 28 (1966), 447–476.

Abu-Manneh, Butrus. "The Christians between Ottomanism and Syrian Nationalism: The Ideas of Butrus al-Bustani," *International Journal of Middle East Studies* 11 (1980), 287–304.

'Aflaq, Michael. *Choice of Texts from the Ba'th Party Founder's Thought* (Florence: Cooperativa Lavoratori, 1977).

Ahmed, Leila. *Women and Gender in Islam: Roots of a Modern Debate* (Yale University Press, 1992).

Akhavi, Sharough. "The Dialectic in Contemporary Egyptian Social Thought: The Scripturalist and Modernist Discourses of Sayyid Qutb and Hasan Hanafi," *International Journal of Middle East Studies* 29 (1997), 377–401.

al-Ahsan, Abdullah. *Ummah or Nation? Identity Crisis in Contemporary Muslim Society* (Leicester: The Islamic Foundation, 1992).

al-'Alawi, Sa'id Bin Sa'id (ed.). *al-Mujtama' al-madani fi al-watan al-'arabi wa dawruhu fi tahqiq al-dimuqratiyya* (Civil Society in the Arab World and Its Role in the Realization of Democracy) (Beirut: Center for Arab Unity Studies, 1992).

Allah, Muhammad Ahmad Khalaf (ed.). *al-Qawmiyya al-'arabiyya wa al-islam: buhuth wa munaqashat al-nadwa al-fikriyya* (Arab Nationalism and Islam: Intellectual Studies and Roundtable Debates) (Beirut: Center for Arab Unity Studies, 1981).

Amin, Qasim. *The Liberation of Women and the New Woman: Two Documents in the History of Egyptian Feminism*, tr. Samiha Sidhom Peterson (Cairo: The American University in Cairo Press, 2000).

    Qasim Amin: tahrir al-mara wa al-tamaddun al-islami (Qasim Amin: The Liberation of Women and Islamic Civilization) (Beirut: Dar al-wahda, 1985).

al-Anani, Khalil. "Brotherhood Bloggers: A New Generation Voices Dissent," *Arab Insight: Emerging Social and Religious Trends* (Washington, DC: World Security Institute, 2008), vol. II, no. 1, 29–38.

Arif, Nasr Mohamed. "Political Parties in Egypt: The Problems of Existence, Legitimacy and Function," *Strategic Papers* 14 (January 2005).

al-'Awa, Muhammad Salim. *Fi al-nizam al-siyasi lil-dawla al-islamiya* (Alexandria: al-Maktab al-misri al-hadith, 1975). Translated as *On the Political System of the Islamic State* (Indianapolis: American Trust Publications, 1980).

al-'Ayid, Khalid. "The Movement of Islamic Jihad and the Oslo Process: An Interview with Ramadan 'Abdallah Shallah," *Journal of Palestine Studies* 28 4 (1999), 61–73.

Ayubi, Nazih. *Political Islam: Religion and Politics in the Arab World* (London: Routledge, 1991).

al-'Azim, Sadik Jalal. "Orientalism and Orientalism in Reverse," *Khamsin* 8 (1981), 5–26.

al-'Azm, Sadiq Jalal. *al-Naqd al-dhati ba'd al-hazima* (Self Criticism after the Defeat) (Beirut: Dar al-Tali'a, 1968).

    al-Naqd al-fikr al-dini (Critique of Religious Thought) (Beirut: Dar al-Tali'a, 1969).

al-Azmeh, Aziz. *al-Turath wa al-sulta* (Heritage and Power) (Beirut: Dar al-Tali'a, 1990).

Badran, Margot. "Feminisms and Islamisms," *Journal of Women's History* 10 (1999), 196–204.

    "Gender Activism: Feminists and Islamists in Egypt" in Valentine M. Moghadam (ed.), *Identity Politics and Women* (Boulder: Westview Press, 1994), 202–227.

Baker, Raymond William. *Islam Without Fear: Egypt and the New Islamists* (Harvard University Press, 2003).

    Sadat and After: Struggles for Egypt's Political Soul (Harvard University Press, 1990).

al-Banna, Hassan. *Ila al-shabab wa ila al-talaba khassa* (To the Youth and Especially the Students) (Cairo: Dar al-da'wa, n.d.).

    Risa'il al-thalatha (Three Letters) (Cairo: Dar al-tiba'a wa al-nashr al-islamiyya, 1977).

    Risala al-mu'tamar al-khamis (Letter of the Fifth Conference) (Cairo: Dar al-kitab al-'arabi, nd).

al-Baytar, Nadim. *al-Iydiyulujiyya al-thawriyya* (The Revolutionary Ideology) (Beirut: al-Mu'assasa al-jami'iyya, 1982).

al-Bazri, Dalal, Hani al-Hurani, Husayn Abu Rumman. *al-Mar'a al-'arabiyya wa al-musharaka al-siyasiyya* (The Arab Women and Political Participation) (Amman: Dar Sinbad, 2000).

Bin Sa'id, Sa'id (ed.). *al-Mujtama' al-madani fi al-watan al-'arabi wa dawruhu fi tahqiq al-dimuqratiyya* (Civil Society in the Arab World and Its Role in the Realization of Democracy) (Beirut: Center for Arab Unity Studies, 1992).

Binder, Leonard. *Islamic Liberalism: A Critique of Development Ideologies* (University of Chicago Press, 1988).

al-Bishri, Tariq. "Bayn al-'uruba wa al-islam: al-mawqif min 'ghayr al-muslimin' wa min al-'ilmaniyya" (Between Arabism and Islam: The Position of Non-Muslims and Secularism), *al-Sha'b*, May 27, 1986.

al-Haraka al-siyasiyya fi misr, 1945–1951 (The Political Movement in Egypt, 1945–1951) (Cairo: al-Haya al-misriyya al-'amma lil-kitab, 1972).

al-Haraka al-siyasiyya fi misr, 1945–1951 (The Political Movement in Egypt, 1945–1951) (Cairo: Dar al-shuruq, 1983).

Ma hiyya al-mu 'asira (What is Modernity) Cairo: Dar al-shuruq, 1996.

Sa'd Zaghlul mufawidan: dirasa fi al-mufawadhat al-misriyya al-britani-yya, 1920–1924 (Sa'd Zaghlul Negotiating: A Study of Egyptian-British Negotiations, 1920–1924) (Cairot: Dar al-Hilal, 1998).

Sa'd Zaghlul yufawidhu al-isti'mar: dirasa fi al-mufawadhat al-misriyya al-britaniyya, 1920–1924 (Sa'd Zaghlul Negotiates the Colonization: A Study of Egyptian-British Negotiations, 1920–1924) (Cairo: al-Hay'a al-misri-yya al-'amma lil-kitab, 1977).

al-Bishri, Tariq (ed.). *Bayn al-islam wa al-'uruba* (Between Islam and Arabism: The Position of Non-Muslims and Secularism) (Cairo: Dar al-shuruq, 1988).

al-Hiwar al-qawmi al-dini: awraq 'amal wa munaqashat al-nadwa al-fikriyya (National-Religious Dialog: Working Papers and Intellectual Roundtable Debates) (Beirut: Center for Arab Unity Studies, 1989).

al-Muslimun wa al-aqbat fi intar al-jama'a al-wataniyya (Muslims and Copts in the Framework of a National Society) (Cairo: al-Hay'a al-misriyya al'amma lil-kitab, 1980).

Brand, Laurie A. *Women, the State and Political Liberalization: Middle Eastern and North African Experiences* (Columbia University Press, 1998).

Braungart Margaret M. and Richard G. Braungart. "The Effects of the 1960s Political Generation on Former Left-and Right-Wing Youth Activist Leaders," *Social Problems* **38** (1991), 297–315.

Browers, Michaelle. "The Centrality and Marginalization of Women in the Political Discourse of Arab Nationalists and Islamists," *Journal of Middle East Women's Studies* 2 (2006), 8–34.

Democracy and Civil Society in Arab Political Thought: Transcultural Possibilities (Syracuse University Press, 2006).

"The Egyptian Movement for Change: Intellectual Antecedents and Generational Conflicts," *Contemporary Islam: Dynamics of Muslim Life* 1 (2007), 69–88.

"Origins and Architects of Yemen's Joint Meeting Parties," *International Journal of Middle East Studies* 39 (2007), 565–586.

"The Secular Bias of Ideology Studies and the Problem of Islamism," *Journal of Political Ideologies* **10** (2005), 75–93.

Burgat, François. *Face to Face with Political Islam* (London: I. B. Tauris, 2003).

Burrowes, Robert D. and Catherine M. Kasper. "The Salih Regime and the Need for a Credible Opposition," *Middle East Journal* **61** (2007), 263–280.

Buti, Muhammad Sa'id Ramadan and Tayyib Tizini. *al-Islam wa al-'asr: tahaddiyat wa afaq* (Damascus: Dar al-fikr al-mu'asir, 2000).

Carapico, Sheila. *Civil Society in Yemen: The Political Economy of Activism in Modern Arabia* (Cambridge University Press, 1998).

Center for Arab Unity Studies. *The Future of the Arab Nation: Challenges and Options* (New York: Routledge, 1992).

Clark, Janine A. "The Conditions of Islamist Moderation: Unpacking Cross-Ideological Cooperation in Jordan," *International Journal of Middle East Studies* **38** (2006), 539–560.

Clark, Janine and Jillian Schwedler. "Who Opened the Window? Women's Struggle for Voice within Islamist Political Parties," *Comparative Politics* **35** (2003), 293–312.

al-Dajani, Ahmad Sidqi. *Madha ba'd harb Ramadan? Filistine wa al-watan al-'arabi fi al-'alim al-ghad* (What is after the Ramadan War? Palestine and the Arab Nation in the World of Tomorrow) (Beirut: Arab Center for Studies and Publishing, 1974).

"The PLO and the Euro-Arab Dialogue," *Journal of Palestine Studies* **9** (1980), 81–98.

al-Quds wa intifada al-aqsa wa harb al-'awlama (Jerusalem, the al-Aqsa Intifida and the War of Globalization) (Giza: Markaz al-i'lam al-'arabi, 2002).

Rasa'il al-mu'tamar al-qawmi al-islami bayna kharif 1994 wa rabi' 1997 (Letters of the National-Islamic Conference Between the Fall of 1994 and the Spring of 1997) (Cairo: Markaz yafa, 1997).

Wahdat al-tanawwu' wa hadarah 'arabiyya islamiyya fi 'alam mutarabit (The Unity of Diversity and the Arab-Islamic Civilization in a Destitute World) (Cairo: Dar al-mustaqbal al-'arabi, 1990).

'Uruba wa islam wa mu'asara (Europe, Islam and the Future) (Beirut: Manshurat filastin al-muhtalla, 1982).

al-Dajani, Ahmad Sidqi, *et al. Tajdid al-fikr al-siyasi fi itar al-dimuqratiyya wa huquq al-insan: al-tayyar al-islami wa al-markisi wa al-qawmi* (The Renewal of Political Thought in the Framework of Democracy and Human Rights: Islamic, Marxist and Nationalist Trends) (Cairo Center for Human Rights Studies, 1997).

Dresch, Paul. *A History of Modern Yemen* (Cambridge University Press, 2000).

"The Tribal Factor in the Yemeni Crisis" in Jamal S. al-Suwaidi (ed.), *The Yemeni War of 1994* (London: Saqi Books, 1995), 35–55.

Dresch, Paul and Bernard Haykel. "Stereotypes and Political Styles: Islamists and Tribesfolk in Yemen," *International Journal of Middle East Studies* **27** (1995), 405–431.

Dunne, Michele Durocher. *Democracy in Contemporary Egyptian Political Discourse* (Amsterdam: John Benjamins Publishing Company, 2003).

al-Duri, 'Abd al-'Aziz. *The Historical Formation of the Arab Nation: A Study in Identity and Consciousness*, tr. Lawrence Conrad (London: Croom Helm, 1987).

The Rise of Historical Writing among the Arabs (Princeton University Press, 1983).

Elad-Altman, Israel. "Democracy, Elections and the Egyptian Muslim Brotherhood," *Current Trends in Islamist Ideology* **3** (2006), 24–37.

Elmessiri, Abdelwahab. "Secularism, Immanence and Deconstruction" in John L. Esposito and Azzam Tamimi (eds.), *Islam and Secularism in the Middle East* (New York University Press, 2000), 52–80.

Enloe, Cynthia. *Bananas, Beaches and Bases: Making Feminist Sense of International Politics* (University of California Press, 1989).

Fikri, Yahya. "Ayyuha al-munadhilun al-yasiriyyun al-shurifa dakhil al-tajammu': irhalu 'anhu … wa indhamu ilayna" (Attention Esteemed Leftist Fighters Within the Tagammu': Leave it Alone and Leave it to Us), *Awraq ishtiraqiyya* **9** (2005), 45–48.

Flores, Alexander. "Egypt: A New Secularism?" *Middle East Report* **153** (1988), 27–30.

Freeden, Michael. *Ideologies and Political Theory: A Conceptual Approach* (Oxford University Press, 1998).

Ideology: A Very Short Introduction (Oxford University Press, 2003).

Freeman, Amy. "Re-locating Moroccan Women's Identities in a Transnational World," *Gender, Place & Culture* **11** (2004), 17–41.

al-Gawhary, Karim. "'We are a Civil Party with an Islamic Identity': An Interview with Abu 'Ila Madi Abu 'Ila and Rafiq Habib," *Middle East Report* **199** (1996), 30–32.

Huquq al-muwatana: huquq ghayr al-muslim fi al-mujtama 'al-islami (The Rights of Citizens: The Rights of Non-Muslims in Islamic Society) (Herndon, VA: International Institute of Islamic Thought, 1993).

Ghannouchi (Ghannushi), Rashid. "The Participation of Islamists in a Non-Islamic Government" in Azzam Tamimi (ed.), *Power Sharing Islam?* (London: Liberty Publications, 1993), 51–63.

al-Ghazzali, Muhammad. *Our Beginning in Wisdom*, tr. Ismail al-Faruqi (Washington, DC: American Council of Learned Societies, 1953).

El-Ghobashi, Mona. "The Metamorphosis of the Egyptian Muslim Brothers," *International Journal of Middle East Studies* **37** (2005), 373–395.

Gibb, H. A. R. *Studies on the Civilization of Islam* (London: Routledge & Kegan Paul, 1962).

Glosemeyer, Iris. "The First Yemeni Parliamentary Elections in 1993: Practising Democracy," *Orient* **34** (1993), 439–452.

Gluck, Sherna Berger. "Palestinian Women: Gender Politics and Nationalism," *Journal of Palestine Studies* **24** (1995), 5–15.

Habib, Rafiq. *Awraq hizb al-wasat al-misri* (Papers of the Egyptian Wasat Party) (Cairo: n.p., 1996).

Hadara al-wasat (The Culture of the Center) (Cairo: Dar al-shuruq, 2001).

al-Umma wa al-dawla: bayan tahrir al-umma (Nation and State: Manifesto on the Liberation of the Umma) (Cairo: Dar al-shuruq, 2001).

Haddad, Yvonne Yazbeck and Jane I. Smith. "Women in Islam: 'The Mother of all Battles'" in Suha Sabbagh (ed.), *Arab Women: Between Defiance and Restraint* (New York: Olive Branch Press, 1996), 137–150.

Hafez, Mohammed M. and Quintan Wiktorowicz. "Violence as Contention in the Egyptian Islamic Movement" in Quintan Wiktorowicz (ed.), *Islamic Activism: A Social Movement Theory Approach* (Indiana University Press, 2004), 61–88.

Hale, Sondra. "Activating the Gender Local: Transnational Ideologies and 'Women's Culture' in Northern Sudan," *Journal of Middle East Women's Studies* **1** (2005), 26–52.

Hamzawi, Amr, Marina Ottaway, and Nathan J. Brown. "Islamist Movements and the Democratic Process in the Arab World: Exploring the Gray Zones," *Carnegie Paper No. 67* (March 2006).

Hanafi, Hassan. *al-Din wa al-thawra fi misr: al-Harakat al-diniyya al-mu'asira* (Religion and Revolution and Egypt: The Contemporary Religious Movement) (Cairo: Madbuli Bookstore, 1988).

"Madha ya'ni al-yasar al-islami" (What Is the Meaning of the Islamic Left?), *al-Yasar al-islami* **1** (1981), 5–48.

Min al-'aqida ila al-thawra (From Doctrine to Revolution) (Cairo: Madbuli Bookstore, 1988).

Muqaddima fi 'ilm al-istighrab (Introduction to the Science of Occidentalism) (Cairo: al-Dar al-fanniyya, 1981).

"The Relevance of the Islamic Alternative in Egypt," *Arab Studies Quarterly* **4** (1982), 54–74.

Hasib, Khayr al-Din. "al-Bayan al-khatami: dawra 'mukim al-janin' lil-mu'tamar al-qawmi al-islami, al-dawra al-rabi'a" (Concluding Declaration: The 'Camp Jenin' Round of the National-Islamic Conference, Round Four) *al-Mustaqbal al-'arabi* **281** (2002), 151–161.

Hassan, Riaz. *Faithlines: Muslim Conceptions of Islam and Society* (Oxford University Press, 2002).

Hasso, Frances. "The 'Women's Front': Nationalism, Feminism and Modernity in Palestine," *Gender & Society* **12** (1998), 441–465.

Hatem, Mervat. "The Pitfalls of the Nationalist Discourses on Citizenship in Egypt" in Suad Joseph (ed.), *Gender and Citizenship in the Middle East* (Syracuse University Press, 2000), 33–57.

Hatem, Mervat. "Secularists and Islamist Discourses on Modernity in Egypt and the Evolution of the Postcolonial Nation-State" in Yvonne Yazbeck Haddad and John L. Esposito (eds.), *Islam, Gender and Social Change* (Oxford University Press, 1998), 85–99.

Hatem, Mervat. "Toward the Development of Post-Islamist and Post-Nationalist Feminist Discourses in the Middle East" in Judith E. Tucker (ed.), *Arab Women: Old Boundaries, New Frontiers* (Indiana University Press, 1993), 29–48.

Hatina, Meir. *Identity Politics in the Middle East: Liberal Thought and Islamic Challenge in Egypt* (London: Tauris Academic Studies, 2007).

Hatina, Meir. "The 'Other Islam': The Egyptian Wasat Party," *Critique: Critical Middle Eastern Studies* **14** (2005), 171–184.

Hermassi, Elbaki (ed.). *al-Din fi al-mujtama 'al-'arabi* (Religion in Arab Society) (Beirut: Center for Arab Unity Studies, 1990).

Hijab, Nadia. *Womenpower: The Arab Debate on Women at Work* (Cambridge University Press, 1988).

Hourani, Albert. *The Emergence of the Modern Middle East* (University of California Press, 1981).

Huband, Mark. *Warriors of the Prophet: The Struggle for Islam* (Boulder: Westview Press, 1999).

Hudson, Michael. "Bipolarity, Rational Calculation and War in Yemen" in Jamal S. al-Suwaidi (ed.), *The Yemeni War of 1994: Causes and Consequences* (London: Saqi Books, 1995), 19–32.

Husayn, 'Adil. *al-'alaqat al-iqtisadiyya bayna misr wa isra'il* (Economic Relations Between Egypt and Israel) (Beirut: Institute for Palestinian Studies, 1984).

Iqtisad al-misri min al-istiqlal ila al-taba'iyya, 1974–1979 (The Egyptian Economy: From Independence to Dependency), 2 vols. (Beirut: Dar al-kalima lil-nashr, 1981).

"Islam and Marxism: The Absurd Polarisation of Contemporary Egyptian Politics," *Review of Middle East Studies* 2 (1976), 71–83.

al-Jabha al-'arabiyya al-iraniyya didda al-hilf al-amriki al-sihyuni, 1991–1993 (The Arab-Iranian Front against the American-Zionist Alliance) (Cairo: Arab-Islamic Center for Studies, 1998).

Nahwa fikr 'arabi jadid, al-nasiriyya wa al-tanmiyya wa al-dimuqratiyya (Toward A New Arab Thought: Nasirism, Development and Democracy) (Cairo: Dar al-mustaqbal al-'arabi, 1985).

al-Tatbi': al-mukhatta al-sihyuni lil-haymana al-iqtisadiyya (Normalization: The Zionist Plan for Economic Hegemony) (Cairo: Madbuli Bookstore, 1985).

Huwaydi, Fahmi. *Muwatinun la dhimmiyyun* (Citizens not Protected Peoples) (Beirut: Dar al-shuruq, 1985).

Ibrahim, Saad Eddin and Ahmad Sidqi al-Dajani (eds.). *al-Sahwah al-Islamiyya wa humum al-watan al-'arabi* (The Islamic Awakening and the Concerns of the Arab World) (Amman: Arab Thought Forum, 1988).

'Id, 'Abd al-Razzaq and Muhammad 'Abd al-Jabbar. *al-Dimuqratiyya bayn al-'almaniyya wa al-islam* (Damascus: Dar al-fikr al-mu'asir, 1999).

al-'Imara, Muhammad. *Hal al-islam huwa al-hal? limadha wa-kayfa?* (Is Islam the Solution? Why and How?) (Cairo: Dar al-shuruq, 1995).

al-Islam wa al-mara fi ray al-imam muhammad 'abduh (Islam and Women in the View of Imam Muhammad 'Abduh) (Cairo: al-Qahirah lil-Thaqafah al-'arabiyya, 1975).

al-Islam wa al-sulta al-diniyya (Islam and Religious Authority) (Cairo: Dar al-thaqafa al-jadida, 1979). *Qasim Amin: tahrir al-mara wa al-tamaddur al-islami* (Qasim Amin: The Liberation of Women and Islamic Civilization) (Beirut: Dar al wahda, 1985).

al-Tahrir al-islami lil-mara: al-rad 'ala shubhat al-ghula (The Islamic Liberation of Women: A Reply to Doubts Raised by Extremists) (Cairo: Dar al-shuruq, 2002).

al-Tafsir al-markisi lil-Islam (The Marxist Interpretation of Islam) (Cairo: Dar al-shuruq, 1996). International Crisis Group. Reforming Egypt: In Search of a Strategy Middle East/North Africa Report Notes 41. (October 4 2005).

Islah (Yemeni Reform Gathering). *Masira 'ata, April 1993-April 1997* (Account Presented, April 1993-April 1997) (Sana'a: al-Afaq lil-tib'a wa al-nashr, 1997).

Ismail, Salwa. "Confronting the Other: Identity, Culture, Politics and Conservative Islamism in Egypt," *International Journal of Middle East Studies* **30** (1998), 199–225.

Rethinking Islamist Politics: Culture, the State and Islamism (London: I. B. Tauris, 2003).

"State-Society Relations in Egypt: Restructuring the Political," *Arab Studies Quarterly* **17** (1995), 37–52.

al-Jabri, Muhammad 'Abid. "Badal al-'almaniyya: al-dimuqratiyya wa al-'aqlaniyya" (The Alternative of Secularism: Democracy and Rationalism), *al-Yawm al-sabi'* **224** (August 22, 1988).

al-Din wa al-dawla wa tatbiq al-shari'a (Religion, the State and the Application of Islamic Law) (Beirut: Center for Arab Unity Studies, 1996).

Ishkaliyyat al-fikr al-'arabi al-mu'asir (Problematics of Contemporary Arab Thought) (Beirut: Center for Arab Unity Studies, 1989).

Masala al-huwiyya: al-'uruba wa al-Islam ... wa al-gharb (The Question of Identity: Arabism, Islam ... and the West) (Beirut: Center for Arab Studies, 1995).

Nahnu wa al-turath (The Heritage and Us) (Beirut: Dar al-tiba'a lil-tanwir wa al-nashr, 1980).

al-Jabri, Muhammad 'Abid and Hasan Hanafi, *Hiwar al-mashriq al-maghrib: talih silsila al-rudud wa al-munaqashat* (East-West Dialog: Followed by a Series of Replies and Debates) (Casablanca: Dar al-tubqal, 1990).

al-Jifri, Abdul Rahman Ali. *A Paper on the Yemeni Crisis.* Department of Politics, University of Exeter (October 29, 1997).

Joffé, E. G. H, M. J. Hachemi, and E. W. Watkins (eds.). *Yemen Today: Crisis and Solutions* (London: Caravel Press, 1997).

Katulis, Brian and David Emery. *"Yemen," Countries at the Crossroads 2006: A Survey of Democratic Governance* (New York: Freedom House, 2006).

Khomeini, Ruhollah. *al-Hukuma al-islamiyya* (Islamic Government) (Cairo: n.p., 1979).

Jihad al-nafs, aw al-jihad al-akbar (Struggle with the Self, or the Greatest Jihad) (Cairo: n.p., 1980).

Kostiner, Joseph. *Yemen: The Tortuous Quest for Unity, 1990–1994* (London: The Royal Institute of International Affairs, 1996).

Krämer, Gudrun. "Cross-Links or Double Talk? Islamist Movements in the Political Process" in Laura Guazzone (ed.), *The Islamist Dilemma: The Political Role of Islamist Movements in the Contemporary World* (Reading: Ithaca Press, 1998), 39–67.

Kurzman, Charles. *Liberal Islam: A Sourcebook* (Oxford University Press, 1998).

Lahoud, Nelly. *Political Thought in Islam: A Study in Intellectual Boundaries* (New York: Routledge-Curzon, 2005).

Lee, Robert D. *Overcoming Tradition and Modernity: The Search for Islamic Authenticity* (Oxford: Westview, 1997).

Lynch, Marc. "Young Brothers in Cyberspace," *Middle East Report* **245** (2007), 26–33.

Mandaville, Peter. *Global Political Islam* (London: Routledge, 2007).

Mansur, Bilqis Ahmad. *al-Ahzab al-siyasiyya wa al-tahawwul al-dimuqrati: dirasah tatbiqiyya 'ala al-yaman wa bilad ukhra* (Political Parties and

Democratic Transformation: A Study Applied to Yemen and Other Countries) (Cairo: Maktabat Madbuli, 2004).

Mansur, Mahmud. "al-masar al-tatbiqi lil-tajriba al-dimuqratiyya fi al-yaman wa mu'ashshirat al-mustaqbal" (The Practical Democratic Course in Yemen and Indications of the Future), *Markaz dirasat al-mustaqbal* **3** (1998), 68–80.

al-Maqalih, Muhammad Muhammad. *Man qatala jar allah 'umar: al-jarima bayn al-din wa al-siyasa* (Who Killed Jarallah 'Umar: The Crime Between Religion and Politics) (Sana'a: Markaz al-'abadi, 2004).

al-Maqrami, Muhammad 'Abd al-Rahman. *al-Tajammu' al-yamani lil-islah: al-ru'ya wa al-masar – dirasa fi al-nash'a wa al-tatawwur* (The Yemeni Reform Gathering: Vision and Path: A Study of the Origin and Development) (Sana'a: Yemeni Reform Gathering, 1998).

Maududi (Mawdudi), S. Abul A'la. *Political Theory of Islam*, tr. Khurshid Ahmad (Lahore: Islamic Publications, 1968).

Rights of Non-Muslims in Islamic State, tr. Khurshid Ahmad (Lahore: Islamic Publications, 1961).

Unity of the Muslim World, tr. Khurshid Ahmad (Lahore: Islamic Publications, 1967).

Meijer, Roel. "History, Authenticity and Politics: Tariq al-Bishri's Interpretation of Modern Egyptian History," *Occasional Paper* 4 (Amsterdam: Middle East Research Associates, 1989).

Quest for Modernity: Secular Liberal and Left-Wing Political Thought in Egypt, 1945–1958 (London: Routledge, 2003).

Muruwa, Husayn. *al-Naza'at al-maddiyya fi al-falsafa al-'arabiyya al-islamiyya* (Materialist Tendencies in Arab-Islamic Philosophy) (Beirut: Dar al-Farabi, 1975).

al-Mutawakkil, Muhammad 'Abd al-Malik. *al-Tanmiyya al-siyasiyya* (Political Development) (Sana'a: n.p., 2004).

Nafi, Basheer M. "The Arab Nationalists and the Arab Islamists: Shadows of the Past, Glimpses of the Future," *Middle East Affairs Journal* **6** (2000), 109–128.

Najib, Samih. *al-Ikhwan al-muslimun: ru'aya ishtirakiyya* (The Muslim Brotherhood: A Socialist View) (Cairo: Center for Socialist Studies, March 2006).

al-Ishtirakiyya alati nadfa' 'anha: ru'aya al-ishtiraki li-taghyir misr (The Socialism We Defend: The Perspective of the Revolutionary Socialist Trend for Changing Egypt) (Cairo: Center for Socialist Studies, March 2006).

Najjar, Fauzi M. "Islamic Fundamentalism and the Intellectuals: The Case of Nasr Hamid Abu Zayd," *British Journal of Middle Eastern Studies* 27:2 (2000), 177–200.

Narayan, Uma. *Dislocating Cultures: Identities, Traditions and Third World Feminism* (New York: Routledge, 1997).

Nashir, Sadiq. *Jar allah 'umar yatakallam: qisa hayat min shahqa al-milad ila rasasa al-mawt* (Jarallah 'Umar Speaks: The Story of a Life from the Breath of Birth to the Bullet of Death) (Sana'a: Markaz al-'abadi, 2003).

Noonan, Rita K. "Women against the State: Political Opportunities and Collective Action Frames in Chile's Transition to Democracy," *Sociological Forum* **10** (1995), 81–111.

al-Qaradawi, Yusuf. *Awlawiyyat al-haraka al-islamiyya fi al-marhala al-qadima* (Cairo: Maktaba wahba, 1991). Translated as *Priorities of the Islamic Movement in the Coming Phase* (Swansea: Awakening Publications, 2000).

Ghayr muslimin fi al-mujtama' al-islami (Non-Muslims in Islamic Society) (Cairo: n.p., 1975).

al-Halal wa al-haram fi al-Islam (Cairo: 'Isa al-babi al-halabi, 1960). Translated as *The Lawful and the Prohibited in Islam* (Kuala Lumpur: Islamic Book Trust, 2001).

al-Hulul al-mustawrada wa kayfa janat 'ala ummatina (How Imported Solutions Disastrously Affected our Community) (Cairo: Maktaba wahba, 1977).

al-Ijtihad al-mu 'asir bayna al-indibat wa al-infirat (Contemporary Independent Reasoning between Discipline and Dissolution) (Cairo: Dar al-tawzi' wa al-nashr al-islamiyya).

al-Islam wa al-'almaniyya, wajhan li-wajh: radd 'ilmi 'ala duktur fu'ad zakariyya wa jama' at al-'almaniyya (Islam and Secularism, Face to Face: A Scientific Reply to Dr. Fu'ad Zakariyya and the Group of Secularists) (Cairo: Dar al-sahwa, 1987).

Sahwah al-Islamiyya bayna al-juhud wa al-tatarruf (Qatar: Ri'asa al-mahakim al-shar'iyya wa al-shu'un al-diniyya, 1981). Translated as *Islamic Awakening Between Rejection and Extremism* (Herndon, VA: International Institute of Islamic Thought, 1990).

Qutb, Sayyid. *Social Justice in Islam*, tr. John B. Hardie and Hamid Algar (New York, Octagon Books, 2000).

Ramadan, Sa'id. *Ma'alim al-tariq* (Signposts of the Way) (Damascus: n.p., 1955)

Rizq, Hani and Khalis Jalabi Kanju. *al-Iman wa al-taqaddum al-'ilmi* (Faith and Scientific Progress) (Damascus: Dar al-fikr al-mu'asir, 2000).

Roy, Olivier. *The Failure of Political Islam*, tr. Carol Volk (Harvard University Press, 1994).

Sa'dawi, Nawal and Heba Raouf Ezzat. *al-Mara wa al-din wa al-akhlaq* (Woman, Religion, and Ethics) (Damascus: Dar al-fikr al-mu'asir, 2000).

Sa'id, Rifa't and 'Adil Husayn. *al-Hiwar bayn rif' at al-sa 'id wa 'adil husayn* (Dialogue Between Rifa't sa'id and 'Adil Husayn) (Cairo: al-Ahli, 1995).

Saif, Ahmed. *The Yemeni Parliamentary Elections: A Critical Analysis* (Dubai: Gulf Research Center, 2004).

Salem, Paul. *Bitter Legacy: Ideology and Politics in the Arab World* (Syracuse University Press, 1994).

Salvatore, Amando. "The Rational Authentication of *Turath* in Contemporary Arab Thought: Muhammad al-Jabri and Hasan Hanafi," *Muslim World* **85** (1995), 191–214.

al-Saqqaf, Faris (ed.). *Mustaqbal al-hizb al-ishtiraki al-yamani fi dhaw mu'tamaru al-rabi'* (The Future of the Yemeni Socialist Party in Light of Its Fourth Congress) (Sana'a: Markaz dirasat al-mustaqbal, 2002).

Sargent, Lydia. *Women and Revolution: A Discussion of the Unhappy Marriage of Marxism and Feminism* (Boston: South End Press, 1981).

al-Sayyid, Ridwan. "Islamic Movements and Authenticity" in Roel Meijer (ed.), *Cosmopolitanism, Authenticity and Identity in the Middle East* (London: Routledge, 1999), 103–114.

Schwedler, Jillian. *Faith in Moderation: Islamist Parties in Jordan and Yemen* (Cambridge University Press, 2006).

"The Islah Party in Yemen: Political Opportunities and Coalition Building in a Transitional Polity" in Quintan Wiktorowicz (ed.), *Islamic Activism: A Social Movement Theory Approach* (Indiana University Press, 2004), 205–228.

"Yemen's Aborted Opening," *Journal of Democracy* **13** (2002), 48–55.

Schwedler, Jillian and Janine A. Clark. "Islamist-Leftist Cooperation in the Arab World," *ISIM Review* **18** (Autumn 2006), 10–11.

Sela, Avraham. "Politics, Identity and Peacemaking: The Arab Discourse on Peace with Israel in the 1990s," *Israel Studies* **10** (2005), 15–71.

Shafiq, Munir. *al-Dimuqratiyya wa al-'ilmaniyya fi al-tarjriba al-gharbiyya* (Democracy and Secularism in the Western Experience) (London: al-Markaq al-maghribi lil-buhuth wa al-tarjama, 2001).

Fi al-wahda al-'arabiyya wa al-tajzi'a (On Arab Unity and Fragmentation) (Beirut: Dar al-Tali'a, 1979).

al-Fikr al-islami al-mu'asir wa al-tahaddiyat: thawra, haraka, kitaba (Contemporary Islamic Thought and the Challenges: Revolution, Movement and Writing) (Kuwait: Dar al-qalam, 1986).

'*Ilm al-harb* (Science of War) (Beirut: al-Mu'assasa al-'arabiyya, 1972).

al-Islam fi ma'raka al-hadara (Islam at the Center of Civilization) (Beirut: Dar al-kalima, 1982).

al-Islam wa tahaddiyyat al-inhitat al-mu'asir: qadaya al-tajzi'a wa al-sihyuniyya–al-taghrib wa al-taba'iyya (Islam and the Challenges of the Current Despair: The Issue of Fragmentation and Zionism – Alienation and Dependency) (London: Dar Taha, 1983).

al-Marksiyya al-lininiyya wa nazariyya al-hizb al-thawri (Marxist–Leninism and the Theory of Revolutionary War) (Beirut: Dar al-Tali'a, 1971).

al-Nizam al-duwali al-jadid wa al-khiyar al-muwajaha (The New World Order and the Alternative Choice) (Beirut: al-Nashir, 1992).

al-Qawmiyya al-'arabiyya bayna waqi 'al-tajzi'a wa tatallu'at al-wahda (Arab Nationalism between the Reality of Breakdown and the Aspirations of Unity) (Jerusalem: Wakalat Abu 'Arafat, 1980).

Sha'rawi, Muhammad Mutawalli. *Fiqh al-mara al-muslima* (Jurisprudence for Muslim Women) (Cairo: al-Dar al-'alimiyya lil-kutub wa al-nashr, 1998).

Sharif, Abdu H. "Weak Institutions and Democracy: The Case of the Yemeni Parliament, 1993–1997," *Middle East Policy* **9** (March 2002), 82–93.

Shukr, 'Abd al-Ghaffar. *al-Tahalufat al-siyasiyya wa al-'amal al-mushtarak fi misr, 1976–1993* (Political Alliances and Joint Action in Egypt, 1976–1993) (Cairo: Markaz al-buhuth al-'arabiyya, 1994).

Sivan, Emmanuel. "Arab Nationalism in the Age of Islamic Resurgence" in Israel Gershoni and James Jankowski (eds.), *Rethinking Nationalism in the Middle East* (Columbia University Press, 1997), 207–228.

Snow, David A., E. Burke Rochford, Jr., Steven K. Worden, and Robert D. Benford. "Frame Alignment Processes, Micromobilization and Movement Participation," *American Sociological Review* 51 (1986), 464–481.

Soueid, Mahmoud. "Islamic Unity and Political Change: Interview with Shaykh Muhammad Hussayn Fadlallah," *Journal of Palestine Studies* 25 (1995), 61–75.

Stacher, Joshua A. "Post-Islamist Rumblings in Egypt: The Emergence of the Wasat Party," *Middle East Journal* 56 (2002), 415–432.

Sulayman, William, Tariq al-Bishri, and Mustafa al-Fiqi. *al-Sha'b al-wahid wa al-watan al-wahid: dirasat fi al-usul al-wahda al-wataniyya* (One People and One Nation: Studies of the Sources of National Unity) (Cairo: al-Ahram Center for Political and Strategic Studies, 1982).

al-Surimi, Khalil Muhammad. *Lamhat min masira al-islah al-yamaniyya* (A Brief View of the Journal of Yemeni Islah) (Sana'a: n.p., 2004).

Taleb, Hassan Abou (ed.). *The Arab Strategic Report* (Cairo: al-Ahram Center for Strategic and International Studies, 2005).

Talib, Saadaldeen Ali. "A Decade of Pluralist Democracy in Yemen: The Yemen Parliament After Unification, 1990–2003" in Ali Sawi (ed.), *Parliamentary Reform* (Cairo: Konrad Adenauer Stiftung, 2003), 176–211.

Tarabishi, George. *Madhbaha al-turath fi al-thaqafa al-'arabiyya al-mu'assira* (The Massacre of the Heritage in Contemporary Arab Culture) (London: Dar al-Saqi, 1993).

al-Muthaqafun al-'arab wa al-turath (Arab Intellectuals and the Heritage) (London: Riyad al-rayyis, 1992).

Taraki, Lisa. "Islam is the Solution: Jordanian Islamists and the Dilemma of the 'Modern Woman,'" *British Journal of Sociology* 46 (1995), 643–661.

Tibi, Bassam. *Arab Nationalism: Between Islam and the Nation-State*, 3rd edn (New York: Saint Martin's Press, 1997).

Tönnies, Ferdinand. *Community and Society*, tr. Charles P. Loomis (Michigan State University Press, 1957).

Turabi, Hasan. *Awlawiyyat al-tayyar al-islami li-thalathat 'uqud qadimat* (Priorities of the Islamic Trend in the Coming Three Centuries) (Umm Durman: Bayt al-ma'rifa lil-intaj al-thaqafi, 1991).

al-Ittija al-islami yuqddimu al-mara bayna ta'alim al-din wa taqalid al-mujtama' (The Islamic Trend on Women, Between the Teachings of Religion and the Traditions of Society) (Jeddah: al-Dar al-sa'udiyya, 1984). Translated as *Emancipation of Women: An Islamic Perspective*, 2nd edn (London: Muslim Information Centre, 2000).

'Ulaymi, Rashad Muhammad and Ahmad 'Ali Bashari. *al-Baramij al-intikhabiyya lil-ahzab wa al-tanzimat al-siyasiyya fi al-jumhuriyya al-yamaniyya: dirasa muqarana* (Electoral Programs of Political Parties and Organizations in the Yemen Republic: A Comparative Study) (Sana'a: Majallat al-Thawabit, 1993).

Utvik, Bjø'rn Olav. "*Hizb al-Wasat* and the Potential for Change in Egyptian Islamism," *Critique: Critical Middle Eastern Studies* 14 (2005), 293–306.

Waardenburg, Jacques. "Reflections on the West" in Suha Taji-Farouki and Basheer M. Nafi (eds.), *Islamic Thought in the Twentieth Century*, (London: I. B. Tauris, 2004), 261–295.

Wajih, Tamir. "al-tahadda alathy tuwajihah kifaya" (The Challenge Facing Kifaya), *Awraq ishtiraqiyya* **9** (2005), 38–41.

Weinbaum, Batya. *The Curious Courtship of Women's Liberation and Socialism* (Boston: South End Press, 1978).

Wickham, Carrie Rosefsky. *Mobilizing Islam: Religion, Activism, and Political Change in Egypt* (Columbia University Press, 2002).

Zayd, 'Ala Abu. *al-Mar'a al-misriyya fi al-ahzab al-siyasiyya* (The Egyptian Women in Political Parties) in 'Ala Abu Zayd (ed.), *al-Mar'a al-misriyya wa al-'amal al-'am: ruya mustaqbaliyya* (The Egyptian Woman and Public Work: A Future-Oriented Perspective) (Cairo: Center for Arab Unity Studies, 1995), 47–70.

al-Zayyat, Muntasir. *The Road to al-Qaeda: The Story of Bin Laden's Right-Hand Man* (London: Pluto Press, 2004).

Zubaida, Sami. "Islam, Cultural Nationalism and the Left," *Review of Middle East Studies* **4** (1988), 1–32.

Law and Power in the Islamic World (London: I. B. Tauris, 2003).

"Trajectories of Political Islam: Egypt, Iran and Turkey," *Political Quarterly* **71** (2000), 60–79.

Index

Cambridge Middle East Studies